THE DOGS ARE EATING THEM NOW.

GRAEME SMITH
THE DOGS ARE EATING THEM NOW.
OUR WAR IN AFGHANISTAN

COUNTERPOINT | BERKELEY

Copyright © 2015 Graeme Smith
First published by Alfred A. Knopf Canada

All rights reserved under International and Pan-American Copyright
Conventions. No part of this book may be used or reproduced in any manner
whatsoever without written permission from the publisher, except in the case of
brief quotations embodied in critical articles and reviews.

Images courtesy of the author.
Maps by Sean Tai.

Library of Congress Cataloging-in-Publication Data Is Available

ISBN 978-1-61902-479-3

C O U N T E R P O I N T
2560 Ninth Street, Suite 318
Berkeley, CA 94710
www.counterpointpress.com

Printed in the United States of America
Distributed by Publishers Group West

10 9 8 7 6 5 4 3 2 1

FOR MY SISTER

CONTENTS

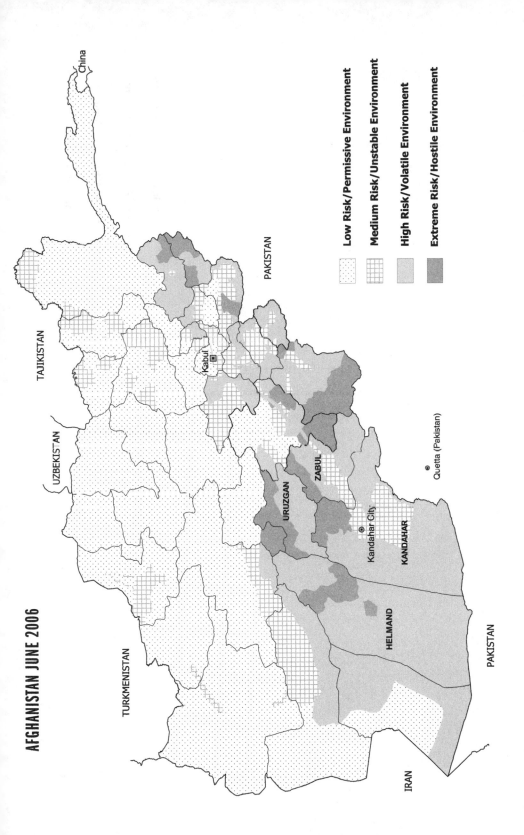

AFGHANISTAN JUNE 2006

Low Risk/Permissive Environment

Medium Risk/Unstable Environment

High Risk/Volatile Environment

Extreme Risk/Hostile Environment

CHINA

TAJIKISTAN

UZBEKISTAN

TURKMENISTAN

Kabul

PAKISTAN

URUZGAN

ZABUL

Kandahar City

KANDAHAR

HELMAND

Quetta (Pakistan)

IRAN

PAKISTAN

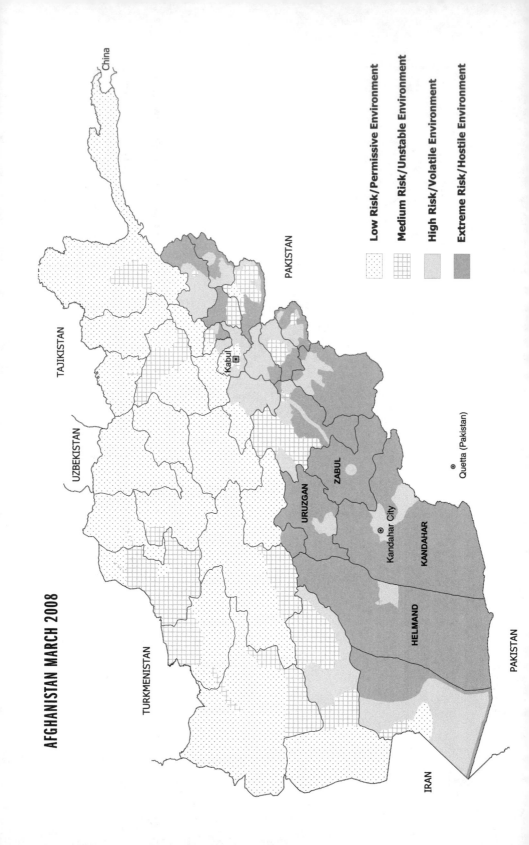

AFGHANISTAN MARCH 2008

Low Risk/Permissive Environment

Medium Risk/Unstable Environment

High Risk/Volatile Environment

Extreme Risk/Hostile Environment

China

TAJIKISTAN

UZBEKISTAN

TURKMENISTAN

IRAN

PAKISTAN

PAKISTAN

Kabul

URUZGAN

ZABUL

HELMAND

KANDAHAR

Kandahar City

Quetta (Pakistan)

FOREWORD

Years ago, when the United States was intensely focused on Afghanistan, I was invited to a meeting at CIA headquarters. It was unusual for the agency to open its doors for a scruffy Canadian journalist, but the Americans were desperate to understand the war. The mission was already turning into a debacle in 2008, and the security apparatus was preparing a surge of reinforcements that would triple the size of the 35,000-strong U.S. deployment. Thousands of young soldiers would be patrolling mud villages in the dangerous southern provinces of the country; as the only Western journalist based in the south, I was suddenly popular with U.S. officials eager to hear about the local politics and history.

I was ushered through the white marble foyer, past the stars chiseled into the wall to honor the dead, and into an elevator where my chaperone warned me not to touch any buttons. He pointed at a camera in the ceiling and told me the elevator would automatically take us to the correct floor. Past a heavy door, a gleaming conference table was set with little bowls of snacks and miniature glass bottles of Pepsi. Somebody must have measured the distance between the sodas, arranged with precision at regular intervals. I was surprised by the number of intelligence analysts who sat down opposite me: about a dozen, and many of them showed an impressive grasp of the politics in desolate places on the other side of the world. They would mention the name of an obscure tribal leader from a distant river valley and ask me which of his sons seemed most qualified to assume leadership after his recent death. These were sophisticated questions, underpinned by an unspoken assumption that America could defeat the Taliban if the U.S. devoted enough careful attention to the fight.

The United States and its allies have now given up on the idea of pushing back Afghanistan's insurgents—and mostly avoid talking about the war. These days, nobody organizes meetings for detailed analysis of tribal dynamics in the south. America is now focused on the logistics of withdrawal, about how to shut down nearly all the 800 international military bases once scattered throughout the country. The U.S.-led International Security Assistance Force will formally end its mission on December 31, 2014. It started thirteen years ago as a small force authorized by the United Nations to maintain security in Kabul and the surrounding areas and grew into a behemoth with a peak strength in 2011 of about 140,000 foreign soldiers. The military push was supported by more aid dollars than the U.S. spent on the Marshall Plan that revived Europe's economy after the Second World War. (The U.S. committed more than 109 billion dollars to Afghanistan, compared with 103 billion for the Marshall Plan, adjusted for inflation.)

Today, the number of deployed troops has been reduced to 34,000 and will get cut to fewer than half that strength in 2015 as a lingering presence with a narrow mandate to "train, advise, and assist" the Afghan security forces. Most of the remaining forces will be American, as U.S. diplomats struggle to persuade their NATO allies to contribute about 5,000 additional troops; right now, only about 2,000 non-U.S. troops are committed. When I talk to ambassadors in Kabul or the foreign ministers of Western countries who sent troops to join the U.S.-led coalition, there's a profound sense of exhaustion with the entire topic of Afghanistan. A senior advisor to one of the largest donors took off her glasses during one meeting and rubbed her eyes: "Mr. Smith," she said, "how can we stop pouring our money down a hole?" At a briefing in Brussels, an official interrupted my speech about how to improve the situation. The worsening trajectory of events cannot be halted, he argued: "Right now, it's all about containment." Later, he apologized that several of his colleagues could not attend the meeting because they were busy with more urgent discussions of Iraq and Syria. Recently, a senior U.S. official confided that he personally believes the surge of troops in Afghanistan was "a huge mistake."

Even as the West becomes disillusioned and turns away, the war grows more ferocious. This single fact should hang over any discussion of the country: the situation in Afghanistan—bad to begin with—has deteriorated further in the last two years. The number of violent incidents in the country increased about 15 to 20 percent in 2013 from the previous year and further escalation will almost certainly make 2014 the most violent year since the arrival of foreign troops. By one estimate, the number Afghan forces killed and injured was about 8,200 in 2013, as compared with about 9,500 insurgents, which far exceeded the body counts of previous years. We're still waiting to see the totals for 2014, but a Western security official told me the numbers this year have doubled, on both sides. A growing number of women and children are getting caught in the crossfire. The United Nations reports that civilian casualties rose 24 percent in the first half of 2014, compared with the same period a year earlier. For the first time since the UN started tracking numbers, more civilians are getting killed in ground battles than in other violence such as bombings—reflecting the growing confidence of the insurgents, who are increasingly confronting government forces in face-to-face firefights and relying less heavily on guerilla tactics.

So far, the largest battle with Taliban insurgents remains Operation Medusa in 2006, when international forces destroyed the bases and tunnels of Taliban entrenched west of Kandahar city. Ever since that moment, the insurgents have avoided massing in formations that could be targeted by air strikes—until now, as the Americans reduce their forces. We're seeing hundreds of insurgents swarm over the walls of remote outposts. Kandahar province, which serves as the main setting of this book, has followed the national trend of rising violence and slow erosion of government territory. Only about two dozen of the country's 400 district administration centers have been seriously challenged in the latest fighting season, but that number will probably increase as U.S. aircraft become less visible in the skies. I've often heard the Taliban rhetoric: an insurgent is asked if he would continue fighting without the presence of a foreign enemy and responds emphatically, "No." Unfortunately, that appears to be empty propaganda. It would be nice to imagine the Taliban giving up their war after the infidels go away, but so far it's not happening.

Nobody knows how the Afghan government will survive the growing conflict, and the prospect of anarchy or escalating civil war looms darker than ever on the horizon. Afghan security forces are still holding the insurgency at bay, for the moment, but they're getting pushed back into urban centers. America and its allies have built the Afghan forces into a bulwark against the rising insurgency, with perhaps 370,000 personnel on the payroll. A force of that size might be capable of maintaining at least the skeleton of the state, holding major cities and retaining enough firepower to blast through roadblocks on the highways. Yet it's unclear how much longer the U.S. government will continue supplying most of the $6 billion required each year for the Afghan security apparatus, and I'm afraid of what will happen when we stop paying the bills for thousands of armed men. Even if Congress decides to keep pouring money into the war, the security forces might collapse under the pressures of corruption and ethnic factionalism. I can't see any sign of that catastrophe right now—the number of offensives reported by the Afghan security forces is holding steady, meaning that officially there's no faltering in their willingness to fight—but it's hard for an outsider to read the fault lines. The other day I stood in line at the airport behind an

Afghan defense official whose wife was carrying a designer handbag worth about as much as a car. Could their wealth be connected to the complaints I hear from soldiers and police who say that bullets, fuel, and other supplies are sold on the black market? If so, would such corruption become fatal, or just lamentable? It's impossible to know until the fissures deepen.

Ethnic conflicts may also deepen in the coming years. Afghanistan got through the first round of presidential elections in April 2014 without much polarizing rhetoric, but the second round in June turned into a bruising squabble between ethnic factions. Most of the Pashtun support went to Ashraf Ghani, a Pashtun, while the Tajiks rallied around the half-Tajik candidate Abdullah Abdullah. This summer I watched young men racing through Kabul in cars spray-painted with graffiti, leaning out the windows with automatic rifles and green-white-and-black flags that represented a former government run by northern warlords. Those warlords, now transformed into politicians, were getting into minor gun battles as they feuded over the electoral contest. More serious violence almost happened in July, after Abdullah accused the Ghani camp of widespread fraud, and Abdullah's supporters pushed him to seize power by declaring a parallel state. Abdullah refrained, however, and ultimately conceded to Ghani in September after two visits by U.S. Secretary of State John Kerry, who secured deals between the two candidates on the formation of a unity government with Ghani as president and Abdullah in the freshly invented role of "chief executive officer." The fact that President Hamid Karzai surrendered power to Ghani—with Abdullah's participation—makes this process one of the most peaceful transitions of leadership in the history of Afghanistan. But we are still in the early days of the new presidency. Many analysts are worried that Ghani faces too many challenges: the treasury is almost empty, the insurgency is growing, and the new president has a worrisome number of enemies inside government. If the Taliban don't bring him down, his own allies might.

On the other hand, who cares about Afghanistan? This question was hardly ever raised when Osama bin Laden was alive, while Al-Qaeda remained the focus of our nightmares. We should recognize that the inferno in this country was, at least partly, fueled by a gnawing paranoia at the heart of Western society. The war against terrorism was not rooted in any rational calculation of how to handle the threat of major attacks such as 9/11. It was more about the ancient fear of barbarians outside the city gates, about our uneasy relationship with people who have different values, about the wealthy refusing to accept any violence spilling over their high walls. A cynical reading of the last dozen years would be that the rich world struggled, and failed, to contain the problems emanating from the poor.

Our failures in Afghanistan will remain as a stark example of a strategy that doesn't work. The U.S. intelligence analysts who spoke with me in that surreal meeting room in the summer of 2008, like everybody else in the war effort, probably did not have a realistic chance of success. No matter how well they studied their diagrams of prominent families in rural Afghanistan, no matter how carefully they read the history books, a basic assumption of the mission was flawed. They were relying on counter-insurgency theories that suggested American soldiers could walk into the world's most conservative villages, make friends, hunt their enemies, and build a better society. None of that proved successful. Perhaps it wasn't ever possible, after all.

Graeme Smith, Kabul
October 2014

INTRODUCTION

THE PROPHET'S CLOAK

We lost the war in southern Afghanistan and it broke my heart. When I started following the surges of troops into Kandahar and surrounding provinces in 2005, I felt excited by the idea that the international community could bring the whole basket of civilization to the south: peace, democracy, rule of law, all those things. Now the foreign troops are withdrawing. We have abandoned our lofty goals. Now it's all about damage control, about exercising options that limit embarrassment. The years when our armies pounded their way into the south will be remembered for heights of violence that exceeded the gruesome body count of the Taliban wars in the 1990s. Every wave of foreign troops coincided with more skirmishes, more assassinations, more bloodshed. Our attempts to set up a moderate Afghan administration gave birth to a regime that resembled neither a fully democratic government nor a group capable of ruling its entire territory. It failed the basic test of statehood: monopoly on the legitimate use of violence. Ordinary people turned to Taliban courts in search of justice less corrupt than the system imposed by outsiders. The insurgents were not defeated. We killed thousands of them, but their movement would not die.

It's not just that the foreigners gave up on dreams of a better future for southern Afghanistan, but that we're leaving a dangerous

1

mess. Like the old bombs and landmines buried all over the stricken landscape, the south is now waiting to explode. Many expect another civil war; others fear anarchy.

This moment when we hold our breath, watching anxiously as the foreign troops pull back, should serve as a time of reflection about our mistakes. Far away from the air-conditioned headquarters where the foreigners made their plans, all of the good intentions collided with reality. The result was tragic, and comic, and should be studied carefully. As this phase of the war lurches to a bitter conclusion, we might also pause to lament.

That kind of self-reflection is not likely to happen inside the North Atlantic Treaty Organization, because NATO claims victory. The greatest military alliance in human history will probably fail to think clearly about the biggest action it has ever attempted outside its own territory. It will say, accurately, that its soldiers fought bravely. Glossy brochures will get filled with images of aid projects. Photographs of smiling children in the green valleys of the north will misrepresent NATO's legacy, however, as long as violence rages in the dusty south. The historical fact is that nobody has ever ruled Afghanistan without holding Kandahar, the largest city in the southern region. This vital part of the country remains an open wound, needing somehow to get stitched up.

But what kind of surgery can repair a country? Our modern techniques resemble the early days of medicine, when the human body was poorly understood and doctors prescribed bloodletting, or drilled into skulls to treat madness. With the same ignorant faith in our methods, we now invade a country with crushing force and try to drain away ideas that we find dangerous, as if bombs and bullets could cure the illness of extremism. Not all intervention is misguided, of course; I was standing in Benghazi when the tanks of Colonel Moammar Gadhafi rolled toward us in the spring of 2011, and I've never felt so relieved to hear that NATO decided to take action. The Libyan war may yet emerge as a success story for the nascent science of healing sick countries with military force. Afghanistan looks like the opposite case: the patient may survive, but the doctor wasn't much help.

I wasn't always so skeptical about the effort. A different metaphor lured me into war: an idea that gave me real enthusiasm about the Afghan mission. Somebody told me a story of ancient mapmakers who struggled with the blank spaces on their vellum charts, the emptiness of places never visited by cartographers. They drew monsters at the edges of the known world, inventing fables about lions, serpents and basilisks that might devour an unwary traveller. "Here be dragons" read the most famous inscription. I can't remember the name of the soldier who told me this, but his words remain clear: "The thing about modern civilization," he said, "is that we can't stand those empty spots. The dragons fly out and bite you in the ass."

These blank spaces were what attracted me to southern Afghanistan. Once upon a time, the theory goes, it didn't matter if a state failed. Whole empires collapsed without affecting countries on the other side of the planet. Now the world is looped and threaded with shipping routes, flight paths, optical fibres across the sea floor. The fabric of civilization cannot tolerate frayed edges. You cannot leave a blank space like Afghanistan of the 1990s, ruled by zealots and neglected by the international community. You cannot scribble "Here be dragons" and walk away. The country gets infested by terrorists. Hijacked planes come streaking out of the sky. The dragons bite you in the ass.

I was vulnerable to that kind of grand vision, only twenty-six years old when I started covering Afghanistan as a newspaper correspondent, part of a generation of journalists whose careers started after September 11, 2001. I had visited many countries but always felt disappointed that none of them seemed foreign; there was always a Starbucks or a McDonald's around the corner. Afghanistan was excitingly different, a place where credit cards and calendars meant almost nothing. In the years after 2001, the country became a bustling hub for spies, aid workers and other ambitious expats. They appeared to be involved in something important, and during my first swoon of interest in the country I started to believe they were mending the tapestry of our globalized society; I hoped that their projects would draw the world toward a basic system of law and order. After the fourth or fifth round at a bar in Kabul, foreigners would make bets on which trouble spots we would tackle next. We took it for granted that modern ideas about health, education and agriculture could lift any society out of poverty. We assumed that those efforts could be protected against any threat by our glorious armies, the most sophisticated forces ever fielded. Any foreign journalist who claimed to be a dispassionate observer was kidding himself. The project involved "us," in the broadest sense. As reporters, we may have used the third person in our text, but in conversation we slipped easily into a collective "we" that included the whole panoply of foreigners.

More than forty countries contributed forces, and people from dozens of other countries were part of the civilian reconstruction effort. They talked enthusiastically about the latest theories on counter-insurgency and social development. This was not Vietnam; these were not grunts thrashing in the jungle. We had professionals. They mapped every inch of terrain with satellite guidance, turning badlands into databases with the precise location of battles, rumours, the names of leaders today and a thousand years ago. The officers read all the important books about Afghanistan and took notes in ruggedized laptops. When they squinted out at the mountains and valleys, they looked with electronic eyes. They watched feeds from robot planes drifting overhead, whose cameras panned smoothly even as the landscape below erupted with explosions. They swore constantly. They shit in bags and drank water the temperature of warm urine. But for all the hardships they rarely had reason to question their own supremacy. They smashed Taliban bases every day, while the opposite almost never happened. Most of the time, our guys went out and kicked ass, ticking the boxes on their mission objectives.

Military planners knew the difficulty of such wars and did not repeat history out of ignorance. Many of them could recite the lines written a century ago by Rudyard Kipling, about the lopsided math of guerilla war: "Two thousands pounds of education drops to a ten-rupee *jezail*." When a soldier heaved a rocket onto his shoulder and sent the device thundering down by remote control, he muttered, "There goes a Porsche," because the rocket cost about as much as a luxury car. Meanwhile, forensic teams catalogued the cheap ingredients of insurgent bombs: plastic pails, crop fertilizer, old mortar shells, a pressure switch made from a rusty carpenter's saw. It cost almost nothing to make a bomb that could throw a multi-ton vehicle like a child's toy, a marvel of engineering sailing into the empty sky. When fallen soldiers flew home to graveyards far away, their replacements needed years of expensive training, vastly more than the "two thousand pounds of education" required in Kipling's day. But insurgents buried their dead quickly, in shallow trenches; sons and brothers replaced them immediately.

The costs were high—but we had money to burn, or to make something burn. The United States had enjoyed the longest economic boom in its history during the 1990s, and its allies had likewise flourished. It's easy now to forget the fear that pervaded the Western world—but in September 2001, I stopped at a gas station in rural Pennsylvania on my way toward the field where the fourth hijacked plane had plowed into the earth, and the guy who filled my tank made a prediction: "We gonna kill some ragheads." He was right, and a lot of the killing would happen in Afghanistan.

The war may have felt justified in our guts, but it played out in southern Afghanistan like a farce. The foreign troops seized control of the former hideouts used by Osama bin Laden and his followers, and yes, it felt satisfying to clamber around the rubble of the al-Qaeda camp that we all recognized from grainy images of jihadi training videos on the evening news. We posed for pictures on the crumbling ruins of Tarnak Farms and wondered if the stories about bin Laden plotting the attacks within those very walls were true. But the al-Qaeda camps had long since disappeared by the time I arrived in the south, following a massive influx of NATO troops. The world's great armies were not gathering in southern Afghanistan to chase a bunch of terrorists. They set themselves a more sweeping agenda: to bring a measure of calm, to improve lives, to establish law and order. Sometimes they succeeded: child mortality declined, more women survived childbirth. A new generation of Afghans now enjoys much greater access to education than its predecessor, despite the fact that many of the new schools have been burned down or converted into livestock sheds. A cascade of foreign aid brought some of the trappings of modernity to parts of the country that had never seen television, cellphones and the Internet.

Not much of the progress feels enduring, however. The Afghan economy is a bubble created with war money. It's impossible to drive the streets without seeing advertisements for quixotic development projects, long forgotten, the flaking paint on the misspelled placards having outlasted any local memory of what the foreigners were trying to achieve. I met a brave American farmer who accepted a US government contract to plant pomegranate trees in dangerous areas, an operation he nicknamed "combat farming." Each sapling was duly counted as progress toward the goal of promoting legal agriculture instead of opium cultivation, but the farmer was under no illusions about whether his little trees would survive long enough to bear fruit. The slightest disturbance churned the dirt into dust, like feathery plumes of talcum powder, and most disturbances in Kandahar were not minor. Aircraft dropped bombs; the Taliban planted crude explosives underground; military convoys broke across the fields to avoid the mined roads. War erases progress, leaves no trace of improvement.

As the violence climbed, a military spokesman or general would often try to explain by saying, "We're kicking the hornet's nest." Yet another metaphor, in a land of storytellers, and the logic of it always bothered me. At one point I interrupted a senior general and asked,

"Sir, is there any time in real life when it would make sense to kick a hornet's nest?" The general laughed. "Clearly you've never owned a cottage," he said, and I went away wondering how many owners of vacation properties actually make this mistake. It was amazing how often the military repeated this message: after the death of a soldier, his superiors would solemnly face the television cameras and explain that his unit had been involved in urgent work to clear a path for peace and democracy, and that sometimes kicking the hornet's nest gets you stung. I'm always reminded of this whenever I hear the latest news about faltering peace talks with the Taliban. We're trying to negotiate a graceful exit, and the key phrase has become "political solution." But how do you negotiate with an angry swarm, after the nest is kicked?

Nobody who deals with these questions does so without looking tired or angry, and some of the greatest minds on Afghanistan policy are also the most depressed. I met a former US Marine recently, with his wife and daughter, three months old, burbling in her mother's arms. We talked about how our experiences of war had opened our eyes, and I repeated something I had read about Plato's ideal education, that young men must see the battlefield as part of their grooming for adulthood. The Marine looked at me skeptically. There's something about Afghanistan that requires colourful figures of speech, so I offered this one: "It was like living in a kindergarten and toddling out into the hallway and down the stairs and into the boiler room, leaving the nice pretty world and seeing all of the dark scary machines underneath." The soldier nodded and said: "Yeah, but here's a better way of saying it. The whole thing was like eating at McDonald's, and then going and visiting a slaughterhouse." He added: "Because it was a meat grinder." By coincidence, I had ordered a hamburger at the restaurant where we were sitting, which arrived moments later. I ate with difficulty.

Writing this book tears me apart sometimes. I keep typing curses into the text, streams of invective that I go back and delete, feeling ashamed of my failure to find better words than *fuck fuck fuck*. But I also need you to feel the profanity, because there is something profane about the errors we committed in Afghanistan. The Pennsylvania gas jockey was probably right: a certain amount of killing was inevitable after 9/11. Al-Qaeda started a fight, and anybody who lives in Afghanistan would understand the logic of punishing misdeeds. Southern tribes limit the scale of their revenge, however; similar to that ancient law, "an eye for an eye," tribal rules usually keep the retribution to a crude ratio of one-to-one. We have more complicated rules of war these days, with legal definitions of "proportionality," or "excessiveness," and we can argue endlessly about international law— but it was impossible to live at the throbbing heart of the war, falling asleep to the sound of helicopters and woken by explosions, without feeling like the whole thing was too much. It did not seem like an effective way to achieve our goals, but merely a recipe for fighting and fighting, and more fighting. Over a decade of war in Afghanistan has settled nothing, and that in itself is profoundly unsettling.

It's impossible to grasp the sheer stupidity of the war with detached analysis. I have laughed out loud at charts listing the number of Taliban forces arrayed against Afghan troops and international forces; so many of those numbers are wild guesses. I've even had a look at some of the US Central Intelligence Agency's district-by-district assessments of the situation, containing only somewhat more educated guesses. Nor can you get much of a picture by thinking about these things on the level of theory, or metaphors—dragons, hornets or surgeons. When friends and family asked about Afghanistan, I often found myself with my mouth open, not making a sound, caught on the edge of speech.

My usual excuse is that I'm not qualified to talk about the whole country, only the troubled south. I visited southern Afghanistan seventeen times from 2005 to 2011, working independently of the international forces and also spending time with US, Canadian, British and Dutch troops. None of that experience gives me the right to summarize the broader situation in the country, but the southern region does serve as a useful case study. It's where the war became most intense; it's where policymakers focused much of their attention; it's where the policy most obviously went wrong. The world needs to understand what happened and draw lessons from this debacle—and the only way of reaching those conclusions is by visceral immersion. You must get down in the dust and shit. I spent a lot of days smelling the death, getting sunburns. The charred flesh of suicide bombers got stuck in the treads of my shoes. I was shot at, bombed, rocketed, mortared, chased through narrow streets. I took photographs, recorded audio, filled a suitcase with leather-bound notebooks. I filed the material into folders on my computer, and later took a leave of absence from my job so I could sit quietly and let the echoes settle. I tried to pick out scenes and bits of dialogue that might help you understand. This was a healthy process. The nightmares faded, and I stopped obsessing about the tactical properties of every room. Eventually I could attend a fireworks show without feeling nauseous. My anxiety eased, not only because I spent time away from the battlefields but also because this writing project left me feeling less burdened. I could stop giving angry speeches about the war as I distilled my experience into these pages.

Looking back on my time in Kandahar, trying to make sense of it, I often think about a meandering conversation I had while researching the holiest object in the south: the Prophet's Cloak. Outsiders often wondered why the insurgents fought so fiercely for Kandahar, why a ramshackle city of maybe half a million people was considered the spiritual heart of the country. Part of the answer is locked in a silver box, itself nested inside two wooden chests, hidden from public view inside a sealed shrine in the middle of the city. It's a cloak, reputedly presented by God to the Prophet Mohammed. The founder of Afghanistan, Ahmad Shah Durrani, took the cloak during one of his sweeps through Central Asia and brought it back to what was then his capital city, Kandahar, in 1768.

The cloak played a central role in Afghanistan's history, and continues to hold symbolic power, but getting a clear description of the cloth itself proved incredibly hard. Mullah Omar, leader of the Taliban, is among the few politicians who has removed the cloak from its box, brandishing the cloth in front of his followers in 1996, but few people involved in that ceremony remained in Kandahar, or wanted to talk about it. The only person I could find who had touched the cloak was Mullah Masood Akhundzada, who inherited the duty of protecting the sacred object from a line of ancestors who have guarded the ornate blue-tiled shrine for more than two centuries. Known officially as Keeper of the Cloak, the solemn young man was only in his thirties but already had grey in his beard. I asked him: How big is the cloak? "Large," he said. Bigger than your outstretched arms? "It changes shape." He claimed that the cloak was woven from the hair of the "Camels of Paradise," and did not have any seams. "It's hard to describe," he said. "It's very soft, like silk. You cannot say what colour it is, because many people see different colours."

By the time of my conversation with the Keeper of the Cloak, I'd spent enough years in Kandahar to feel that his answers were appropriate for such an inscrutable part of the world. Of course the holiest object in this land would be described to an outsider as shapeless, seamless and colourless. It was something that must be witnessed first-hand, like so much of Kandahar. The same thing applies to the war itself. I have no clear policy recommendations, no succinct lessons about the conduct of foreign interventions. I have only these memories, shapeless and seamless. It's something you must see for yourself.

Highway 1 to Kandahar

CHAPTER 1

THE ROAD TO KANDAHAR SEPTEMBER 2005

A grim lineup waited for the flight to Kabul. The passengers were short, dark men with fake leather jackets and broken noses, and many could have used a shower. I'd never seen such a bedraggled crowd in an airport; the plane itself looked like a survivor, too, as if the aircraft had been roughed up by thugs. My seat cushion slipped from its frame, and something dripped from the air vents. I would later recognize this as typical scenery aboard Ariana, the national airline of Afghanistan. I tried to ignore it, and focus on my reading.

My editors at *The Globe and Mail* had assigned me to cover the 2005 parliamentary elections, and like many correspondents who drop into the country for quick visits, I clutched a stack of printouts in hopes of cramming the story into my brain. My reading materials from that day reveal the naïveté of the international community in the early years of the war. Nobody wrote much about the Taliban at that point, dismissing them as a broken movement, reduced to small bands of gunmen scattered in the mountains. Instead, my sheaf of reports focused on the foreigners' optimistic vision of a new Afghanistan. The lead sentence of a *Washington Post* feature declared that "the country is gearing up enthusiastically for a massive exercise in postwar democracy." A United Nations map showed how millions of refugees were streaming back across the border, returning home after decades of civil war. I'd even found a paper titled "Safeguarding Afghanistan's Audio-Visual Heritage," in which the Ministry of Information and Culture declared an "urgent" need to scan digital copies of government archives as part of the effort to build a new, efficient, modern bureaucracy in Kabul.

It's painful to read those papers now, years later. They capture a moment in history when foreigners and Afghan-born expatriates crowded into Kabul to build a democracy. In those initial years after the United States and its allies expelled the Taliban from the capital in 2001, a dream blossomed. It was the fervent hope that one of the world's poorest countries, savaged by a generation of war, might flourish with a heavy dose of foreign assistance. Once upon a time in Afghanistan, it wasn't crazy to say that one of Kabul's top priorities should be digital recordkeeping.

At the time, most critics said the international effort should be bigger and tougher. There was a widespread feeling that the Iraq War had distracted the United States, leaving Afghanistan without enough troops to enforce the central government's rule. Nobody believed that remnants of the former Taliban regime could fill the power vacuum in the countryside; instead, most attention focused on the warlords who had helped US forces defeat the Taliban. "Warlords, militias, and brigands dominate the entire country," declared the most sharply written paper in my stack of readings, a report by Human Rights Watch. Like many others, the advocacy group claimed that the lawless zones needed to be filled with foreign troops. Under the heading, "Wanted: Peacekeepers," the report said that villagers would welcome a major deployment of forces in the rural countryside. "Afghans outside Kabul have been clamoring for two years to share in the benefits of international security assistance." That statement seemed logical. Why wouldn't villagers want the same advantages enjoyed in the capital?

I paused my reading to squint out a window for my first look at Afghanistan. The descent into Kabul was steep because of concerns about surface-to-air missiles, and while no passenger aircraft had been shot down in recent history, the pilots were taking no chances. We stayed low over the mountains, close enough to see the texture of the white snowcaps, then swept across a rocky landscape rich with colours: rust, grey, orange, pink, sage green and endless shades of brown. I had pictured Afghanistan as a moonscape of rocks and dust, so it was surprising to see that farmers had carved terraces into the mountain slopes and that trees dotted the crests. Lush fields surrounded the rivers. There was a beautiful moment as we hurtled toward the runway, when I could see an expanse of farmland on the outskirts of Kabul and mountains rising into the hazy distance. I climbed down from the plane feeling confident that my in-flight readings had given me a handle on the story. This was a country recovering from war. Foreigners were helping, but they needed more troops. It was wonderfully simple.

A soft-spoken young man, the cousin of a colleague's acquaintance, met me at the airport and took me to the Mustafa Hotel, a busy place in those days before suicide bombs scared off most of the customers. The bartender showed me the tattoo on his neck, a dotted line with the words *Cut Here*, a reference to the videos of beheadings we had all seen on the Internet. He proudly pointed to the bullet holes that decorated his establishment. Kabul seemed like a Wild West outpost from a boy's imagination, a chaotic town at the edge of the world. A flak jacket was waiting for me at the hotel, and after I tore open the courier package I snapped a photo of myself looking like a real war correspondent, I thought— standing in a snowdrift of foam packing. I seem excessively clean in that photograph: other journalists had advised me to get scruffy, grow a beard so I could blend in among Afghans, but on that first visit I wasn't fooling anybody. My translator told me not to worry: foreigners in Kabul didn't require disguises in those days, and certainly no flak jackets. It was safe to walk around in jeans and a T-shirt.

Not that the city was entirely calm. The next day, I visited the headquarters of the Electoral Complaints Commission (ECC), which had responsibility for the most controversial part of the upcoming vote: deciding which candidates to disqualify because they refused to give up their private armies. This was a difficult task, because many of the candidates were notoriously violent characters, and the United Nations established the ECC only four months before voting day. The staff looked at thousands of complaints and disqualified a small number of low-profile candidates, but didn't touch the big players. The head of the commission, a veteran United Nations consultant named Grant Kippen, cheerfully admitted that he didn't have enough resources, but said the electoral process was going ahead smoothly under the circumstances. He invited me into his courtyard for a lunch of rice, chicken and diet soda. Relaxing under parasols beside flowering bushes, it was easy to think that this white-haired diplomat had the situation under control. Mr. Kippen, a dignified man in a pressed shirt and dress pants, described the election as part of the broader effort to make the Kabul government the only legitimate authority in the country. Yes, he said, many of the candidates stood accused of horrible crimes—election posters and billboards advertised newly minted politicians who had killed hundreds of people in civil wars—but the international community seemed ready to accept these militia leaders into government in hopes of disarming them and making them part of the system. Afghanistan was making a transition from a patchwork of fiefdoms where strongmen hold sway, Mr. Kippen said, into a country where rule of law applies in the whole territory.

As he spoke, however, the rule of law appeared to be fraying in the streets, and his words were drowned out by shouts as somebody screamed into a loudspeaker. A crowd was chanting *Allahu Akbar*, God is great, and uniformed Afghan police clomped around the metal roofs of the ECC buildings. The officers yelled from the rooftops and pointed their guns down at the crowd, while Mr. Kippen squinted up at the wall bristling with barbed wire that separated him from the protesters, as if calculating the odds of a protester—or maybe a hand grenade—coming over the top. A well-muscled security advisor with a flat-topped haircut approached our table.

"So how many unhappy candidates do we have outside?" Mr. Kippen asked. "Two?"

"No, three," said the advisor with a German accent, adding: "I'm just glad I know where the American military rations are hidden in the basement."

The commission staff was kept inside for their own safety, but I went outside to see the protesters. They were supporters of disqualified candidates, minor figures but still capable of raising a ruckus. Pickup trucks and sport-utility vehicles jammed the downtown street, honking. A throng of men pushed down the dirt alley that led to the ECC's entry gate, resisted by a swarm of police and plainclothes Afghan security agents. Officers formed a human chain across the alley, linking arms and trying to hold the mob, as women and children peeked from behind the curtains of nearby houses. I wriggled my way toward a man who was obviously leading the protest, a big guy with a salt-and-pepper beard who was sweating and screaming at police officers. The argument grew more heated until they were physically tussling, with officers grabbing the man's white robes and holding his arms. I thought he was being arrested until they abruptly released him and he retreated to the main road, still shouting, and his supporters dispersed.

Walking away from the fracas, he mopped his brow with a handkerchief and introduced himself to me. He said that he was trying to make the authorities understand that election officials had wrongly disqualified his brother. Like so many other candidates, the man's brother had been a militia leader who fought against the Soviet occupation in the 1980s, but claimed to have given up his weapons to comply with the election rules. That probably wasn't true, as most strongmen kept their gun stashes, but his brother complained with justification that bigger militia leaders were allowed to remain on the ballot. "They robbed people's homes, they killed lots of people. And they're still on the lists. How can that be?" he said, before climbing into a pickup truck and roaring away.

Mr. Kippen's local Afghan staff was reluctant to translate what the protesters had been chanting, until they finally admitted that one of the slogans was "Death to Grant Kippen." But he saw the protest as proof that the ECC was doing its job, removing disruptive figures from the election. For me, the lesson was more visceral. Inside the walls of Kabul's institutions, among the rose bushes and trim lawns, it was easy to imagine a functioning state. Outside, where the police sweated through their uniforms and struggled to keep control, state-building looked more difficult.

I wanted to get out of Kabul and see the country. Nobody knows what percentage of Afghans live in cities because the last census, in 1979, was never finished, but it's a fair guess that most of the population is rural. The capital city did not represent Afghanistan, with foreigners crammed into the downtown, blocking traffic with their sport-utility vehicles, doing business inside sandbag fortifications and drinking at bars with no admittance for Afghans. There was talk about an upcoming surge of NATO forces into the south, so I planned to go that way. I stayed up late writing a story, and fell asleep in my clothes for a couple of hours before my translator woke me in the dimness before dawn. He wanted to get an early start because Highway 1 was considered safe in the daylight but he worried about robbers after sunset. I struggled to the car in the same blue linen shirt I'd been wearing for two days. That shirt clearly marked me as a foreigner, and is a detail of the story that surprises people working in Afghanistan these days. In the following years it became unthinkably dangerous for a foreigner to drive from Kabul to Kandahar, much less wearing Western clothing and taking snapshots with a big Nikon.

A wave of nostalgia hits me now, looking at my photographs from that road trip. We sailed along fresh asphalt, one of the foreigners' biggest gifts to the country, an artery between major cities paved smooth at a cost of hundreds of millions. The road stretched down out of the jagged foothills of the Hindu Kush and into the scrublands of the south. As the land became flatter, and the air hotter, my translator turned around in the front seat with a big grin. "Now you are seeing the real Afghanistan," he said, gesturing at a vast tract of nothing. He wasn't talking about the landscape, of course; he was expressing the feelings of many Pashtuns, that their homelands in the south and east somehow represent a more authentic side of Afghanistan. Members of the biggest ethnic group in the country sometimes even refer to this zone with a different name— Pashtunistan—and many feel patriotic about this country that does not exist. Our driver said the journey to Kandahar had previously required twice as much time, a bruising ordeal along rutted tracks, and he seemed pleased that international aid had cut the drive to an easy five or six hours. (In the following years, blast craters and checkpoints pushed the travel time back up, to ten or eleven hours.)

My translator didn't seem worried about drawing attention to ourselves as I dangled my camera out the window, although as we reached the outskirts of Kandahar city he suggested that I slip into local clothing. My clumsy fingers made a mess of the traditional cloth belt, so my pants kept falling down. I insisted on wearing my leather hiking boots, which spoiled the disguise, but nobody seemed to mind the presence of such a strange foreigner. My photo archive from those days show I was free to roam around the south without fear, pausing to watch grinning boys leap into a canal, and spray each other with water hoses at a gas station. Further southeast, in the border district of Spin Boldak, I spent a full two hours walking the streets and taking pictures for a story about the disputed border between Afghanistan and Pakistan. Wandering that town without protection would later become a serious risk for foreigners, but in 2005 what drove me onward was not fear but, surprisingly, boredom.

In fact, most of the stories I researched on that trip seem unimportant in retrospect. I wrote about the struggles of an aspiring local filmmaker, photographed soldiers giving plastic jewelry to girls and earnestly reported the pronouncement of a top Canadian commander who claimed the insurgency could be defeated within two years. Nobody talked about the armed opponents of the government as a serious obstacle. Military officials preferred to discuss their plans for boys' soccer camps, or girls' essay contests. I initially slept within the secure confines of a military base on the northeast side of Kandahar city but eventually moved into a guesthouse. It was the sort of place where I could stroll out the front gates and bump into colleagues at a nearby restaurant, or browse the carpets for sale at a downtown shop. Catering to foreign visitors, the shops displayed carpets with American flags and woven scenes of planes hitting the twin towers. The only security advice from my translator was, "Mr. Graeme, please do not walk the streets at night."

I even paused for some tourism on my final day in the city, slipping off my boots and padding around in my socks on the marble floor of a mausoleum for Mirwais Khan Hotak, one the ancient rulers of Afghanistan. Shafts of sunlight came through the pointed windows, playing on the intricate designs in blue, green, orange and gold. Later in the afternoon, I lounged on a terrace of trim grass near a bridge over the Arghandab River. My translator took me up the Forty Steps, an ancient stairway carved into a small mountain west of the city. The steps seemed built for giants, and I clambered on all fours like a child on a staircase, up the spine of the rocky outcrop. At the top we found a cave hacked into an open-sided cube, the walls chiselled with ancient Persian script, apparently a tribute to Mughal conquests. On that day, two Afghan soldiers sat near the precipice and poured each other tiny glasses of tea from a brass pot. They had a couple of Kalashnikov rifles, but the weapons were nestled among cardboard boxes at the back of the cave. Their job was to watch for signs of trouble, but they hadn't bothered to turn on their military radio, a bulky device in a canvas knapsack. Instead, they seemed content to sip their tea as afternoon sun slanted over the expanse of green fields. Kandahar looked peaceful.

Still, I wondered if the foreign presence was useful. That evening, back in my guesthouse, I flipped on my voice recorder and made a note. "I've had a song stuck in my head for the last week or so," I said. "It's by Laurie Anderson, the New York performance artist. She pauses for a moment in the song, then says, 'And what I really want to know is: Are things getting better, or are they getting worse?'" Before leaving, I put that question to one of my new Afghan friends. In those days, 2005, it was a relevant topic of debate: some people still seriously argued in favour of the new government, while others felt nostalgia for the Taliban. I asked my friend to collect his thoughts for an audio recording. He stopped to think, then gestured at me to turn on the machine. "By the name of God," he started, and gave his full name, identifying himself as a doctor at the city hospital. "Now I'm going to tell you some advantages and disadvantages of the Taliban leaving Afghanistan." Speaking in a well-organized essay format, he listed the benefits of the foreigners' presence: cellular telephone networks; education for boys and girls; new paved roads; freedom to watch television and movies; and economic prosperity. He took a breath and continued with the disadvantages of the current system: inflation, corruption and drug addiction. He went on at length about how violence had recently increased, along with blackmail, robbery and extortion. Such problems were rare during the Taliban regime, he said, but he concluded that the balance was positive. "It will be good," he said. "I think it's getting a little better."

My heart aches, now, listening to his careful optimism. There was a twinkle in his eyes in those days. He looked good, his hair neatly trimmed, and he spent his evenings at a local gym to slim the belly that he considered an embarrassing sign of middle age. He had a wife and two children, a small family by Afghan standards. He was proud of his wife's literacy. He had an opportunity to take a second wife, an attractive nurse at the hospital, but he preferred Western-style monogamy. ("It is better to have peace in the family," he said.) The fact that he discussed his domestic life with somebody outside his family, much less an infidel foreigner, was a sign of his willingness to break with tradition. He represented a fresh generation of professionals that prospered in the new Afghanistan. He could name every bone in the human body in five languages and still hungered for knowledge, asking me to bring medical books on my next visit. He opened a pharmacy in the city, and his brother set up an engineering firm. I spent happy afternoons with his nephews as they practised English and discussed the fighting styles of Jackie Chan and Spider-Man.

But later, as the killings increased, his brother the engineer shut his office on the edge of Kandahar city and moved toward the safer heart of downtown. Over the following years he moved again, and again, and finally ended up in a high-walled compound near a US special forces base. Even there, in the shadow of the foreign troops, the engineer wasn't safe from the rising chaos. One of his nephews was kidnapped, and his family had to pay a heavy ransom—hundreds of thousands of US dollars, a sum that impoverished his clan. My friend the doctor carried the ransom money himself, handing over the cash to a masked man and receiving in return a hand-drawn symbol in a corner of a crumpled note—which he later traded for his nephew at a different location. Another of his relatives was shot by unknown assailants, but survived. The engineer had already retreated from projects in the rural districts, limiting his work to the safer confines of the city, but the kidnapping and shooting drained his energy. Finally he shuttered his Kandahar business and moved to Kabul. The doctor pulled back, too, slowly becoming less visible on the streets, and the last time I saw him in Kandahar, in early 2009, he looked like an old man. His hair was greasy and unkempt, and his eyes suggested he hadn't had a proper sleep in weeks. He spoke urgently about moving away. The simple prediction he gave me four years earlier—"It will be good"—turned out to be false.

I met him again in 2011, after he escaped to Dubai with his family. We strolled through a shopping mall and he seemed to enjoy the stretches of polished marble, the giant aquariums, the coloured fountains that danced to music. He showed me his favourite ride at the mall's amusement park, a flight simulator, but refused to join the children who screamed past on roller coasters, which he considered "too dangerous." Kandahar had exhausted his appetite for risk. Having saved himself from Afghanistan, he looked back at the foreigners' intervention with none of the equivocation he felt in 2005. He concluded that the benefits were outweighed by drawbacks: violence, instability, corruption and the dangerously fragile nature of the new regime. On a recent trip home, he had noticed Afghan soldiers cruising the roads in new air-conditioned vehicles with the windows rolled up, something he saw as a metaphor for the security forces' lack of concern for anything except their own comfort. "The army men should have the windows open, looking at the city and seeing what is happening," he said. "Instead they are enjoying themselves." The same attitude permeated the Kabul government, he said, noting that many of the top officials had visas and passports that would allow them to leave Afghanistan. "If something bad happens they will run away," he said. With only a hint of self-reproach, he added: "They will run away, like me."

The young translator who first welcomed me in 2005 and took me on that road trip to Kandahar has also escaped the country. (He now lives in Canada.) The astonishing freedom we enjoyed on that initial journey can only be understood in contrast with the way conditions deteriorated on the Kabul–Kandahar highway in subsequent years. By the spring of 2006, my translator looked at me like I was joking when I suggested a road trip. No, he explained, the Taliban have started running checkpoints on the main highway. Gunmen stop cars and frisk passengers, looking for evidence of collaboration with the so-called infidel occupation; you would be kidnapped or killed. But he reluctantly agreed that it might be possible to travel by bus, because in those days the Taliban did not have a strong grip on the highway and didn't want the hassle of searching bus passengers, most of whom would be ordinary Afghans. This time I couldn't wear Western clothing because he was worried that our fellow passengers might use their cellphones to tip off the Taliban. So I shambled up to the bus station without looking anybody in the eye or speaking a word, fully disguised in local clothing. My translator shepherded me onto the old coach like a mentally impaired child and tucked me away in a window seat near the back. We sat tense and silent for several hours, watching the beige emptiness of the south give way to rolling hills as we drove into the central region. When my translator recognized the landscape of Wardak province he visibly relaxed and informed me that Taliban were no longer a threat. We started chatting in English, which caused a sensation among the other passengers. People turned around in their seats to stare at the strange presence of a Westerner who had passed himself off as an Afghan. Some of the looks weren't welcoming, but my translator assured me that we had emerged from the danger zone, having escaped Taliban territory and entered the security bubble around Kabul. The final hour of the drive passed easily.

That was my last road trip between Afghanistan's two main cities. By the following year, 2007, I didn't need to ask my staff about security on the highway. Wardak province was no longer a place where people relaxed, as the growing violence littered the road with burned hulks of military vehicles and fuel tankers. That province became such a Taliban stronghold that an insurgent later bragged to me that his men had burrowed tunnels into Wardak's mountains and lined them with fresh concrete to hold all their weapons and ammunition. Foreigners travelled by plane when going to southern Afghanistan.

The foolhardy ones who risked the roads quickly became examples of the rising danger, as happened in July 2007 when the Taliban captured a busload of Korean missionaries on the highway to Kandahar and held them for ransom. Two were killed and twenty-one released, with the Taliban reportedly getting about a million dollars for each of them. The highway also became risky for Afghans whose jobs brought them into contact with foreigners, and they started taking extraordinary precautions to avoid getting caught at insurgent checkpoints. An Afghan who managed a professional office in Kandahar once pointed to a wicker basket on his desk that contained nothing but three cellphones. Before travelling, he explained, his employees stripped themselves of any item that could identify them and put on shabby wristwatches and shoes. They removed the memory chips from their cellphones and replaced them with new ones whose contact lists contained only three names, and each number rang one of the phones in the basket. His employees introduced themselves as religious students, and the manager said he was accustomed to taking calls from Taliban checkpoints, responding with a gruff impersonation of a mullah who doesn't like being bothered to confirm the bona fides of his followers. He chuckled at his own cleverness, but he looked tired every time I saw him. Despite the precautions, his employees were still getting killed on a regular basis.

For those of us who survived Afghanistan, the bright shine of the early years remains haunting. All of the old hands have stories about the freedoms they enjoyed in that golden period, roughly 2002 to 2005, and many have regrets about how events later unfolded. At a dinner party a few years ago, I sat across from Francesc Vendrell, who served as the European Union's special representative to Afghanistan after the collapse of the Taliban regime. He ranked among the most senior diplomats in the country by the time of his departure in 2008, with access to the inner workings of Kabul. By all accounts he was a voice of conscience, but I was still curious about whether he felt sadness about his role in the machinery of war. Our dinner companions grew quieter as Mr. Vendrell fingered the stem of his wineglass. "Not sadness," he said. "Anger." Many people around the table, all of them with years of experience in Afghanistan, nodded their heads. It wasn't only the war hawks who called for a large-scale invasion of the south and other areas beyond Kabul; many big-hearted humanitarians had pushed for intervention. But whose dreams were we chasing in southern Afghanistan? Ordinary people in the country did not care about projects such as safeguarding their "audio-visual heritage," and most importantly, Afghans outside of the capital were not clamouring for "the benefits of international security assistance." The road to Kandahar was paved with the best intentions, but the foreigners had no idea what Afghans wanted. That disconnect was about to have horrendous consequences for the south.

Afghan security contractor injured in a suicide bombing

CHAPTER 2

THE SURGE APRIL 2006

Kandahar felt menacing when I returned in spring. Police check-points appeared on the streets I had wandered so casually on my previous visit, and military vehicles chugged past with soldiers yelling at people to keep their distance. Thousands of troops from NATO countries were arriving to reinforce the Americans, and the whole city vibrated with their energy. I was sleeping in a tent at Camp Nathan Smith in Kandahar, in quarters then located right beside a helicopter pad, and my earplugs did nothing against the sound of rotors that was more like a body massage than something audible. The caffeine was keeping me awake, too. I had started what would become my standard routine in Kandahar, visiting local business-men, elders and other notables, and the ritual was usually the same: take off your sandals, sit down on the floor and drink something caffeinated. I got suspicious looks when I asked for sweet milk tea, which I enjoyed in northern Pakistan; it turned out that people in Kandahar prefer green tea, and they also felt certain that Pakistani agents were lurking around, stirring up trouble—so I stopped asking for milky tea. Usually I didn't need to ask for anything, because they assumed a foreigner would drink Pepsi. Either way, it was a steady chemical buzz. There was also an adrenaline buzz, from my first real taste of war. It would later seem normal to hear explosions in the city, but the first time it happened I slammed my laptop shut and rushed out of my tent. Brown smoke was rising in the hot air, several storeys high. This was still such a novelty for the foreign troops that a Canadian soldier was standing on the roof of a concrete bunker nearby, shading his eyes and peering over the barricades for a better view, and I scrambled up to join him. We couldn't see much, so I jumped down, called my driver and rushed toward the column of smoke. Only two minutes' drive from the base, the blast had left a giant hole in a mud wall and mangled a police car. Nobody survived. Firemen had just finished soaking the wreck, and it steamed in the harsh light of early afternoon. I would see a long parade of similar scenes in the years that followed, but at the time the drama of the bombing provoked a gush of words in my diary about the sense of urgency that comes with working so close to danger:

> *Everybody is risking their lives, and everybody believes they're saving Afghanistan—and, frankly, saving the world from the kind of Afghanistan that has proven to be so dangerous in the past. At the moment, it's unclear whether they're winning the war. But the stakes are high, the battle is on, and the whole camp seems to vibrate with an energy like the thudding rotors of a helicopter. There's no time for sleep.*

Those were heady days for the NATO surge. The Canadians went first, sending twenty-three hundred soldiers to Kandahar, while Britain was preparing thirty-three hundred troops for neighbouring Helmand province. NATO had not yet assumed formal responsibility for southern Afghanistan, so the planeloads of troops fell under the command of US Operation Enduring Freedom. (Standard joke: "How are you?" "Enduring freedom.") This first wave started with something called "shaping operations," trying to clear a path for other European troops who would arrive in the coming months. American commanders worried that NATO would take a soft approach, so they picked fights with Taliban in every corner of southern Afghanistan before the handover from US to NATO leadership of the mission. Canadian and US troops roamed hundreds of kilometres in search of enemies, and after one such hunting expedition, the commander of the Canadian battle group sounded disappointed when his forces came back without meeting resistance. "We actually were very surprised so far that they have not shot at us," said Lieutenant-Colonel Ian Hope. The colonel then suggested that the insurgents ran away when they saw the "professional bearing" of his heavily armed troops.

The surge also brought an influx of special forces, who appeared to operate with even more blithe confidence. One evening at Kandahar Air Field (KAF), a female contractor told me she had a stash of Singaporean beer in her compound and would be drinking with some US commandos who had been helping her build a wooden deck for her living quarters. It wasn't typical for America's elite forces to volunteer for handyman jobs in remote corners of the camp, but they seemed eager to please a good-looking woman. The commandoes were not supposed to speak with reporters, but after a few beers they started to talk about a set of military orders known as the Rules of Engagement, or ROEs, which describe when a soldier may attack. The commandoes' stories indicated that they saw the ROEs as *suggestions*, not laws. They described an Apache helicopter flying near a mountain, where a special-forces team had spotted an armed man lurking in the crags. The team on the ground got there first, shooting him in the face and chest. The Apache gunner felt cheated of a kill, however, and as he watched the man tumbling down the mountain, his rifle still strapped to his body and flopping randomly, the gunner declared over the radio that the corpse had aimed a weapon at the aircraft—allowing him, under his rules of engagement, to blast it. Bullets sawed the body in half. The special forces guys thought this was hilarious. I had to ask for an explanation of the joke: If a soldier could shoot an Afghan for being in the wrong place, why did the Apache gunner need to worry about identifying a pointed gun? A heavily muscled commando cracked a beer and replied: "Different rules for us. We basically shoot a guy if we don't like the way he's scratching his face."

That kind of swagger was also displayed in background briefings. A senior British officer at the multinational brigade headquarters clicked through slides showing the military analysis of every district in the south, dotted with multicoloured symbols indicating the strength of the Afghan government in six categories: politics, military, economy, information, infrastructure and social issues. Many of the dots were coloured green or orange, showing a positive assessment of the situation, with some outlying areas shaded grey to acknowledge that the military didn't know their status. "Broadly, it's not a bad picture," the officer said. NATO's analysis at the time was not particularly different from the broad consensus, because most sources agreed that the security environment was not terribly dangerous at the start of 2006. That was the last time journalists were shown the military's assessment of those metrics in the south, as the situation began deteriorating and NATO started to carefully ration information about its analysis of the war, but during that initial period we got a clear view of the military's hubris. The NATO troops radiated a missionary zeal for bringing the modern world to backward villagers. Officers described Afghans as so ignorant that they reacted to NATO's armoured vehicles by mistaking them for new Russian equipment—implying the locals had not heard about the withdrawal of the Soviet occupation almost two decades earlier.

Perhaps the best example of the NATO forces' breezy approach came during a briefing on narcotics policy. The troops needed to win favour with the local population and didn't want to upset farmers by destroying their opium poppies, the largest source of cash income in the region. At the same time, the international community wanted to fight a war on drugs in Afghanistan—so eradication teams would slip into areas secured by NATO troops and raze the fields, without telling anybody they were sent by the foreigners.

"So from the point of view of the poppy farmer, they won't know that we're paying for the poppy fields to be ripped up and burned?" I asked one British officer (whom I can't name due to the conditions of the briefing).

"No, they won't know that," the officer said. "I mean, the level of sophistication? They can hardly read."

This caused some skepticism among the journalists. Sitting around a boardroom in the NATO command centre, a modest one-storey structure with plywood walls and concrete blast barriers, it wasn't possible to know Afghan farmers' reaction to this policy. But we could guess they weren't stupid; they would probably understand that eradication was the foreigners' idea. The troops were trying to make the villagers believe that the poppy eradication was an Afghan government program, with no connection to the foreign troops, the British officer said. "The soldiers on the ground, the first message, when they go into a shura [village council], one of the things they're saying is we're not here as part of the eradication. Because the Afghans elders will often say, 'Are you here to do it?' And we say, 'No we're not.'"

"And you're not worried they will figure that out?" I said.

"No."

There was a brief silence.

"Is it duplicitous for us to say that we have nothing to do with that?" a Canadian officer asked, rhetorically.

After another pause, somebody offered: "Yes."

"Hey, duplicity is a reality," said the British officer, provoking laughter. "We're not on some libertarian lovely sort of thing here," he said, before reminding us that this was a background briefing, in which journalists would not be allowed to name the participants. Then he added: "This is realpolitik. . . . If you want to play in the big league, get into some realpolitik."

A tall man with bright blue eyes, the British officer seemed to have quick answers for everything. But he fell quiet when asked: "Does anybody have a grand vision for what could be Afghanistan's largest industry instead of poppy?"

A Canadian military officer said, "Saffron is big."

"USAID is taking the lead on this," said a Canadian diplomat, referring to the US Agency for International Development.

"The other thing is roses," a military official said.

"Roses grow quite well here, yes," the British official said. "Okay, moving on."

The journalists asked hard questions, but for the most part we accepted the soft answers. These officers were talking about Afghans as if they were clay to be molded, but we all failed to understand how profoundly the people would resist. Even when I sat down with a poppy farmer a few days later, I didn't grasp the seriousness of the reaction. He was an ordinary man in his thirties, wearing a blue turban, from a village outside of Kandahar city. The farmer told me that Afghans would take up arms against foreign soldiers who interfered with the opium trade. I asked him whether he himself had weapons, and my translator looked at me like I was stupid: "In your country, you have a car in every driveway," the translator interjected. "Here, everybody has an RPG [rocket-propelled grenade]." But the farmer seemed so gentle and soft-spoken that I had trouble picturing him dusting off an old grenade launcher and fomenting rebellion. I wrote a brief item about drug policy and moved on to other issues without quoting the poppy farmer; I was one of the many visitors to Afghanistan who failed to see the coming uprising.

If anything, the streets seemed calm during that trip into Kandahar city, and I told my translator that I was enjoying the light traffic and mild April breezes. His response was that the empty roads were a bad sign. The arrival of new foreign troops, and the rising violence, were encouraging people to stay home. Business was slow, he said. This turned out to be a perennial complaint in the following years as people fled the war, but at the time it was newsworthy. I walked into the central market, which looked like an old souk except for the modern items on display, from the latest cellphones to boxes of military rations gone missing from US storehouses. We ducked into a low alcove and met a twenty-three-year-old shopkeeper. He looked affluent, wearing crisp white clothes and heavy gold rings—but his sales had dried up. Leaning back against cases of Winston cigarettes and Pepsi, he explained that his family distributed dry goods, but this was becoming difficult as the roads grew dangerous. Sales were down 50 per cent in recent months. Other merchants had similar stories. Landlords told me rents had fallen, and properties lost value. Kandahar has been a crossroads for centuries, a stop along the silk route between Europe and China, so it made sense that business-men were fixated on the issue of moving trucks along the highways. Driving north to Kabul was not yet a serious problem, but truckers said things were getting worse on the road west into Helmand prov-ince, as British troops started construction on a vast military base in the desert, Camp Bastion. Threats from insurgents and police shakedowns were becoming commonplace.

Even the streets of downtown Kandahar were getting more risky. I still felt comfortable shuffling around the dusty laneways in my Afghan clothes and sandals, but my conversations with shopkeepers were routinely cut short by the need to keep moving. My translator worried that news of a foreigner in the market would reach Taliban sympathizers, so we never stayed in any public spot longer than an hour. (By the following year, it was standard practice for television crews to spend no longer than ten minutes in any public location.) The same fears were starting to infect ordinary people, too. At a hairdresser's salon in the heart of the city, across the street from police headquarters, a stylist told me that his business had suffered because nobody wanted to sit near his windows, exposed to the street. Suicide bombings were becoming more frequent, and the police sta-tion was a well-known target. Like so much else in Kandahar, the haircutter's shop had flourished in the initial years after the fall of the Taliban regime in 2001: after years of boring haircuts and long beards required by the Taliban, there was a rush of customers looking for new styles. Many young men wanted their hair cut to resemble Leonardo DiCaprio in the movie *Titanic*, which became wildly popular when bootleg video discs finally appeared in Kandahar's bazaars, years after the film's release. The stylist decorated his shop with a poster of DiCaprio, along with inflatable beach balls and plastic flowers. His walls also contained the most salacious images I'd seen in Kandahar: a series of posters showing beautiful women, with headscarves demurely knotted under their chins, their faces not veiled by the traditional burkas. But by 2006 his decorations looked as worn as the ripped linoleum that covered only half the floor of the salon. After the initial enthusiasm, he said, foreign styles were going out of fashion, and customers who had shaved their beards in 2001 were now growing them back. Elsewhere in the market, a turban vendor described a similar trend: some people took off their turbans after the Taliban government was chased out of Kandahar, but the turban business had recovered in recent months as the insurgency grew. The old vendor saw it as a sign of things returning to normal: "Now, more people are buying turbans, because this is the original culture of this area," he said. "We accept the laws of the government but we will never change our culture."

Shortly afterward, I climbed aboard a military convoy headed southwest of Kandahar city. Most of the soldiers were Canadians, except for a US civil-affairs officer whose task was to teach the new arrivals what he had learned as he wrapped up a tour of duty. Our first stop was Panjwai District Centre, which at the time was a lightly guarded fort in the heart of Bazaar-e-Panjwai, the biggest town in the districts west of the city. Inside the outpost, the American officer pushed his dark sunglasses up onto his brush cut and hugged a grey-bearded man in a turban. This was the master of the fort, the district chief, a representative of the Kabul government. The Americans had showered the district with aid money, and the Afghan officials welcomed us like high rollers in a casino. "I feel like the Godfather," said one Canadian soldier as we sat down for tea with a group of elders. After some conversation, the district leader started complaining that NATO should put more pressure on Pakistan, claiming that troublemakers were coming over the border. An elder tried to interject—"The fighters who come from Pakistan, they get their weapons here in Afghanistan, the problem is here"—but he was ignored by the district leader, who continued pressing the foreign troops as to why they did not hunt down Taliban across the border. When asked about local problems in his own district, the leader conceded that a few clerics were preaching against the international troops, instructing their followers to avoid collaborating with the occupation. But he emphasized that local government officials supported the foreigners. "We tell people, NATO is not like the Russians," the Afghan official said. "They're not here to occupy."

We thanked him for his hospitality and returned to the military vehicles. As we strapped on our helmets, the American officer explained that this was a relatively safe district. "Panjwai is a success story because it's got the strongest district council in the province of Kandahar." He advised us to travel cautiously as we continued west, however, because Taliban had started infiltrating neighbouring areas. Panjwai would later become the most violent region of the south, but for the moment the soldiers were visibly relaxed. Even as we travelled further afield, I was considered lucky to get a spot in the Canadians' most lightly armoured vehicle, because it had comfortable seats and big windows. The flat roof of the jeep also served as a bed as we spent the night camping in the open desert, and a soldier kindly loaned me his waterproof bivvy bag when a thunderstorm swept in across the dunes of the desert to the south. I went to sleep with the sound of raindrops on the nylon sheet wrapped around my head, the warm air moist and electric. It cleared by morning, but a haze loomed on the horizon. We drove northwest, straight into the wind, and soon the world disappeared. I'd never experienced an Afghan dust storm, and it was astonishing to see the universe reduced to a sandy void. The only reminder that we weren't alone in the howling oblivion was the crackle of the radio.

Then we heard a boom, and the radio chatter became more urgent.

"It looks like one vehicle is absolutely decimated, with another one pretty screwed up as well," said a soldier from a lead vehicle. We were reassured to hear his voice because his radio call from the front of the convoy meant that the Canadians were not hit. "Looks to me like a suicide car bomb," he said.

The convoy halted. Soldiers walked up the road, their guns at the ready. In the brown haze they found scattered ordnance—an artillery shell, a hand grenade with a rusty pin—and fragments of metal. We stepped carefully over chunks of human flesh: foot, leg, charred torso. The blast site became visible, with flames dancing in the remnants of the bomber's car. We saw a man with a bloody face shuffling aimlessly. Medics pulled him behind a truck, away from the wind, and treated his wounds. His uniform, spattered with blood, was standard issue for Afghan police, but he identified himself as a private security contractor for US Protection and Investigations (USPI), an American firm that hired local mercenaries to guard convoys, among other duties. His red sport-utility vehicle was riddled with shrapnel holes. The soldiers guessed that the suicide bomber had chosen his victim at random, and our convoy might have been targeted if we had ventured down the road a few seconds earlier. Soon the local USPI boss, Jack Savant, appeared out of the storm, yelling at the Canadians to say he had the situation under control. Mr. Savant was a storybook character, a balding American in running shoes with a bulletproof plate flapping over his belly and a Kalashnikov in his meaty fist. He claimed to be a retired US special forces sergeant, and he disliked the media—the last time we'd met, his men held me at gunpoint while he examined my press credentials. (He seemed popular with the Canadian soldiers, however, and they wrote tributes to him after he died in another suicide bombing that year.) Soldiers doused the flames with fire extinguishers and

Mr. Savant waved goodbye. The whole thing was over so quickly that I didn't even find out how many men died in the blast. The wreckage disappeared in the rear-view mirror, and we plunged forward into the storm.

I was still new to war, but I'd later realize that this happens a lot in conflict zones: something appears, and disappears, and you rarely get a chance to go back and figure out what happened. Usually it's not that storms obscure the view in any literal sense, it's just that chaos makes the facts hazy. Even when returning to the scene of an incident, as I was about to discover in the coming hours, it's often impossible to piece together any semblance of truth.

The storm passed as we continued along the highway, and an Afghan interpreter pointed at a line of trees near the road. "We were here last week," he said. This unit of soldiers had been down the same road seven days earlier, arriving late to a firefight between insurgents and members of the Afghan National Army (ANA) and Afghan National Police (ANP). I was familiar with the battle, because senior commanders had touted it as a victory. We'd heard that the Canadians arrived to help the ANA and ANP, and together they killed forty-one insurgents. We'd heard rumours that troops mistakenly fired at Afghan forces, but a military commander had flatly denied it. I described these denials to the interpreter, who shook his head sadly. "We didn't realize they were ANA or ANP so we started firing at them," he said. The Canadians had accidentally shot at their own allies as they hunkered under thick foliage along a canal, but it wasn't clear whether any deaths or injuries had resulted from friendly fire.

Now the same unit had the unpleasant task of visiting an Afghan police outpost to repair the soldiers' relationship with the local forces they had inadvertently shot up. The Canadians stayed on alert as they rolled up to the gates of Maywand District Centre, and our convoy was welcomed with hard stares from the Afghans as they opened the metal doors. Soon after pulling into the police compound, the

Canadians' senior officer, Major Nick Grimshaw, strode into a disgruntled crowd. I joined them, and heard the Canadian officer speaking slowly and clearly for the sake of his interpreter. "Hopefully we can coordinate much better, next time we show up," he said.

The district leader refused to be placated.

"We've been fighting twenty-five years, and we never lost so many men in one battle," he said. "Seven men! This is because of bad coordination with the Canadians and Americans."

Major Grimshaw nodded gravely. "There was bad coordination," he agreed.

"My sub-commanders were brave!" the Afghan official shouted.

"Yes, I'm sorry we lost them," Major Grimshaw said. "You have no problems in this area now?"

"No," the Afghan said. "If they come, we will fight them. For now, we are not so fortunate that they would face us."

"Yeah, that would make it too easy," said the Canadian, with a wry smile.

Dusk was falling as they spoke, and the soldiers decided to camp inside the Afghan police compound. We set up canvas cots under the cedars and pines. A warning circulated among the soldiers: The Afghan police are angry, the soldiers whispered; Don't take off your body armour. The outpost had high walls topped with barbed wire, but the Canadians took more precautions than they did when sleeping in Taliban territory. Extra patrols crunched along the gravel driveway and sentries manned the gun turrets. The Afghan leader invited some soldiers into his makeshift command centre, a modest room furnished with cushions and a television that played a grainy version of the movie *Gladiator*. Policemen with automatic rifles crowded around the screen, watching swordfights. The district chief ignored the movie and needled his guests with complaints. His men didn't have any radios, he said, and only three cellphones. The phone networks were weak, so the signal died when his officers took cover in the fields. But his biggest problem appeared to be a shortage of ammunition; he was reduced to buying bullets in the market with his own money. Maybe this was true, or not; I heard stories about district chiefs selling ammunition to the Taliban and faking battles to explain their dwindling stockpiles. The notoriously corrupt Ministry of Interior might also have sold off the supplies before they reached the district.

"I tell our problems to the governor. I list them, one-two-three. But he just bows his head," the Afghan leader said.

"The governor has aged in the last ten months, I think," said the US officer.

The Afghan chuckled. "This is Kandahar. It will kill you."

Then he reached into the folds of a dirty blanket and pulled out a small diary. He opened it, revealing a cracked mirror on the inside cover and pages full of handwritten names and telephone numbers. The diary was discovered on the body of a dead Taliban fighter, he said, and contained contact information for insurgent leaders. Most of the numbers started with the prefix 0300, used by Pakistani phones, a clear indication that insurgent leaders were taking shelter across the border. The soldiers thanked the Afghan for the intelligence and wished him a good night. One of the military interpreters stayed behind to help me continue talking, even after the generator quit for the evening and the room fell into darkness. I strapped on a headlamp so I could keep taking notes.

"The Canadians say, let's sit down and plan the next battle," the district leader said. "They talk and talk, but I'm not sure. I have a lot more information I could give them, but I don't know if I can trust them." Apparently the feeling was mutual: a Canadian soldier appeared in the doorway to insist that I say goodnight—"Right now, for your own safety."

A couple of weeks later, I assembled the photos and audio from that trip into a multimedia presentation, describing the dust storm, the suicide bomber and the allegations of friendly fire. At the end of the narration, I added this comment:

It's important for people in Canada to understand the broader picture, which is that Afghanistan will descend into chaos if the foreign troops leave now. Everybody I speak with—diplomats, journalists, soldiers, ordinary Afghans—seem to agree on that point. Many of them say Afghanistan actually needs much more help.

This was technically correct, but wrong in spirit, like telling an obese person with an eating disorder that they will die if they stop consuming food: a biological fact, but misleading. Doubling the number of foreign troops in southern Afghanistan in the early spring of 2006 had only served to highlight self-defeating policies that would continue to plague the rest of the mission: the absurd war against poppy fields; NATO's troubled relationship with Pakistan; and the difficulty of working shoulder to shoulder with untrustworthy Afghan forces, among many others. None of these challenges were ignored by the international troops. The British officer who tried to explain the narcotics policy always seemed on the verge of breaking into laughter at the insanity of his own words. The troops understood much of this, but somehow the understanding on the ground never percolated up the chain of command, or the information never got digested into an effective change in direction, or all of the negative signals were drowned out by the noise of the soldiers' habitually positive thinking. Once set in motion, NATO pressed forward with a sense of inevitability. My next trip would be a case study in the resilience of that military brand of optimism.

Canadian soldier in a sandstorm

CHAPTER 3

OPTIMISM JUNE 2006

The first bang rocked our troop carrier and bounced my helmet off the metal interior. I fumbled in the pocket of my flak jacket for an audio recorder, and switched it on just in time to register the screeching crash of a second jolt as everybody inside the vehicle tumbled sideways. People were shouting in the dark cabin—"Are you okay?" and "We're okay!"—as the diesel engine cranked up to a high pitch and our driver raced us away from Kandahar's latest suicide bombing. Only when the motor whine died down did the Canadian soldiers pause to check for damage. I heard somebody say: "He's bleeding from the mouth a little, but it's nothing too serious, no teeth lost." After a few minutes we kept moving, pressing toward the objective for the day.

The mission was to transport journalists to a victory ceremony (of all things) in the Panjwai valley, where international troops believed they had defeated a major Taliban offensive. Recent fighting had been surprisingly intense, with an estimated nine hundred killed in the first six months of 2006—half of them in the month of May—the first of many record-breaking heights of violence. Several of the most serious battles happened in Panjwai district, the region southwest of Kandahar city where I had been drinking tea with local elders on my previous visit—the district that a US military officer had described as a model for the rest of southern Afghanistan. Now it was erupting into violence. As the back hatch of our vehicle creaked open and we stumbled into the sunlight, I could see that things had changed: the town of Bazaar-e-Panjwai now had extra roadblocks on the main street, and Afghan security forces had new firing positions among piles of sandbags on the roofs of government buildings. Our convoy was blackened and scarred by the explosion. Charred pieces of human flesh stuck to the armour. A television reporter wrinkled her nose at the sight, and I asked her: "Can you believe they were trying to sell me a story about how things have gotten better in Panjwai?"

The human remains spattered on the vehicles probably belonged to the suicide attacker, but may also have been remnants of the four civilians who died in the blast. The bomber had been lurking in an alleyway before ramming his black sport-utility vehicle into our convoy near a major intersection in Kandahar city. Many of the journalists were angry about the incident, feeling that civilians would not have died if the military hadn't been dragging us around the battlefield for a photo op. We figured the announcement would. be cancelled anyway, because it would look ridiculous to declare victory against such a gruesome backdrop. Surprisingly, the event went ahead. "We beat them," said Lieutenant-Colonel Ian Hope, describing a series of recent battles in the Panjwai valley. "Four successive strikes against the Taliban broke the back of their insurgency here."

He was speaking on June 4, 2006. If you chart the violence in southern Afghanistan, the line graph resembles mountains, soaring peaks growing higher and higher. Military commanders boldly predicted that each brutal ascent was the final push before reaching Shangri-La. This always led to disappointment, but the idea of success hidden just beyond the next peak of violence proved an enduring feature of military thinking. The same weekend of the surreal press conference in Panjwai, I sat down with NATO's top southern commander, Canadian Brigadier-General David Fraser. I asked him what he expected to happen as the number of foreign troops almost doubled in the coming month. "We've got more firepower," Brigadier-General Fraser said. "In the short term, it might appear as if it's getting worse. But in the mid-term and long run, I think it actually will make things better." (One of my colleagues asked me to summarize the general's outlook, and I answered only half-jokingly: "Rivers of blood, rivers of blood . . . but it's a good thing.") That kind of optimism went straight down through the ranks, for the most part. A few days earlier, I had visited an outpost where Canadians troops were recovering from a Taliban ambush. Insurgents had opened fire on their convoy in the middle of the night, injuring five soldiers. I talked to a young man who had saved his friend's life by applying a tourniquet below his bleeding hand. "I shined my light on his hand and it was like a red pulp," he said. "He had two fingers but the rest was mashed, like it was squished by something." The soldiers fought all night, but were preparing to resume patrols the same afternoon without sleep. A charismatic sergeant, Patrick Tower, told me the troops could sense the insurgents growing desperate. "I think they're feeling the breaking point coming," he said. "It's just around the bend."

His friend, a master corporal from New Zealand, nodded in agreement. "No matter how many extra fighters they've thrown into this fight in the last two weeks, I mean, they throw in a hundred and we've destroyed more than that."

"Yeah," Sergeant Tower said. "No matter how many they bring in, they cannot pile on the numbers we can pile on, and they don't have the resources we have to sustain a fight."

I asked: "So you think they just can't keep this up?"

"No," the Canadian said, without hesitation.

"There's no way they can," added the New Zealander. "They're running scared, they're falling apart, their leadership is collapsing. People are sick of them. I think they're in their last final effort."

That summer of battle killed nine soldiers from their rotation. Patrick Tower would endure such heavy fire, and perform so bravely, that he was later awarded the Star of Military Valour, the highest decoration earned by a Canadian soldier in half a century. He wasn't the only soldier who underestimated the Taliban, however. Almost everybody I met at the filthy patrol bases in Kandahar seemed to think they were about to defeat their opponents. They were equally convinced that average Afghans supported their cause: "The Taliban represents such a minute percentage of the population here," Sergeant Tower said. "I think the average Afghan wants nothing to do with the Taliban." Villagers were reporting insurgent weapons caches and offering other useful tips, he added, suggesting that I might witness this spirit of co-operation when we visited tribal elders that afternoon.

Hours later, after trudging past a field of marijuana, I found myself sitting with several grey-bearded old men in traditional Afghan clothes. They perched in bare feet under the shade of a mud wall and looked with bemusement at a balding Canadian commander who took off his helmet, dropped his weapon, and squatted down in front of them.

"I see you're quite prosperous with your fields here," the commander said. "Everything is working nicely? Yeah? Good." Then he got down to business, telling the elders that his soldiers had been ambushed nearby on the previous night, when five troops were injured. His men had also been attacked the night before in the same area, and the night before that. The commander made it clear that his patience was wearing thin. "We've seen a lot of Taliban activity," he said.

The elders murmured their disagreement.

"We know there are Taliban in this area but we don't see them," said the villagers through an interpreter, a teenager with the slightest fuzz of moustache on his upper lip.

"So there's no criminal activity here, no interfering with your lives?"

"No."

"So as village elders you know not only your own village but also nearby villages, correct?"

"They know people from those villages, sir."

"So you know there are Taliban, then. When was the last time you saw Taliban in this area?"

"Since the government of Taliban changed they haven't seen any," the interpreter said, referring to the collapse of the previous regime in 2001. The commander put a hand on his hip and stared at them, incredulous that anybody could have missed the armed insurgents swarming through the valley. He continued in the same vein for several minutes, getting the same denials, then broke into a monologue:

"The best option for everybody here is for Taliban to give themselves up to coalition forces, so we can get rid of that menace," he said, more loudly than necessary. "The second option, if they don't give up? They will die an early death," he continued. "We will find them, will hunt them down, and will kill them like the cowards they are. Because they are cowards. We know they're cowards. They hide behind women and children. They use your young men to go fight for them for personal gain while they hide off in the mountains, while they hide off in these houses here, behind your own families."

The interpreter struggled to keep up. Many of the young men hired as field translators were unmotivated, poorly paid considering the risks, and weren't familiar with local dialects of Pashto. It often seemed that only a small fraction of the words spoken in any of these meetings were understood by both parties. In this case, the interpreter gamely tried to convey the gist of the commander's words, but gave up when the villagers broke into a chorus of complaints. After a few minutes, he managed to summarize the elders' message: air strikes had killed women and children during recent fighting, and some people were abandoning the village out of fear.

"What's this?" asked a soldier who was scribbling notes.

"They're saying the bombing affects their families," the commander said. "And I imagine it would," he continued, turning back to the elders. "But the more the villagers get onside, those attacks will stop."

"In our village there is no Taliban, nothing," they replied.

"If there are no Taliban here we won't shoot your village, it's as simple as that," the commander said. He continued threatening and cajoling, reminding them that he was willing to pay for information. They gave him nothing, only complained and spat in the dust. Flies buzzed around the tiny puddles of spittle, competing for drops of moisture. The afternoon light was fading. After another fruitless half hour, the troops returned to their outpost.

I was disappointed by that excursion, and wrote nothing about the trip in the newspaper. In an e-mail, I told a friend:

```
We were supposed to be on a combat mission but the Taliban
didn't show up to fight, so I literally spent two days playing
rummy, eating rations, listening to BBC podcasts and
challenging the guys to rock-throwing contests where we tried
to hit a cardboard box from thirty metres away. I got pretty
good after, oh, five or six hours of practice. One thing I've
learned about soldiers is they make boredom into an art.
```

This was the first battle group of Canadian soldiers to arrive in southern Afghanistan, and most of the soldiers remained upbeat even as they realized their task was going to be harder than expected. It was only as we drove back to Kandahar Air Field that I heard the first whispers of skepticism. I was riding in a G Wagon jeep for the first time since I visited in April; commanders had declared the jeeps too dangerous for civilians but we were breaking the rules because the soldiers were tired and battle-jaded. I was chatting with the driver, talking about how the fighting seemed to be unrelenting. He compared the situation to a Bugs Bunny cartoon: "You know, the ones with the coyote and the sheep dog, and it's always the same thing in the end: 'See you tomorrow, Sam.'" We both stared out into the night, watching mud compounds flash past, driving at maximum speed in hopes that whoever was watching our vehicle wouldn't recognize us as a convoy, and wouldn't have time to attack until we'd already passed. I couldn't see the driver's eyes but his voice sounded far away. "See you tomorrow, Sam," he said.

Panjwai district lost its status as a success story, but many officers still pointed to the nearby province of Zabul as a sign of hope. It had been considered a Taliban stronghold just two years earlier, and was the first province where insurgents felt confident enough to formally declare a shadow government. (Shadow administrations would later emerge across the country, as the Taliban influence grew.) By the time I arrived in 2006, the Americans believed they had rolled back the insurgents. Diplomats talked about the province as a place that had clearly benefitted from the presence of US troops, and military intelligence considered it the most secure province in southern Afghanistan. Some NATO officers pushed the idea of Zabul as a model because the American operations involved putting millions of dollars in the hands of military units in the field to spend on development and aid projects. This was different from the British and Canadian approach, which funnelled most aid money through notoriously slow-moving civilian agencies. The military was eager to show off its prized accomplishment; days after I mentioned an interest, the press officers arranged a US helicopter to whisk me off to Zabul. I almost got stranded in the desert when the big aircraft dumped a load of supplies at a remote outpost, but I scrambled back aboard in time to catch the second leg of the journey to the capital city, Qalat. Soon after arriving at the small Provincial Reconstruction Team headquarters, I bumped into an energetic man named Lieutenant-Colonel Kevin McGlaughlin, who insisted I call him "Beev." He was commander of the PRT, but seemed to treat everybody like a drinking buddy. "Throw your stuff in a corner and jump in," he yelled, and I found myself being chauffeured around in a Humvee by the man most responsible for Qalat's recent make-over. It's an ancient city near a crumbling fortress, but the recent American presence had graced the settlement with modern updates: roads, wells, schools, bridges, and buildings. Beev was a whirlwind, jogging through half-finished structures and construction sites while keeping up a patter of commentary. He cheerfully admitted that he was trained as a B-52 bomber pilot—more qualified to destroy cities than build them—but he had embraced the urban planning aspect of his new job with the charming can-do attitude of military officers. He was the sort of character who horrified those versed in development studies, who were concerned about military commanders becoming temporary kings of these outposts, splashing money around without plans for the long term, and making public works susceptible to the officers' foibles and inevitable departure. Beev himself seemed to invite this kind of criticism, driving up to a plateau above the city to show off what he described as his biggest mistake. At first I couldn't see anything wrong as Beev led me onto a swath of scrubland, where tracks in the dirt made it look flattened by machinery. He trotted across the empty landscape, kicking up dust that made me cough. Beev finally stopped and asked me what I saw. I wheezed, wiped my eyes and shook my head. "This is a runway for my new airport," he said, gesturing at the open expanse. "And this is my new road. It goes straight through the runway. We got a problem, obviously." He posed for a photo at the intersection of his half-finished runway and his half-finished road. Behind his ballistic sunglasses it was hard to read his expression, and at first I was puzzled about why a soldier would be so eager to show a reporter an embarrassing error. But he seemed to be making a point about the pace of reconstruction in Zabul. So many projects were underway simultaneously that it was hard to keep track of all the activity.

All the US money pouring into Zabul appeared to have purchased a bit of calm. I went for a walk with the provincial governor and was surprised when he stepped out the gates of a US military base and into a main street of the city without pausing his conversation or even checking for traffic. Two police officers trailing along behind his entourage seemed bored, their Kalashnikov rifles hanging at their sides. Other politicians in southern Afghanistan travelled in armoured convoys or helicopters because assassins tried to kill them on a regular basis. I'd never seen a government leader wander so casually in the south, but the governor's aides told me he regularly made excursions on foot. "When I first arrived, we didn't have much control over some districts," he said, referring to his appointment in early 2005. "People told me, 'The Taliban is too strong. Stay inside your offices.'"

He chuckled at the memory. "Now, we are a success," he said.

Foreshadows of what would happen next could be heard in a few corners of the military camps, if you looked hard for the skeptics. A Canadian diplomat told me it was a mistake to rely on the military for reconstruction programs. "We could buy a temporary peace," he said. "But that would be based on bribery, and supporting a mafia-like state. The second you walk away and the funds stop flowing, everything falls apart."

The situation did fall apart in Zabul during the following years. Violence in that province grew exponentially, and much of it became off limits for aid workers. But the same kind of deterioration swept over all provinces in the south, so it's impossible to know whose strategy was better. The commanders who implemented these strategies were literate men, well versed in the history of other insurgencies. Stacks of non-fiction in their offices made them seem like warrior-professors who could spend hours talking about Roman methods of subduing rebellious tribes. Of course, Roman legions never faced roadside bombs. The history books also failed, apparently, to teach the modern officers any lessons about the dangers of convenient hope. Most personnel in the NATO mission seemed to genuinely believe that the insurgents were growing desperate, on the verge of breaking. It was such a stubbornly optimistic atmosphere that a bright young commander could stand near a troop carrier spattered with human remains and declare victory. This same blinkered view of the situation would soon lead the NATO troops, stumbling, into their biggest battle ever.

Canadian soldier in Operation Medusa

CHAPTER 4
MEDUSA AUGUST 2006

A sense of anticipation hung over Kandahar city in late summer, something heavy in the terrible heat. The violence had continued rising through the hottest months of the year, and now all eyes looked nervously west, toward the Panjwai river valley, where hundreds of armed Taliban camped among the lush orchards and grape fields. The gunmen weren't far from downtown, maybe ten kilometres beyond the bridge that marked the city limits, and fears were spreading about a military confrontation in the city streets. Most residents had memories of urban warfare in past decades, and nobody wanted to see that kind of fighting again. My translator kept his car filled with gasoline and his suitcases packed, ready to escape. Others had already fled. The smog of diesel and smoke from cooking fires had thinned; cresting a hill on my way into the city, I enjoyed an unusually clear view of the Eid Gah mosque on the opposite side of town, its dome like a blue egg among the mud buildings. Beyond that, I could see the jagged rock that rises almost vertically to the west and north of the city, small mountains that had made Kandahar a natural fortress for centuries. Now those mountains seemed to offer little defence against insurgents who slipped easily across the landscape. Along the highway, rows of vendors' stalls had lost their bustle. We passed the wreckage of a taxi, with scattered shoes and human gristle in the dust, the remnants of an explosion. Drivers did not pause to gawk, slowing only to avoid holes carved by the blasts. Insurgents attacked so many times with so-called improvised explosive devices (IEDs) that the airport road was nicknamed "IED alley." My driver somehow believed we could avoid the bombs if we drove quickly, making the trip from the airport a terrifying dash through traffic, past herds of goats and the occasional camel. Inside the city, many storefronts were shuttered with locked metal blinds; these were usually businesses marked by the taint of Western influence—medical clinics, computer stores, sellers of audio cassettes and compact discs—whose owners worried the Taliban might not tolerate them. In the years since President Hamid Karzai and his Popalzai tribe had assumed control of Kandahar, merchants had started advertising their connection to the ruling clan by adding the tribal name to their shop signs, and it sometimes seemed as if every bakery and auto mechanic was owned by somebody ostensibly named Popal. But during the sweltering final weeks of summer, the hand-painted "Popal" signs had disappeared. It was better to hide your loyalties in a city on the brink of invasion.

As business slowed, the remaining shopkeepers found themselves with plenty of time to drink tea and complain. Some admitted they were taking out extra insurance against Taliban attack by sending gifts to the well-known insurgent commanders in the fields outside the city. Merchants assembled little packets of cash, or vouchers for cellphone credit, wrapped up in scarves and presented with compliments. I understood this as pragmatism. Who wouldn't want to protect themselves against armed zealots? Almost every building in the city wore the scars of previous wars, and men with missing legs hobbled on wooden crutches or wheeled themselves along the rutted alleyways in hand-cranked contraptions. It made sense that city residents would have psychological scars as well. I did not want to believe that an average person in Kandahar would willingly sponsor the death of foreign soldiers, or that gifts for the Taliban represented votes in favour of the brutal movement. If ordinary citizens were helping the insurgents, I guessed, the climate of fear must be making people crazy.

So I went to see a psychologist. Abdul Rahim Halimyar, forty-eight, ran the only mental health clinic in the city, although it looked more like a drug dealer's lair than a medical establishment. That impression proved correct, in some ways, because Dr. Halimyar's practice consisted mostly of prescribing mind-dulling medication. It was amazing that his dazed patients could even reach his office, up a steep flight of stone steps to the second floor of an old building in the central market. The waiting area was crowded and dirty. Behind a stained lace curtain, in his tiny consulting room, the doctor whisked around with a theatrical air, wearing a white coat and a stethoscope around his neck. His scraggly hair, gap-toothed smile and bloodshot eyes made him look like an avatar for all the madness of the city. I asked him whether anxiety levels were rising in Kandahar, and he strongly agreed. I'd assumed he would criticize the Taliban for causing the distress, but instead he blamed outsiders for meddling in his country. His patients had lost hope for the international mission, he said. "They hear on the radio that the whole world is trying to help Afghanistan, but they see no improvement. I'm a doctor, I'm educated, and they always ask me. I tell them, no, please don't hope. It will get worse." I wanted to chronicle the ways his patients suffered, the psychological effects of slain relatives, smashed homes, harrowing escapes. He preferred to rant about the foreigners' mistakes. "Ninety per cent of women here are happy with the burka," he said. "But the foreigners are saying they're not happy with this clothing." That evening, back in my tent at the military base, I omitted those quotes from my article about his clinic. They didn't fit my story about a city under siege by unwelcome militants.

But, in some ways, a siege mentality had taken hold. I was driving through the northeastern side of the city when I heard an explosion from the direction of a nearby NATO military base. This was followed by a crackle of bullets, and everybody on the street appeared to reach the same conclusion at once: the Taliban had finally started their urban war. People ran for their lives, running so hard they left their sandals behind. I jumped out of my car and walked against the flow, getting closer to the thick column of smoke billowing into the blue sky. I could see foreign soldiers taking shelter behind a mud wall as a flurry of concussions threw up more dust. "The Taliban are attacking the city," a teenager shouted. My driver, a brave ex-soldier, tugged at my sleeve. He didn't speak English but I understood his growl, "*Razi che zhu!*" ("Let's go!") We joined the mob hurrying away.

But we had all misunderstood: it was just another suicide bomber, one of dozens in the city that summer. The bomb detonated near a military vehicle and set it on fire. The rapid pops and banging sounds had been caused by the ignition of overheated ammunition inside the burning vehicle, a phenomenon known as a "cook-off." A soldier was killed in the attack, and the troops who rushed to the scene accidentally shot dead a young boy. The Taliban were not invading after all, but tension in the city had reached a fever pitch.

Everybody knew a battle was coming, but it still felt like high drama when the international troops finally declared war. NATO had formally taken responsibility for southern Afghanistan earlier that month, and Kandahar's main base now included troops from Canada, Britain, Australia, Denmark, Romania, Estonia, Portugal and the Netherlands. But it was an American commander, Colonel Steve Williams, who served as the voice of the coalition during a press conference at the end of August. He warned villagers west of the city to evacuate immediately because of an impending assault. It was easy to guess why the American had been selected to deliver the message: other countries in the NATO alliance were describing their presence as a humanitarian gesture. A British minister infamously predicted the military surge would happen without a shot fired, and the Canadian military was pushing journalists to write about medical programs. By contrast, the Americans advertised their willingness to draw blood. The US colonel aimed his words directly at the insurgents: "If they want to die, stay," he said. "If they don't want to die, give up." This prompted a look of discomfort from a Canadian press officer, who immediately tried to soften the message.

"I would simply add that . . ." he said.

"I thought that answered it pretty good," said the American colonel, with a smile at the journalists. The Afghan press didn't get the joke, however, because to them the differences among the foreigners were hard to understand. They found it difficult to imagine that English-speaking soldiers who wore similar uniforms, carried the same weapons and fought on the same side would have fundamental disagreements about the war. They saw *all* of us as Americans. (For years, people in Kandahar city would look at me and ask, "Amerikayeh?" and it was hard to persuade them I was from Canada—and then, to convince them Canada was a real country.) Besides, the Afghan journalists were more interested to know why the international troops had waited so long before deciding to attack the insurgents, who had been a threat near the city for months. A local correspondent from the Associated Press said bluntly, "How come the coalition forces didn't do anything?"

It wasn't only journalists asking that question: Afghan politicians were also worried about their enemies gathering outside the city. One influential member of the provincial council had recently been forced to evacuate more than sixty members of his family from the Panjwai valley, marking the first time in decades of war that his family had been uprooted. Nor was the pressure coming only from local sources: NATO itself seemed to feel its pride was at stake in the fields west of Kandahar city, as the sudden appearance of massed Taliban coincided with NATO forces taking over control of the south from the Americans. There was talk among military officers about the insurgents testing the resolve of the Canadians and Europeans, and the need for NATO to prove its potency on the battlefield. Military officials described something they called the "weakest link" theory, suggesting that the Taliban was pushing hard against the mixed NATO contingent in the belief that soft liberal democracies would not have the stomach for war. But the threat was also viewed in some circles as a rare opportunity to kill large numbers of Taliban in a single operation: usually preferring guerilla tactics, the insurgents had rarely offered themselves up for a conventional military battle. The prospect excited a generation of military leaders who had spent their lives studying classic manoeuver warfare—but never experiencing it. Like the NATO alliance itself, the soldiers wanted to show their mettle.

That feeling of urgency may have contributed to NATO's missteps in the next few days, during the start of an offensive named Operation Medusa. A detailed analysis of the operation, published a year later by the journalist Adam Day in *Legion* magazine, would conclude that foreign troops rushed the initial stage of the fight with "little if any battle procedure, no reconnaissance and intel that was either insufficient or wildly wrong." The international side of the battle consisted of about fourteen hundred regular troops, mostly Canadian, with smaller contingents of special forces and Afghan soldiers. Estimates of the Taliban ranks were varied, but speculation at the time placed their numbers at roughly half the strength of the foreign troops. The insurgents had tunnelled defensive shelters and anti-tank trenches into the hard earth of the Panjwai valley, and the landscape favoured the defenders, with a warren of irrigation ditches, underground water channels, and vineyards with grapes climbing rows of chest-high troughs in the ground. The mud walls offered unexpectedly good cover: troops were surprised when a blast from their turret cannon, which fires heavy slugs at more than eleven hundred metres per second, failed to punch through a wall constructed of dirt and straw.

To break down those defences, NATO surrounded the Taliban and pounded them with air strikes and artillery. The valley had been blanketed with warnings on radio and leaflets beforehand, and military leaders declared that no civilians likely remained in the target zone, a rectangular swath of roughly twenty square kilometres. Any women and children still inside that part of the Panjwai could be considered "camp followers" of the insurgents, they claimed, noting that thousands of residents had already evacuated. That zone became the most closely monitored patch of earth in Afghanistan, as military surveillance focused on the battlefield, a deployment of intelligence assets that resulted in the first casualties of the operation. Ground troops watched in horror as a British spy plane fell out of the sky in a streak of fire. The crash killed fourteen personnel, the largest single loss for British forces in decades. On the same day, September 2, most of the NATO force was assembling itself in a U-shaped horseshoe pattern around the target area, with the open side of the "U" facing away from Kandahar city. Military commanders at the time boasted about encircling the insurgents, but that was bluster; all signs pointed to a massive push to drive the insurgents away, via the loosely guarded western edge of the battlefield. It was reasonable to think the Taliban would retreat, surrounded on three sides and enduring a barrage of NATO firepower.

I embedded with a unit on the north side of the "U" formation, Bravo Company of the Royal Canadian Regiment, which initially stayed back from the target area. Sitting on the roof of an Afghan police station, I watched the explosions in the valley, making deep sounds like the rumble of a thunderstorm. But soldiers would later complain that some of the planned air strikes never arrived. Even more baffling for them was the decision to rush ahead with the ground offensive on September 3, two days ahead of schedule, skipping forty-eight hours of bombardment. This led to a bloody debacle that has become celebrated in Canadian military lore, in which Charles Company charged north across the Arghandab River into a hail of enemy fire on that Sunday morning at daybreak. Of the fifty soldiers who crossed the river, four were killed, ten were wounded and others required treatment for stress. It was heroic, but they gained nothing. The commanders fed us journalists the usual lines: "It was an extremely successful day," Brigadier-General David Fraser said, after his soldiers retreated.

Despite their casualties, Charles Company was again selected the next morning to lead an assault on the Taliban stronghold. They gathered on a hillside on the south bank of the river in the early mist, but a US warplane accidentally strafed them just minutes before the attack. The American A-10 doesn't so much fire bullets as belch them out like dragon fire, and it makes an eerie prehistoric howling sound in the sky. The errant blast would have killed more troops if the company hadn't already been suited up for battle; even so, it left one soldier dead and a few dozen wounded. I could hear the commander of Canada's battle group, Lieutenant-Colonel Omer Lavoie, who had warned his bosses not to rush the battle, cursing on the radio. "Fuck, we just lost a whole company," he said. Charles Company would later become the most highly decorated unit in the Canadian military, but for the moment it was a shambles.

The plan to attack from the south was scrapped, and officers started to talk about sending Bravo Company from the north. The men seemed nervous. An officer complained over the radio: "I just don't get what's not being understood. We need a lot more resources to do what we have to do, especially after the events of this morning." The Canadians' big artillery pieces, which had been banging shells into the Taliban stronghold for days, were running low on ammunition. In the beginning the soldiers had been cheering as American planes dropped bombs into the valley, payloads so heavy that the sound hit you in the sternum, dusty mushrooms of smoke blotting out the mountains. But now, after the friendly fire, the torrent of air power seemed like just another threat to soldiers on the ground. They took extra care to mark themselves with infrared light emitters in hopes of being noticed by pilots' night-vision gear, using empty water bottles strapped to their vehicles as holders for glow sticks, tubes of plastic that don't give off any light to the naked eye but show up on military sensors. Some soldiers grumbled about sending an even clearer message to the pilots. "We should spray-paint a big circle around us, with an arrow that says, 'Not here, asshole,'" one soldier said.

That day, and the next, and the next, the troops stayed on the fringes of the valley and watched the pyrotechnics of aircraft and artillery strikes. The soldiers woke before dawn every morning and waited for the order to attack, but it seemed the new plan was still being formulated at higher levels. The Taliban sometimes poked out from among the trees and fired toward the armoured vehicles, but the skirmishes didn't amount to much. I got so comfortable on the front lines that I made the mistake of loitering in the open scrubland only a few hundred metres from Taliban positions, and an insurgent took a shot in my direction: it was my first time hearing a bullet go past my ear. The smack of the tiny sonic boom sounded so much like somebody clapping their hands behind my head that I was initially puzzled, and turned around to see which prankster made the sudden noise, only to discover that the soldiers had thrown themselves to the ground. I joined them, embarrassed but lucky. That night, of course, I didn't mention the near miss when I pulled the small satellite dish from my backpack, aimed it at the stars and huddled inside an armoured vehicle to write my sister.

from: Graeme Smith
to: Caitlin Smith
date: Tue, Sep 5, 2006 at 11:35 PM

I woke up shivering this morning after about ninety minutes
of sleep in the freezing desert. Me and my CP [Canadian Press]
friend had to hustle to catch our convoy last night and forgot
our warm sleeping stuff. Ugh. I made a small fire with food
wrappers and cardboard boxes, and kept stoking it until the
sun started to warm things up. I smelled really bad, like burnt

plastic, but at least I stopped shivering. Today I dumped some
water over my head to rinse away some of the carcinogens. But
of course I still smell awful, after four days with no shower.

Ah, the glamorous life.

It *did* feel kind of glamorous, though. I enjoyed the freedom of
camping outdoors: sleeping in the dirt wasn't so bad, and though
I forgot to bring a toothbrush and a change of clothes, nobody
minded. This was a place where a guy could piss where he wanted,
belch when he wanted, and in some ways behave more naturally than
is usually allowed. My mouth tasted awful, and my combat pants
grew crusted with rings of salt from days of accumulated sweat, but
it felt like an adventure.

Every night I rigged up my satellite, checked my newspaper's website and discovered that my bulletins were appearing on the front
page. Soldiers peered over my shoulder to read the stories about
themselves. The media in Europe and North America were generally supportive of the war at the time, and my dispatches often
ran alongside editorials or columns praising the troops and their
actions. The headline across the top of my newspaper's front page on
September 4, 2006, announcing the death of four Canadian soldiers,
was "Bloodied, but unbowed." I made friends with the soldiers, too,
adopted into a platoon that called itself the Nomads. I felt proud
when they gave me a "Nomads" patch for my flak jacket. The soldiers were brave, generous and devoted to their friends. I was basically an excited kid, recording what felt in some ways like a climactic
battle between the forces of barbarism and civilization—but my
notes include scraps of information that I should have investigated
more carefully. My translators called me with reports of civilian
casualties, and I documented some of them, but forgot about many
others. I wrote down the name of a man rumoured to have lost his
entire family in an air strike ("perhaps five sons, two daughters, one

wife killed") but I never found him. Such professional failures would haunt me later when I ranted about the lack of media resources to track events in southern Afghanistan. Some of that anger would be secretly aimed at myself for allowing stories to slip away.

One of those missed stories that still bothers me was passed along from a reconnaissance unit prowling ahead of the front lines at night. The soldiers usually found no trace of their enemies except blood trails disappearing into the undergrowth, because the insurgents were efficient at removing their dead and observing the Muslim custom of a quick burial. But in the chaos of Operation Medusa, some of the bodies were left behind. One night a Canadian reconnaissance platoon decided to use Taliban corpses as bait, dragging them out from the leafy cover of the farmland and marking them with infrared glow sticks. The soldiers hid themselves and waited for the insurgents to collect their dead. Hours ticked by, with the troops poised to fire—but nobody fell for the trap. The stench of death attracted wild dogs, which spent the night ripping chunks off the bodies while the Canadians watched through their gun scopes.

The soldiers casually joked about it afterward; in one of my audio recordings, an officer sounds casual about it. "We hit a couple of guys over here," he said. "Left them out as bait. And the dogs are eating them now."

Those nights and days of tense waiting ended on September 7, when the Canadian and US troops were ordered to resume their offensive. On the north side of the battlefield, Bravo Company scurried out of the scrub into the dense farmland where their comrades from Charles Company had been ambushed a few days earlier. The soldiers used armoured bulldozers to carve new roads across the dry canals and smashed gaps in mud walls, allowing their vehicles to avoid the existing pathways, which were riddled with landmines. As night fell, the soldiers began doing something that international forces had rarely attempted in that rebellious region: digging into new positions, hacking at walls with pickaxes to open firing holes and cutting down trees with chainsaws to clear gunners' sightlines. Foreign soldiers had visited the area many times in the previous months and years, but they had never stayed for long. Operation Medusa was meant to change that pattern, proving that the foreign troops could follow the counter-insurgency mantra of "clear, hold and build." For one glorious evening it almost seemed possible, too, as the troops' initial advance found no resistance. The soldiers relaxed a little and allowed themselves to admire their freshly conquered land.

"See these vegetables and stuff here? You could live for awhile," said Captain Piers Pappin, a Canadian platoon commander. "These are mulberry trees right here. The fruit's already done, but I recognize the leaves from mulberry trees at home. And pomegranates you can see everywhere."

"If I remember my history right, this is the same bit of farmland that supported Alexander the Great's armies when he busted through here." I had been reading and wanted to show off. There was something about the handcrafted walls and gardens in the valley that make them look like illustrations in a book.

"Yep, Kandahar, he did this," Captain Pappin said, referring to Alexander's marches. "All the way through the Hindu Kush to the Oxus."

The valley was so quiet that we could hear the insects buzzing in the grass. The captain took me inside a compound where we would spend the night, and we met a group of soldiers already making themselves comfortable.

"Alright, I guess we'll chill out for awhile," Captain Pappin said.

"What do you want for supper, sir? We got grapes, grapes and grapes," said a soldier.

"And for dessert, raisins," said a young soldier.

"We got some chicken too, sir," said another, eyeing the live fowl in the yard.

An older soldier cut in: "We found a lot of artillery shells and casings in a lot of the buildings."

"They use them as lawn ornaments," said a young corporal, with a broad smile. "We use garden gnomes, they use 155-millimetre shells."

The battle paused through the night but continued the next morning, September 8, when the Taliban made several counterattacks on the advancing troops. A mortar exploded not far from the spot where I was sitting, and later in the day I found myself hunkered down with the Nomads on the roof of a two-storey mud building that had recently been used by a farmer for drying grapes into raisins. This became a bunker as the Canadians exchanged sporadic fire with enemies hidden in a line of trees. We heard the rattle of an old machine gun in the foliage, and the soldiers pounded the spot with a hail of gunfire, brass casings piling up around their boots. As evening fell, the blasts from turret guns looked like red streaks as hot metal slugs flew through the dusk. Over and over, the international forces slammed ordnance into the Taliban positions and the valley fell silent, only to erupt again when a brave or foolhardy insurgent poked out from between the trees.

The soldiers chatted casually during the long breaks between volleys. A Canadian corporal told me he didn't think anybody back home would believe the intensity of the fight: "Our nation is pretty much pacifist, that's what it is," he said. "But we're actually at war, and that doesn't sit well with a lot of people. It's like, 'Yeah? We've got an army?' I actually run into some people who didn't know we had an army."

Later on, a more experienced soldier was in the middle of explaining the sound created by a rocket-propelled grenade, saying it resembles the noise of a toy bottle rocket, when we got a live demonstration. Something whizzed by our heads and exploded.

"Okay, that was close," the soldier said, adding: "See, it *does* sound like a bottle rocket." He grinned like a maniac as gunfire erupted again.

Some of the soldiers clearly enjoyed the full-throated battle. "This is what the boys trained for," said a grizzled warrant officer, watching the troops firing grenades, mortars, cannons and machine guns. "This is the epitome of my career, this moment here."

It felt like a decisive moment, but it wasn't. Few insurgents remained to block the international forces after days of air strikes, but the troops still moved cautiously. During a pause in the fighting, I followed Captain Pappin over to a hill where a US platoon commander was surveying the fields. Lieutenant Ryan Edwards had already spent seven months in Afghanistan, longer than the average six-month deployment for soldiers with the Canadian battle group. After chatting for awhile about their next moves, and staring out at the rustling fields where they suspected the insurgents were hiding, the American turned to the Canadian officer and offered some frank observations.

"The last place we were at," the lieutenant said, "pretty much every day, it was all about survival. My platoon was twenty-seven, twenty-eight [men]. Pretty much every firefight we had they [the insurgents] would have about one hundred at least. We'd just take human wave assaults at our position, just one after the other after the other. And then ambushes every time we left. That was just a dogfight. There was no real ground to keep. It was just who had the most ammo."

The Canadian officer looked concerned. "But if you have a good defensive position?"

"Fortunately we had a good piece of high ground," the American said, nodding and scuffing the dirt with his boot. "Day after day, we'd go out in between attacks and fight them in their territory. They'd come back to ours, we'd go back to theirs. We'd inflict thirty, forty casualties at a time. It was just that. But the problem was, that was where they lived. They didn't have to come in. That's what we found with the strongest points. Taliban weren't coming into it. That's where they lived. So a lot of them we'd kill, their house was ten metres away from it. So you'd have their wife and kids out there going, 'Oh, you killed my husband! He was innocent!' And I'm like, 'So the machine gun in his hands right now? He was innocent?'"

He added, sarcastically, "That place was a jewel."

The officers talked about other topics, but the US lieutenant circled back to his original idea: that the international troops were fighting the Taliban near the insurgents' own homes. This contradicted the public statement from the United States and other NATO governments at the time, which described the insurgents as the nomadic remnants of the Taliban army, wintering in Pakistan and spending the summers fighting in Afghanistan. The international troops wanted to portray themselves as protecting villagers from the marauding invaders—but like so many other soldiers, the American lieutenant had realized he was fighting the villagers themselves.

It was a rebellion, not an invasion.

"There was definitely a lot of casualties on both sides," the lieutenant continued. "That was one of the biggest strongholds they had. And it was not so much a terrain issue, it was like, that's where they lived. So it was just a huge absolute monster fight."

"They were fighting for hearth and home," Captain Pappin said.

"Yeah, so now they're fighting for home," the American continued. "So we basically found a dirt hill right above them, and just moved in. That's where I lived. At that point, nobody supports you, nobody likes you, nobody even wants to get near you. And it was night after night, just constant. And finally we just broke them."

"Killed enough of them, and they fucking . . ." the Canadian said.

"They just finally, yeah, they finally just—we just finally broke their spirits," said the American. "'Cause really it was like we moved in and pretty much 100 per cent of everybody else—we didn't say anything—they just moved out. Entire villages deserted overnight. And we were like, 'Yeah, that's probably not a good sign.' And pretty much from there it was like, 'Let's do it.'"

"Fuck," I interrupted. "Well, it worked." The Canadian and American officers turned to look at me like I was an idiot. The battles described by the US lieutenant had taken place in Zabul, a province I had recently profiled as an example of successful counter-insurgency efforts. I figured those battles had won a measure of calm, but I was wrong. Nobody's spirit was broken. The violence would get worse in Zabul the next year, and the year after, and the year after, and the year after. The exhausted look on the American officer's face should have tipped me off.

Operation Medusa's final assault happened on September 11, 2006, on the fifth anniversary of the 9/11 attacks. On the north side of the battlefield, the commander of Bravo Company gave a rousing speech as troops warmed themselves around garbage fires at dawn. "It's September 11," he said. "Is that symbolic? Damn right, it's symbolic. It's the reason why we're here." More than a week of relentless bombing had left the former Taliban stronghold a shattered landscape of ruined buildings, littered with shrapnel and unexploded bombs. Fires gutted insurgent hideouts and continued to burn. Estimates of the Taliban numbers in those fields had climbed into the hundreds during the operation, but when NATO made its final attack the soldiers expected to find only a handful of insurgents. Still, the intelligence had proven disastrously wrong in the past, so the troops blasted into their objectives with bone-rattling intensity. Engineers ran up to the walls of farmhouses and set up charges using so much plastic explosive that the detonation kicked up rolling clouds that swept over the troops like the end of the world, blotting out the sun and immersing them in an otherworldly universe of filtered light and falling debris. Sometimes the sheer oomph of those explosions made the soldiers shake their heads and swear.

"Jesus," said a soldier, after a particularly big blast.

"Hoooly," said another.

"What the fuck was that?" said Captain Pappin.

"Fucking rain of fucking building," I replied.

Building materials were falling from the sky: wood, stone, mud. A chunk hit a soldier on the wrist and smashed his plastic watch. We hunkered down, listening to the rubble clattering on our helmets. Then we got up and charged through the blast holes. At first, the soldiers went around each corner with their rifles high and ready, lobbing grenades to clear a path. They blew open doors with shotguns and even punched their gloved fists through obstacles. But their pace slowed as the day continued and they found little except abandoned rooms. The group of soldiers I was following paused for a break from the midday sun, sheltering in a leafy courtyard and eating tomatoes from the garden.

"My wife, she doesn't watch the news," a soldier said. "She stopped six or seven years ago. She's like, there's nothing good on the news. Especially for a military wife, right? She'd prefer not to know. She works at a call centre, and there's a shitload of girls who have military husbands. And they're all like, 'Oh my God, you know who died today?' She's like, 'I don't want to know.'"

Another man chimed in: "Yeah, it's always, 'Ahhh, my baby's coming home in a box!' I'm like, no, no, no."

This got some rueful laughter. It's easy to forget how much soldiers laugh. Years later, listening to my audio recordings of firefights, I'd be amazed at how the sound of gunfire was interspersed with gruff merriment. "Blood trail leads into the marijuana," I observed at one point, noticing a bleeding insurgent had staggered into a field of cannabis. "Well, if you were dying, wouldn't you want to go happy?" said a laughing soldier. Maybe we were all giddy from sleep deprivation, or dehydrated by the sun.

Some of the humour also had a darker edge.

"Let's commence with the killing," said a beefy corporal.

"What do you know about killing, fatboy? We ain't killing no burgers here," said another.

Shortly afterward, a soldier sat down heavily and wiped sweat from the lenses of his protective goggles. "Fuck me, I want to shoot somebody. I'm serious. This pisses me off," he said.

"You'll get your chance," I said.

"I already had a chance the other day, and I want more," he said. "I'm in the infantry. I didn't join this to make fucking changes in the world, other than population depreciation."

I laughed at this, too, but I also felt a measure of sadness. These young soldiers might as well have been exploring a distant planet. The Panjwai valley was an alien landscape to these troops, and I started to feel that the sheer magnitude of this dislocation was somehow a part of the conflict. That night as the troops slept, I opened my laptop and tried to understand these feelings by tapping out a few paragraphs. I probably looked like a strange intruder myself as I sat with my computer in a pile of straw, under the arched roof of an Afghan farmer's empty house. Swarms of moths fluttered against my screen, the brightest light in the valley.

This war is tribal, I wrote. *That's the heartbeat of the battle.* Down beneath the layers of ideas and politics, across the world from the leaders who sent the soldiers into battle, in this ancient land of wars, the ceremony of conflict followed old ways. The soldiers who knew the history, the ones who read books when not carrying guns, said they could feel the presence of the Greeks, the British, the Russians, and all the great powers that trampled the same fields. The other soldiers only felt something shiver through them, something that made them fall silent, put away their dirty magazines and stare across the Stone Age landscape, rubbing the plastic stocks of their assault rifles in the same reassuring way that Alexander's men would have handled their spears. Out there, somewhere in the foliage, in soil worked by hands with the same methods for a hundred generations, was a hostile tribe. These enemies behaved differently from us, in a manner so outlandish that it was easy to believe anything about them. They attacked and disappeared. They died and disappeared, too, dragged away by their comrades. Every soldier had heard stories about Russian troops in the 1980s who were captured by insurgents, about the rape of prisoners. Some of the older soldiers laughed scornfully at these tales, but younger ones repeated them with wide eyes. Most of them said they would save their last bullet for suicide. The rest of the bullets were for killing, and the soldiers did want to kill. Of course they also wanted to build Afghanistan into a country, they wanted peace and security and all the nice things they were told to fight for, but the real motivation was more primal. Many of them had friends who died in Taliban ambushes or bombings. The rest of them talked about September 2001, about the challenge to the Western way of life by religious fanatics. Their commanders avoided using words like "revenge" and "payback," but in the ranks they were not so cautious. A dangerous tribe inhabited these fields, and the troops wanted to fight.

Maddeningly, the fights were hard to find. Soldiers waited for days, listening to their radios crackle with rumours and reports of skirmishes. They lolled in the shade of their troop carriers, dazed by the heat and deprived of sleep by their regular shifts to keep watch. They rigged up sound systems inside the armoured shell of their vehicles and hip-hop echoed over the emptiness. Others passed the time watching DVDs, or clipping photos of women from magazines. Their vehicles offered more than protection from bullets, more than powerful weapons; they were life itself, a source of food and electricity and comfort. Soldiers did not even call them vehicles; instead, they were "boats," sailing through desolation. Inside the metal armour was civilization. Outside was terror.

In the end, the operation settled into a search of recently abandoned Taliban bases. The soldiers' trophies were mostly junk: flares, tripwires, ammunition holders, bullets, rocket-propelled grenades, timing devices, gun parts and a mobile phone rewired to serve as a remote trigger for explosives. Most of the insurgents seemed to have been living in Afghan homes, but some excavated tunnels in the hard-baked earth. One of these fortifications started as a trench in a streambed and curved away into a small entrance. I ducked low and scrambled inside on my hands and knees, waiting for a moment inside to adjust to the cool darkness. The trench continued underground, covered by layers of sticks and corrugated metal sheeting, buried under layers of dirt. I groped my way through the tunnel's zigzags, holding out my cellphone to cast light on the rough walls. Eventually the crawlspace opened up into a cavern, lit by shafts of light from chinks in the mud. The floor was covered with garbage, including the sort of water bottles imported to Afghanistan by the international troops. Some of the empty wrappers also suggested that the insurgents had been eating packaged food distributed by well-meaning foreigners. A soldier shouted down, asking what I'd found in the Taliban tunnels.

"Nothing," I said. "Dead end."

Canadian soldier rests during Operation Medusa

CHAPTER 5

MEDUSA'S AFTERMATH SEPTEMBER 2006

"The war's over, dude." That was my wildly incorrect assessment in an e-mail to a friend on September 12, as international forces settled into their freshly conquered swath of farmland in the Panjwai valley. Operation Medusa had been a defining moment for NATO, the largest battle Afghanistan had witnessed since the fall of the Taliban regime. It wasn't officially finished, but it was cooling down. I caught a ride on a supply convoy to a small outpost, where one officer compared the happy atmosphere to that of a classroom near the end of a school year. That evening, I sat with Canada's battle group commander and watched the sun setting over the valley from the same rooftop where I had witnessed a hail of air strikes several days earlier. Leaning back in his metal folding chair, Lieutenant-Colonel Lavoie expressed pride that the combined NATO forces had successfully beaten a major gathering of insurgents. But he still seemed taken aback that so many Taliban had surfaced in the first place. He looked tired.

"After fighting one of the biggest engagements we've seen here in the last four or five years," he said, "I'll be honest, the numbers that came at us surprised me. I'd say their tenacity surprised me as well." The commander tried to explain the Taliban resurgence as a sign of their desperation: as thousands of NATO troops arrived in the south, the insurgents were forced to choose between retreating or attacking, he said. "They're caught between a rock and a hard place." That's how the military leadership viewed their opponents at the time, as hapless mercenaries who were bullied into throwing themselves into the fight, believing they would face punishment from ringleaders in Pakistan if they didn't sacrifice themselves on the battlefield. At the same time, the military also appeared to think the Taliban had global ambitions, and the reach necessary to export terrorism around the world: "I don't look at this purely from the perspective that I'm here to help the Afghans fight an enemy," the colonel said. "Because, yeah, clearly the Taliban are the enemy of the Afghan people. But on a much broader scale, they're also the enemy of most democratic countries and the Western world."

I respected this commander, but his views didn't make sense. It seemed unlikely that villagers in the Panjwai valley would allow their homes to be used as Taliban outposts entirely against their will; in a place where farmers often stashed automatic weapons in their houses for self-defence, I couldn't believe that the locals would be easily intimidated into co-operating. (They were not so easily persuaded to help the NATO forces, for example.) How could the Taliban multiply so astonishingly? And, more broadly, was NATO really fighting—as advertised—the enemies of the Western world, or just a bunch of rebellious farmers? As soon as I'd returned from the battlefield, had a shower and a cheeseburger and a full night of sleep in an air-conditioned tent, I left my body armour in a heap on the floor of the media tent. I changed into more comfortable cloth- ing, and went in search of answers.

In the meantime, Western politicians and military leaders were busy claiming victory. "The Taliban is on the run," proclaimed Canadian prime minister Stephen Harper in a nationally televised address, in which he surrounded himself with families of victims from the 9/11 attacks. US Marine general James Jones, then serving as NATO's most senior commander, told a Senate committee that the Taliban had given international forces a difficult test, and "they passed brilliantly and successfully." In a speech on September 29, President George W. Bush elaborated on the same message, and gave his own summary of Operation Medusa:

We saw the effectiveness of NATO forces this summer, when NATO took responsibility from the United States for security operations in southern Afghanistan. The Taliban saw the transfer of the region from the United States to NATO control as a window of opportunity. They saw it as an opportunity to test the will of nations other than the United States. See, they've been testing our will. And they understand it's strong, and they need to understand it will remain strong.

President Bush waited for applause from his audience, a group of reserve officers, and continued:

So the Taliban massed an estimated eight hundred to nine hundred fighters near Kandahar to face the NATO force head-on. And that was a mistake. Earlier this month, NATO launched Operation Medusa. Together with the Afghan National Army, troops from Canada, and Denmark, and the Netherlands, and Britain, and the United States engaged the enemy, with operational support from Romanian, and Portuguese, and Estonian forces. According to NATO commanders, NATO forces killed hundreds of Taliban fighters. . . . The operation also sent a clear message to the Afghan people: that NATO is standing with you.

The number of Taliban killed in the operation seemed to climb higher as the triumphant speeches continued. Some military officials bragged that US Spectre gunships had hunted fleeing Taliban into the desert and slaughtered them by the hundreds. The lumbering warplanes killed so many insurgents that they ran short of ammunition, the officers said, speaking in awed tones about how the Spectre's smoky flares make the aircraft look like a shining angel of death. Some officials claimed that fifteen hundred or more insurgents died in the operation, prompting breathless media reports that the battle killed off a major portion of the estimated three to four thousand committed fighters in the entire country. I told my boss to remain skeptical about these claims: "For anybody to suggest anything about a certain number of Taliban killed as 'a large chunk of the entire force' tells me that person knows absolutely nothing about this battlefield," I wrote in an e-mail to the newsroom. "The Taliban are a movement, not a discrete number of fighters."

Kandahar's politicians also declared victory. On September 17, Governor Asadullah Khalid summoned journalists to his palace garden, an oasis of manicured grass and rose bushes hidden behind high walls in the heart of the city. "The enemy has been completely eliminated," Mr. Khalid announced. The governor had made his entrance through a trellised archway covered with flowers, flanked by senior Afghan security commanders and NATO's Brigadier-General Fraser. It was all very picturesque, if you ignored the fact that a suicide bomber had rammed a minivan full of explosives into a NATO convoy earlier that morning, suggesting that the Taliban had not, in fact, vanished. All the same, the government's supporters in Kandahar seemed satisfied. The Taliban were no longer camped on the outskirts of their urban enclave, and the threat of major battles in the city streets had faded. The fighting season was coming to an end as autumn approached, and cold rain turned the former battlefields into rivers of mud that literally stopped insurgents in their tracks.

I picked my way through the muddy streets one afternoon, and went to see Haji Mohammed Qassam, a provincial council member. The politician represented a branch of the Barakzai tribe, a group that generally aligned itself with the foreign troops in Kandahar. He lived in a compound on the south side of the city, at the end of a narrow alley. A teenager with a Kalashnikov guarded the mouth of the alley, but he smiled when he recognized me from previous visits. Inside, Mr. Qassam was hosting a group of bearded elders. I slipped out of my sandals at the doorway and gave the ritual greetings as I stepped onto the carpet: *Salam aleikum, tsanga ye?* Peace be upon you, how are you? I only understood a few of the words; the rest was a stream of syllables repeated from memory, part of an elaborate dance required to enter a room politely. I shook hands with every man in the circle before Mr. Qassam waved to a seat beside him on a red velveteen cushion. Sitting cross-legged, I made eye contact with each man in the room and repeated the greetings. I've always appreciated the gentility of these customs; it also gives you plenty of time to assess your companions and decide if they're dangerous. I was grateful to Mr. Qassam for inviting me to sit beside him, because if a busy man banishes you to a low-prestige seat near the doorway you may find yourself waiting for hours as he finishes his business.

Mr. Qassam switched from his own language to a rapid-fire patter of barely intelligible English, hard for me to understand and impossible for the others in the room. "Most people are happy about this fighting," he said. If the Taliban weren't stopped in Panjwai, he said, they would have spilled over into the neighbouring district of Dand, where his own farms were located. He seemed to recognize that his opinion might appear self-serving. "But we have some people in Kandahar with sympathy for the Taliban," he acknowledged, "and they did not like this fight." Either way, nobody thought the fighting in the Panjwai valley was finished, he said. Tens of thousands of local residents who fled their homes now refused to go back, despite NATO's promise to rebuild their villages.

The politician paused for breath, and I slipped in the two questions that were preoccupying me: Why so many Taliban? And, are they really international terrorists, or disgruntled locals? Mr. Qassam started with the second question, saying that some of the insurgents did arrive from religious schools in Pakistan, so in that sense they were operating internationally—but everybody in the south views the Pakistan border as an illegitimate line dividing the Pashtun people, so nobody would see the Taliban as foreigners. The only group of insurgents from far-flung places were probably the members of Hizb-i-Islami, a militia that operates semi-independently in eastern Afghanistan. But those were a tiny minority of the fighters, he said; the heart of the problem was that villagers rebelled against the government. This caught my attention, because it reminded me of Lieutenant Edwards, the US officer who had described the rebellious villagers in Zabul. But why would any villager reject a government that is bringing an avalanche of foreign aid? Mr. Qassam himself was involved with distributing the riches, spending hours sitting with planners who dished out money for bridges, schools and irrigation projects. The politician poked buttons on a few cellphones, stalling for a moment. Finally he said, "We make big mistakes."

He offered several examples of blunders in the months before Operation Medusa, but one event stood out as the biggest: in the summer of 2006, the Afghan government sent a commander named Abdul Razik to stop the Taliban from gaining strength in the Panjwai valley. Mr. Razik had official status as a commander of the Afghan Border Police in a district near the Pakistani border, and sometimes described himself as a "Colonel Razik" (or, later, "General Razik"), but in those days his force resembled an informal militia drawn from members of the Achakzai tribe. Unfortunately, the Achakzai had been feuding for centuries with another major tribe that inhabits the borderland, the Noorzai. The Noorzai are also populous in the river valley southwest of Kandahar city, so when the government dispatched Mr. Razik there in August, the locals did not view the action as an exercise of authority by the central government; instead, they saw an incursion by their tribal enemy. Rumours spread through the valley that the police commander intended to kill not only Taliban but any member of the Noorzai tribe. The issue must have been further confused by the fact that the Panjwai valley was among the Taliban's first strongholds during their sweep to power in 1994, which came with help from powerful backers among the Noorzai. Any campaign to kill off people with Taliban links must have been viewed by the locals as indiscriminate slaughter, because of the sheer density of people with such connections in the area. In any case, Mr. Razik's band of men soon found themselves facing an armed uprising. Locals ambushed them southwest of the district's biggest town, forcing Mr. Razik to retreat, with the bodies of policemen abandoned to rot in the middle of the road. Humiliatingly, the government had to negotiate with local tribesmen for permission to give the officers a proper burial. "This was a bad idea, to bring Abdul Razik," Mr. Qassam said. "One village had ten or twenty fighters against the government before he came—and the next day, maybe two hundred."

I wanted to meet some of those angry Noorzai tribesmen. One of my translators was a member of the Noorzai himself, but that actually made the task more difficult. Only a few members of his family were aware that he worked for the foreign media, and it would have been dangerous to be branded as a collaborator with the infidels. Our interview subjects were also nervous about being observed talking with a foreigner, which made our encounters clandestine. We found one subject squatting at an arranged location in an alleyway, and he led us around the back of his house so he could usher me into his guest room without being noticed. A middle-aged man with a bushy beard, he settled into the cushions while his son poured water from a steel pitcher to wash his father's hands, then ours. He had returned the previous day from the Panjwai valley, where he owned a large farm. His grape vines were dying, he said, because the diesel generator that ran his water pump had broken and no repairman wanted to risk the trip. Insurgents had mined the road to his homestead. One of his field hands had recently noticed two wires sticking out of the dirt; innocently fiddling with the unusual objects, he touched the wires together—and was knocked flat on his back by an explosion as a nearby bridge disappeared in a shower of rubble. "The Taliban were angry with him," the farmer said, chuckling. "He wasted an expensive mine." Still, the insurgents did not punish the worker for ruining their booby trap. The Taliban appeared to be wooing the locals with careful behaviour, forbidding their fighters from looting homes or robbing travellers. "When they came to my farm, they did not eat my grapes without permission," the farmer said approvingly. Not that the Taliban presence meant no risks. He pulled a black leather diary from his breast pocket and showed me where he had scribbled a few phone numbers for government officials. Those numbers could have gotten him killed if the Taliban had found the diary during their regular searches at checkpoints, because the fighters would have assumed he was working with the government. Still, he considered the Afghan police far more predatory. Like other local people, he never used the Pashto word for "police" when discussing law enforcement: instead, he described the security forces as *topakan*, which translates loosely as "gun lord" or warlord. He spit the word like an epithet. The *topakan* had originally been proud mujahedeen, holy warriors who expelled the Soviet forces, but they fell upon each other in a frenzy of civil war from 1992 to 1994, a period of internecine warfare that became the darkest days anybody could remember. Rebels who had defended the country turned into petty marauders—*topakan*—squabbling with each other for territory. For local police to be tarred with the label *topakan* meant they had become the worst sort of brigands in the eyes of the people. These grievances were exploited by the Taliban, who had presented themselves as a way of removing the *topakan* during the establishment of their original regime in 1994. (Taliban is the plural form of *talib*, or student, and the movement has always drawn support from the idea of virtue associated with religious study.) Although wealthy, the landowner I was interviewing dressed shabbily for the sake of paying smaller bribes at checkpoints. His clothes were stained and dirty, his cheap wristwatch losing its gold patina. "You know why the Taliban are increasing day by day?" he said. "The local forces beat people and steal their money."

I heard similar stories in the days after Operation Medusa, as I tried to puzzle through how the battle started. Villagers described police stealing from shops, ransacking storehouses and seizing caches of opium that would never be reported. Some committed arson to cover up their looting and blamed the insurgents for the fires. Shakedowns cost the locals their wristwatches, cellphones, even their vehicles. The police confiscated so many motorcycles that one young man took a novel approach to avoiding the problem. Driving up to a checkpoint one summer evening, he yanked the keys from the ignition of his motorcycle and threw them into the bushes. He rolled gently to a stop at the police roadblock and parked his bike. The officers demanded his keys, but he explained that he'd tossed them away. "They beat him, took his money and his watch. But he kept his bike," said the young man's friend, laughing. It was unclear how the youth later managed to collect his bike, but the stunt turned him into a local hero for outwitting the cops.

The insurgents were celebrated for expelling the police from part of the Panjwai valley in the months before Operation Medusa. The Taliban enforced a harsh order, punishing thieves by chopping off their hands. But the insurgents also relaxed some of the rules enforced by their previous government, which had forbidden any music except Taliban chants. "My brother-in-law had a wedding this summer," a farmer said. "We didn't have any music or drumming. Some Taliban arrived at the wedding, and they said, 'Why no music?' We said, 'Because you have forbidden these things.' They told us, 'No, no, no. Now the Taliban behave like common people.'" He seemed disappointed that foreign troops had driven the insurgents away. After the government regained control of the area, he said, its officers resumed their predations.

I found myself wondering whether Operation Medusa had changed anything. You can hear me searching for a little optimism in the conversation I recorded with Talatbek Masadykov, then serving as head of the United Nations mission in southern Afghanistan. My first question to him was a rambling effort to string together the events of the previous month into a hopeful narrative. I told him about my friends in Kandahar who kept their suitcases packed before Operation Medusa because they expected a Taliban rampage into the city. I talked about how frightened the local residents seemed during the final weeks before the battle, and asked whether the NATO offensive had eased any of those fears. The veteran UN official shook his head. "I don't think so," he said. "The security situation has not improved." Probably no foreigner was better qualified to make such a judgment. With his fresh haircut, lime-green golf shirt and pressed khaki pants, Mr. Masadykov looked too clean to have expertise about the war; a casual visitor might wonder if he ever left the walled gardens of his compound. His appearance was misleading, however; Mr. Masadykov had decades of experience in the region, and was among the rare foreigners who could speak fluent Pashto. During the initial years of his UN job, in 2002 and 2003, he had visited every district of the nine southern provinces, travelling without armed escorts in white UN-marked vehicles, even camping for two nights in the notorious Baghran valley, a Taliban stronghold in northern Helmand province. Such travel was daring, but not suicidal, in the period of relative peace after the collapse of the Taliban government in 2001. But in the years that followed, Mr. Masadykov had watched the situation deteriorate. His security teams began to draw up maps to identify the roads that were still acceptable for travel by UN vehicles. By the time of our conversation in 2006, only two roads in Kandahar remained open. "Slowly, slowly our movement was restricted," he said, his English slightly accented by his native roots in Kyrgyzstan. "Slowly, slowly, every time, we were going to less number of districts, less number of villages." He seemed cynical about whether the deterioration could be halted with operations such as Medusa. In the days before the battle, NATO commanders had promised this attack would be different from previous sweeps into rural Kandahar because they would follow up by holding the Panjwai valley with the assistance of local forces and bring aid to the villagers. But those local Afghan security forces were themselves often the source of trouble, Mr. Masadykov said: "They are misbehaving sometimes, looting, going to search and at the same time stealing everything in the houses. We are receiving a lot of complaints about it." Although he was reluctant to accuse individual police commanders of abuses, he eventually confirmed the story of Abdul Razik, and how the police commander became embroiled in tribal conflict. "The elders said, 'No. Enough is enough. We will take a stand, we will take power.' They were not exactly real Taliban. But in this one moment, these few days, they joined the anti-government elements and started fighting. The cleanup operations in those days killed a lot of people who were Noorzais, who were not really against the government but who were against this commander."

I told the UN chief about my recent conversations with disgruntled tribesmen, and their complaints about the Afghan police behaving like robbers.

"Yes, this a case of bad governance," Mr. Masadykov replied. "I can say now, when we're talking about Taliban, maybe half of these so-called anti-government elements acting here in this area of the south, they had to join this Taliban movement or anti-government movement because of the misbehaviour of these bad guys." He paused for effect, looking intently at me, and then looking at my digital recorder on the table between us. He probably understood that this wasn't good for his career, describing NATO's triumph as the killing of farmers with legitimate grievances. But he continued anyway: "I recently saw the report where they listed the names of the so-called Taliban commanders. Among them, knowing this area more or less—not all of them, of course, but some of them—I saw they are not Taliban. They were listed by internationals because internationals were informed by the local [Afghan] administration.

And still we have the people who are trying to play games, using the Canadians and Brits against their own personal tribal enemies. I saw people who were never Taliban, they're now fighting against some certain tribal elders or certain groups."

Not long after my story was published, under the headline "Inspiring tale of triumph over Taliban not all it seems," the UN chief was transferred away from Kandahar. Mr. Masadykov's boss downplayed his comments, saying they did not reflect the official view of the United Nations.

Whatever official words were used to describe the effects of Operation Medusa, events on the ground conveyed their own message. A steady drumbeat of violence filled the following weeks, unabated by the operation. For the Canadian soldiers who led the charge into the Panjwai valley, the month after their glorious victory would prove more deadly than Medusa itself, with ten soldiers killed by insurgent attacks. The unit of soldiers I had followed into the Panjwai valley, the Nomads, suffered their first death at the end of September, when a twenty-three-year-old private named Josh Klukie stepped on a booby trap. It was probably an anti-personnel landmine stacked on top of a tank mine, because the explosion was big enough to destroy a vehicle. I remembered Private Klukie as a man in peak physical shape, like a guy in a recruiting poster. He'd been walking through the same cluster of villages that we had swept into during Medusa. His unit had avoided the roads during their foot patrol because they knew insurgents buried explosives along the well-travelled routes, but in the early afternoon they started following a makeshift track that I'd watched them bulldozing two weeks earlier. The dust was deep and powdery: a good place to hide a bomb. "We went on the road, and it was that dust, that fine dust, you know?" said one of his friends two days later, when we met beside the runway at Kandahar Air Field. His unit had just loaded Private Klukie's flag-draped casket onto a transport plane, and many of the soldiers had tears in their eyes, but the young corporal was steady enough to give me an account of the death.

The soldiers had been walking in single file. The explosion kicked up so much debris that everybody was blinded in the first moments, and the soldiers called out each others' names until it was clear that Private Klukie wasn't answering. His friend was among the first to discover him, about fifty metres off the path.

"He landed in the vineyard," he said. "He was laying on his back when the American medic and I found him. We immediately started working, without saying anything to each other. He put a tourniquet on his right leg, which was almost completely gone. I put tourniquets on his arm and his other leg. You could tell he couldn't hear anything, but he could recognize me, you know. I was looking right at him. He couldn't say anything. I was just telling him to keep fighting, you know, keep fighting, keep fighting. I had that last tourniquet on him, I grabbed him by the shoulder, I'm like, 'This is nothing, Josh, this is nothing.' He just looked at me, smiled, and that was it."

The corporal paused to reflect on those final moments before his friend's death. "I was just looking at him. I was trying to encourage him as best I could, because there was really nothing else we could do. He fought it for as long as he could, but you know. It was maybe three minutes. He didn't suffer. He didn't feel anything. He wasn't crying out in pain. He was just there, and in shock."

The young soldier had done so many chest compressions that he cracked all the ribs in his friend's ruined body. He continued until the American medic hauled him away. The US soldiers also gathered up some of the scattered body parts—"things that were missing, the messier work"—and then the Canadians lifted the body bag and carried their comrade home. Back at the airbase, Klukie's friend didn't sleep at all on the first night after the explosion. "I thought a lot about it. Initially I was like, 'I've kind of had enough of this. Shooting, rockets, mortars, people trying to kill you.'" But when we talked, after the farewell ceremony, the soldier had changed his mind: "I want to get back out there, and I definitely want to get a grip and get revenge."

There was the word again: revenge. Commanders talked about the war in abstract terms, but the fight became personal for anybody who picked up the charred remnants of a dead friend.

Operation Medusa would later prove to be the biggest gathering of Taliban to directly confront US and NATO forces. But nothing was resolved; this was only the beginning of a bloodier phase in the war. The international community failed to learn the most important lesson of Operation Medusa: the tensions that built up in the summer of 2006 were mostly the fault of the predatory local government. There were widespread complaints about Mr. Razik's militia; instead of scuttling his career, however, his enthusiasm for battle helped him rise to prominence in the following years. Brigadier-General Razik is now the most powerful police officer in southern Afghanistan. Some of his NATO allies have misgivings about his reputation for brutality, but that same reputation is viewed as an asset by military planners looking for Afghan leaders tough enough to survive after the withdrawal of troops in 2014. Western strategists are gambling that everybody I spoke with after Medusa was wrong, essentially, that the rebellion wasn't provoked by harsh policing—or, at least, they are betting that strongmen such as Mr. Razik can stamp out such rebellions.

It's impossible to know who will be proven correct. I hope my instincts are wrong. None of what I learned about the Taliban in the next few months, however, gave me any comfort that the insurgency could be so easily tamed.

A member of Jamiat Ulema-e-Islam pretends to light an American flag on fire

CHAPTER 6

QUETTA NOVEMBER 2006

The Taliban were mysterious. You never knew whether the villager who offered you tea secretly worked for the insurgents. Even when shooting at you, they rarely showed more than a muzzle flash. Every day brought new warnings: two suicide bombers planning to hit military convoys; no, scratch that, five bombers going after UN installations; no, forget it, today you should watch for jihadists posing as taxi drivers. Many of these warnings mentioned Kandahar's most common vehicle, the white Toyota Corolla, so every car on the road seemed like a threat. Military officials took me aside and revealed under the strictest confidence that I should be careful of men whose traditional long shirts were cut square at the bottom, or those with exceptionally large white turbans, or even black turbans. They confided that the insurgents were brainwashed religious students who had been sexually abused by their teachers—emotionally stunted orphans desperate for paradise. Propaganda images posted in the washrooms at Kandahar Air Field warned soldiers about Taliban eavesdropping, with a cartoon version of the insurgent portrayed as a leering devil with green skin and yellow eyes. The foreign troops believed they were fighting monsters.

These images coloured my first meeting with a Taliban gunman, in 2006, at the offices of an Afghan government program called

Peace Through Strength (PTS). In theory, PTS was supposed to broker reconciliation talks with Taliban factions, but its officials were incapable of offering much except surrender; naturally, this made the reconciliation office a quiet place. A few Taliban occasionally straggled into the PTS system, however, and one day my translator got a call from a friend saying we could visit a Taliban fighter if we hurried over. Soon I was shaking hands with a man wearing, contrary to expectations, a small grey turban and a shirt tailored with a rounded cut. My first impression was of a caged animal, a man built like a wrestler who leapt off a couch, shook my hand, and then stalked the room as if hunting for an exit. At one point he reached into his pocket and my translator lurched forward, preparing to throw himself at the fighter—this translator was useful in such situations, heavily muscled and trained in martial arts—but the insurgent only smiled and pulled out a metal box, not a weapon. He twisted the box open and wadded his mouth full of green gunk called *naswar*, a popular kind of chewing tobacco mixed with ash and lime. He chewed with his mouth open, spitting in a metal cuspidor.

He introduced himself as the cousin of a Taliban leader and asked me to call him Malik, a pseudonym. He had surrendered to the reconciliation program in hopes of trading his co-operation for the freedom of his younger brother, who was held captive in a government jail. But the deal fell apart, leaving Malik in limbo, and he had been living for six months under guard himself in a government house—not entirely free but not officially a prisoner. We talked in a comfortable room with an air conditioner and a television playing National Geographic programs. He seemed tired of interrogations, telling me right away that he wouldn't reveal where any Taliban were hiding, and wouldn't give any estimates of insurgent strength. He also cautioned that he would not reveal how the insurgents get weapons or training. I hadn't asked him any of those things, and started with easy questions about his hometown north of the city. I tried to slip a recording device onto the table between us, which most Afghans mistook for a cellphone, but Malik was too savvy. He recognized the recorder and told me to switch it off. We talked for hours, a circular conversation that revealed little, and even after several meetings over a period of weeks, I never gained any valuable insight. He spoke in generalities, repeating the Taliban's usual complaints about civilian casualties and the torture of prisoners. "If the coalition treated prisoners well, if they didn't bombard people and kill civilians, we would never be successful," he said. "We would never have so many recruits."

At times he was friendly, apparently believing that telling his story would help release his brother from prison—but he could also turn nasty. My translator left me alone with him for five minutes, and he started questioning me in rudimentary English: "Jesus or Moses?" He repeated the question over and over, with puzzling intensity, until my translator returned and assured him that I'm a Christian ("Jesus") and not Jewish ("Moses"). The answer satisfied him, and I decided not to attempt a nuanced discussion of spirituality with a hot-tempered killer. We left that meeting with a sense that Malik was a little too curious about me. The office guards checked the road outside for threats, as usual, before signalling that it was safe to drive away—but that precaution didn't stop a white Toyota Corolla from following us. My driver indicated something was wrong by staring in the rear-view mirror and hissing through his teeth. He swerved down side streets, into a jumble of garbage-strewn slums. The tail stayed on us, and we accelerated. The slum roads were narrow, edged by high mud walls and riddled with ruts and hillocks. A group of children watched solemnly as we raced past. I called a friend who lived nearby, and he opened his gates as we approached his well-guarded compound. Our car skidded to a stop in his courtyard and his guards shut the door immediately behind us. We spent a tense afternoon in hiding, but it seemed whoever was following hadn't noticed us slip away.

I never visited Malik again, and stayed away from the Taliban reconciliation office for several months. My next meeting with an insurgent was arranged more informally. It was the autumn of 2006, in the aftermath of Operation Medusa, and one of my translators scheduled a chat with a relative who had participated in the fighting. Like many Afghans, my translator's extended family included both government workers and insurgents. Not all of them disagreed with each other ideologically; sometimes they followed the pragmatic tradition in which Afghan families hedge their bets, sending their sons to serve in a variety of factions in a conflict. We had tea at a friend's compound, but the fighter seemed wary. As with my previous encounter, I found this Talib hard to read. The weathered creases around his eyes seemed permanently crinkled in amusement, even when he was spewing hatred. "No Muslim wants the human garbage of foreign soldiers in beautiful Afghanistan," he said cheerfully, as if this was obvious. He told me several things I didn't find credible, such as his claim that the massed army of Taliban fighters southwest of the city had been a diversionary tactic; I had crawled through the insurgents' trenches, and couldn't believe that anybody would dig those bunkers without intending to defend them. Some of his battle stories also seemed intended to exaggerate his fervour: "I saw eleven Taliban hit by a bomb. Two survived, and they were crying out: 'Why did we survive? Our friends have left us behind! We pray for our chance of martyrdom.'" His voice remained light-hearted as he described his comrades blown to pieces. After an hour of conversation, he thanked us for tea and slipped out the door.

These encounters always left me feeling even more curious. I wanted to go deeper, wanted a better sense of the insurgents' origins. I had seen the Pakistani phone numbers in the diary of a fighter killed earlier that year, and heard complaints from military officials about the insurgents' safe havens across the border. Some insurgent militias that fought alongside the Taliban were believed to operate from bases in the northern parts of Pakistan's borderlands, but I was interested in the main Taliban leadership council, or *rahbari shura*, sometimes called the "Quetta Council," named after the provincial capital of Balochistan, just inside the Pakistani border. I wanted to see the place that reputedly served as the Taliban's headquarters.

We left early on a damp morning in November 2006 and drove to Pakistan. My translator and I were both dressed in Afghan clothing, so we walked across the border using the standard local method, pressing a one-hundred-rupee note (equivalent to one dollar) into a guard's hand. We passed under the Friendship Gate, a hulking three-storey marker constructed by Pakistan in an unfriendly effort to designate a border that Afghanistan has never recognized. We weren't searched, weren't asked for identification, and I ended up in Pakistani territory so quickly that I was disoriented. I'd had only a few hours' sleep the previous night and I found myself a bit lost when my Afghan translator, who was crossing illegally, said goodbye and disappeared back across the frontier. I needed to get my visa stamped because I didn't want to travel without proper documents, but nor did I want to attract too much attention from the crowds of tribesmen. I stepped into a building that looked like a passport office, but it turned out to be an outpost of the Frontier Corps, a paramilitary security force. By the time I realized my mistake, the soldiers had made it clear that I wasn't free to leave. I was detained for a few hours, probably for my own safety, as the soldiers wondered what to do with a young foreigner. I drank several cups of tea with a well-mannered officer before I was rescued by the Pakistani journalist who had arranged to pick me up. He bundled me into a car, and as we climbed up the mountain passes he commented that moving a Western journalist across the border was, in some ways, similar to drug smuggling.

Even before we reached Quetta, I could see that the landscape was marked with signs of a political struggle. Descending from the rocky ledges onto the plains of Balochistan, I saw the colours red, white and green painted on every available surface: houses, placards, even big rocks beside the road. My guide explained these were the colours of Pashtoonkhwa, nationalists from the Pashtun ethnic group who favoured breaking the tribal areas away from Pakistan and forming an independent territory, or joining Afghanistan. They accused the government in Islamabad of helping the Taliban. Meanwhile, their main rivals also had flags everywhere, horizontal black-and-white banners that fluttered over houses and religious schools. These signified the Jamiat Ulema-e-Islam (JUI), a political party sympathetic to the Taliban. We drove past large JUI madrassas that looked more like castles than religious schools; these were suspected of feeding recruits to the Afghan insurgency. I was amazed at how openly people displayed their allegiances. In Afghanistan people camouflaged themselves for safety, while in Pakistan, supporters and opponents of the Taliban hung their advertisements from every lamppost and electricity wire. Their symbols overwhelmed the clutter of commercial billboards, like an election campaign.

This political contest gripped every corner of the city, including the entertainment market. My guide took me into a half-constructed shopping mall, past luggage stores and rug emporiums, up a flight of bare concrete stairs to a row of stalls selling cassette tapes and compact discs. A group of boys playing pool glanced at us suspiciously as we browsed the shops. Glossy posters showed Bollywood girls, glittering in their low-cut blouses and jewelled hair. Next door, more pious shops were plastered to the ceiling with album covers featuring mosques and holy sites in Pakistan and Saudi Arabia. Mullahs with heavy beards glowered from the posters. Under the glass counters, bumper stickers sparkled in Urdu, Pashto and English: "Down with Bush! Down with Clinton! Down with the foreign enemies!" A vendor happily talked about his discs with Islamic prayers and speeches, but he was not eager to discuss his Taliban videos. He denied selling any such thing, but when pressed he acknowledged, "Well, maybe one or two." He reached into a stack and pulled out an unmarked disc. We found several hours of Taliban propaganda at the market, some for less than a dollar per disc, which my translators searched for useful information.

The footage usually contained an author's note: "Published by the Islamic Emirate of Afghanistan," using the Taliban's name for their former regime. The videos were amateurish, but offered scenes of insurgents' lives: A Taliban commander inspects trenches, test-fires a machine gun, even bakes some bread. A gang of armed fighters enjoys a boat ride near the Kajaki Dam—a site supposedly guarded by foreign troops—and a smiling gunman leans over the gunnel to taste the waters. The videos were edited to avoid giving away too much information, however, and were often deceiving. One of my translators noticed text scrolling across the video, announcing the Taliban had obtained Stinger missiles, and to my uneducated eye the dark metal object on a fighter's shoulder *did* resemble one of the US anti-aircraft missiles that had proven formidable against the Soviet in the 1980s. I urgently sent copies of the image to weapons experts, but they responded unequivocally: No, that was not a Stinger missile. It was a cheap Russian-designed weapon called a Strela-2m, or SA-7B, common on the black market and easily fooled by flares. Still, it was proof that the insurgents had obtained surface-to-air missiles.

These bits of insight made it worthwhile to keep scrutinizing the Taliban videos. We kept going for several months, buying discs and churning through them for bits of news, but it was too distressing. The Taliban propaganda showed a sickening taste for blood. Many sequences included footage of bomb attacks, with military vehicles blown to pieces. Other clips were snuff films, as Afghan men confessed to collaborating with the foreign occupiers and then suffered slow beheadings. The victims writhed in agony while their captors sliced and sawed, until the Taliban finally held up the severed heads in triumph. One of the shots lingered on the blood spreading in long rivulets, the streams of red almost supernaturally bright in the Afghan sun. The onslaught of these images made me feel like crying, my chest and stomach tightening. My translators' faces would twist with emotion as well, and eventually they needed to stop and compose themselves. We tried to fast-forward through the grisly parts, but we still kept seeing awful things. For journalists who risked falling into Taliban hands almost every day, it was too easy to imagine ourselves in those videos. We stopped watching.

Years later, a friend revealed how the Taliban would use the bloodthirsty imagery to taunt their opponents. A messenger left a package containing a video disc at the front gates of the Kandahar governor's palace one morning in 2007. It showed a boy, maybe twelve years old, wearing a camouflage jacket and a white headband. In his childish voice, the boy denounces a blindfolded man as a traitor and a spy for the Americans. Then he kneels over the captive and slices at his throat with a knife, decapitating him. The child executioner would later make headlines as viewers around the world expressed shock that a small boy would be drawn into such depravity, but an important detail was never reported in the news. Kandahar's governor at the time, Asadullah Khalid, had personally known the victim—who was, in fact, a spy. The hand-delivered video informed the governor that his agent was dead.

I tried to avoid being noticed in Quetta. I didn't take many photographs, and slouched around the city disguised as an Afghan tribesman. In a city known as the Taliban's headquarters, I figured it was best to look like one of them. This only made my acquaintances nervous, however, and my guide told me that I looked like a suicide bomber. He removed my Kandahari cap and shawl, and took me drinking. His social group turned out to be a raucous mix of intellectuals, businessmen and old communists. Many of them spoke English, and they consumed impressive amounts of liquor, in private. Listening to them tell crude jokes and chat with their mistresses on their cellphones, I was struck by how different these men seemed from the Taliban planners who almost certainly lived in the same neighbourhoods. It was like the Bollywood girls on display in the market, right beside the extremist mullahs. Quetta was a city invaded not only by Taliban fighters, but also by Western culture. New stores sold video games decorated with girls in revealing white tank tops, while nearby women covered their faces with burkas. The same contrasts exist in many parts of the Muslim world, but in Quetta the differences seemed especially sharp. A cultural war ran parallel with the actual war.

While my guide was trying to arrange a meeting with the Taliban, we passed the time by attending a Pashtoonkhwa political rally, where several of the speeches touched on Taliban culture. The rally seemed well organized, with trucks and busses ferrying people to an empty tract outside the city. Some people were wearing brand-new Pashtoonkhwa baseball caps, which made me wonder who was donating so much money to the Taliban's political enemies. A party leader gave a rousing critique of the pro-Taliban religious parties. Shouting into the rasping loudspeaker, he pointed out that a senior figure from one of the conservative groups had two educated daughters in parliament, and yet supported Afghan insurgents who fought against female education. "If someone goes to school, they beat them up, they throw acid, they say, 'This is not Islam.' But what kind of Islam is this? In Pakistani universities there is co-education, but they don't want the same thing for Afghanistan."

Party organizers became curious about me, the only foreigner in the crowd, and afterward the main speaker invited me back to his headquarters. Sipping tea, he sketched out his understanding of how the Taliban are funded. I drew a diagram of his explanation in my notebook:

ISI ——→ DRUG MAFIA ——→ TALIBAN SHURA ——→ FIGHTERS

The politician's understanding was that Pakistan's biggest spy agency, Inter-Services Intelligence (ISI), allowed drug smugglers safe passage through Pakistan's territory in exchange for cash payments to the Taliban shura, or leadership council, which was believed to be based in Quetta. I would later meet a smuggler who confirmed this business model; he claimed to have witnessed drug dealers making payoffs to Taliban leaders, noting that the crisp bricks of money still had their original bank seals. But later interviews also suggested other ways the Taliban earned money, which would lend themselves to different diagrams:

ARAB SYMPATHIZERS ⟶ PAKISTAN'S RELIGIOUS PARTIES ⟶ TALIBAN
AFGHAN SYMPATHIZERS ⟶ FIGHTERS ⟶ TALIBAN
CRIMINAL ACTIVITY ⟷ TALIBAN
CORRUPT OFFICIALS IN AFGHANISTAN ⟷ DRUG MAFIA ⟷ TALIBAN

It was quite complicated, in reality, but on that first trip to Quetta, drinking tea late into the evening with my hosts from the Pashtoonkhwa, the local politician made it sound deceptively simple. Pakistan's government was nervous about the rebellious tribes in the borderlands, he said, so they were trying to divide and rule by funding militants whose anger was directed at Kabul—not Islamabad. "The Taliban don't exist, it's just the ISI, the Pakistani government," he said, adding that he was perplexed about why America was not attacking the regime in Islamabad for supporting terrorism. "We are financing and harbouring. So what are you waiting for?" Like many people in the region, he addressed his comments to me personally— "What are you waiting for?"—as if I represented the West and its military power.

That misunderstanding, common in this part of the world, was especially dangerous when I visited people who hated the foreign troops. Three days later, I went to see the white-bearded provincial leader of the JUI, the main opponent of the Pashtoon nationalists and the religious party most associated with the Taliban. This was the party whose black-and-white flags I had seen everywhere around Quetta, and judging by the presence of their colours and the number of seats they held in the provincial assembly, they were winning the political contest. New religious schools operated by the JUI were being constructed so quickly that party officials at their local headquarters claimed they couldn't keep track of them. When pressed, they estimated that the JUI had "thousands" of schools in the province, with at least four or five hundred around the city of Quetta alone. Their leader denied that his party was helping the Taliban, however, or that his schools were training militants. He also denied that Pakistan's government had any role in helping the insurgency; on the contrary, he complained that the authorities sometimes arrested Taliban leaders. I asked him to name any insurgent leaders arrested in Quetta. He demurred, and launched into an attack on his critics: "Pashtoonkhwa and others are opposing the Taliban and the religious parties, they are supporting the Americans, so they blame us, or the ISI, saying we support the war in Afghanistan," he said. "But they don't have any proof." Still, he didn't bother to hide his sympathy for the Taliban. His office was decorated with anti-American posters, depicting a man firing an automatic rifle from behind fluttering JUI and Taliban flags, with the bullets aimed at a burning American flag. There was another American flag painted in the parking area of the compound, so the faithful could drive over the stars and stripes as they parked their motorbikes. A party member, seeing my camera, rushed to pull out another crudely painted US flag and demonstrate how it could be used as a shoe mat. In case the point hadn't been understood, he crouched down and pretended to burn the flag with a pocket lighter. He waited patiently as I photographed the scene from several angles. He kept the lighter going for the sake of my pictures but never touched the flame to the flag; I was only one journalist, after all, and he was probably saving it for bigger crowds.

After days of hanging around Quetta, and a final night of hard drinking, my guide woke me early one morning. "The Taliban are ready to meet you," he said.

We drove out of the city, into the ramshackle suburbs. I promised not to reveal the location, but this hardly mattered because my hangover made it difficult to stay alert. Our car left the main road and bumped along a narrow path, finally reaching a compound. This was neutral ground, the secret outpost of a Baloch strongman. Like the Taliban, the Baloch Liberation Army runs insurgent operations in the tribal areas, and like the Taliban they're well armed and officially considered terrorists—but unlike the Islamist militants, the Baloch don't usually kill Westerners. Our host was a jovial strongman with enough firepower to make sure the Taliban didn't show up with guns, though in fact, the Taliban who arrived for the meeting looked as if they rarely handled weapons. Wearing pinstripe vests, gold watches and neatly trimmed beards, the two men looked different from the fighters I had encountered in Kandahar. The front-line insurgents were farmers, rough men with dirt under their fingernails, but these Taliban had manicured hands painted with henna. We greeted each other politely and sat down on a carpet, listening to the birds in the garden. One of them spoke a little English, and claimed to have worked in the Taliban government before 2001. (I later checked him out; he had indeed served as a bureaucrat in Kabul and as a diplomat at the Taliban embassy in Islamabad.) He claimed to have visited Panjwai district three times that year to assist with the fighting against US and Canadian troops. Before the climactic battles of Operation Medusa, he said, the insurgents had thousands of men gathered in Panjwai. Now, he declared, the Taliban had decided on a new strategy: breaking their forces into smaller teams of five to seven fighters and choosing less ambitious goals. This fit with the patterns I was seeing, and these Taliban continued to gain my trust with a few other things that I could corroborate. They confirmed that ammunition shipped by the government to remote districts of Kandahar regularly ended up in Taliban hands, as low-level administrators traded bullets for protection. This matched the observation of a US military officer who had told me a couple of months earlier that supplies for the Afghan army often went missing. ("Sometimes you get to see the ammo again," the officer told me with grim humour. "Except you're not on the giving end.") The Taliban also confirmed my suspicion that the conflict was driven, in part, by tribal feuds. They listed the tribes associated with the Karzai government, and complained that a few tribes were monopolizing the spoils of the foreign invasion. This caused resentment among the disenfranchised tribes, which brought recruits to the insurgency. "This is not a fight between the Taliban and the government," one of them said. "This is the tribes defending themselves." I saw these as important statements, although my translator looked bored; these dynamics were well known locally.

After telling the truth about things I could easily confirm, however, the Taliban offered bits of malicious gossip about their enemies. This was a trick I would later recognize as standard practice, but—unfortunately—this time I fell for it, earnestly scribbling notebook pages full of claims that major Afghan politicians were secretly helping the insurgents. This was probably a disinformation campaign; while political figures on both sides of the conflict regularly talked with each other, two of the people mentioned in that interview as secret allies of the Taliban were later killed by insurgents.

As they finished their sweet green tea and looked pointedly at their watches, I asked them a final question. What about the rumour that the Taliban is backed by Pakistan's Inter-Services Intelligence agency?

The insurgents laughed. "Everybody knows the situation," one said.

He was about to elaborate, but his friend cut him off and they excused themselves. One of them asked my guide if we could offer him a ride into Quetta. This made me uneasy, so I sat in the backseat and gave him the front. If I was going to share a car with a Taliban organizer, I wanted to keep an eye on him. He saw my concerned expression in the rear-view mirror and reacted with amusement, muttering something to my guide with a smile. I asked for a translation.

"He says, 'We won't kill you,'" my guide said. "'We'll just kidnap you and sell you.'" This would have been a real possibility if my guide, a Pakistani journalist, had been less trustworthy. Such a venture might have netted him tens of thousands of dollars, more than the modest sum I was paying him. But like many of the local reporters who generously offer their help to foreign correspondents in those tough corners of the world, he was a true believer in journalism. This particular translator had been working as a journalist in Pakistan for decades, never reaping much profit but becoming famous on the streets as a fair-minded narrator of current events. The kidnapping joke was laughed away, we dropped off our Taliban acquaintance, and my trip home went smoothly.

I had other meetings with Taliban in the years that followed, and even stayed in touch with the insurgent who had jokingly threatened me. He appeared in Kandahar several times and met for interviews in the backseat of my car as we drove around the city. But the bedrock of any relationship between a source and a journalist is trust, and trusting him was difficult as killings and abductions became more frequent. In the following years I would invent a better way of studying the Taliban, but in the meantime I stopped trying to cultivate them as sources. The last time I saw that insurgent with the manicured hands, he was vanishing into a street in Kandahar city, wrapped in a shawl that looked exactly like the others in the crowd.

I did stay in touch with some friends in Quetta, however, and returned there for a week in 2011. Almost four years after my first visit, the Taliban's haven remained mysterious. Pakistan discouraged foreign journalists from spending too much time in the city, regulating their visits with a system of "no objection certificates," paperwork required for any reporting from the borderlands. Pakistani intelligence also kept a close watch over the city's main hotels, and had a history of harassing people who spoke with outsiders. I obtained a visa that exempted me from the certificate system, and wanted to avoid the hotels by staying at a friend's house, but this proved tricky. The roads had grown more dangerous since my first trip, so I arrived in Quetta by air, and when the authorities saw a foreigner's name on the passenger manifest and did not see any corresponding registration at a local hotel, the intelligence agencies went on alert. After a few days of wandering the city, a local journalist warned me that I should check into a hotel where I could be more easily watched. The next day, an ISI colonel visited my room and demanded a list of all the people I had visited. He was friendly and immaculately groomed. We chatted for perhaps three hours. I tried to emphasize the most innocuous parts of my visit, such as my research about Pakistani's mining industry, but he pushed me to account for every hour I'd spent unsupervised. I wasn't exactly under arrest, he said, but it would be safer for me if I remained inside my hotel room. He apologetically explained that the streets had become too dangerous for foreign journalists because of protests against a US raid a few hours earlier in the northern city of Abbottabad. Some locals apparently believed that American commandos had killed Osama bin Laden, the intelligence officer said, rolling his eyes with the condescension Pakistani authorities often show the uneducated masses. "We will never really know what happened," he concluded.

That was a breaking point, for me. Until that day, I had carefully included both sides of the story about Pakistan's involvement with the Taliban when I wrote about the allegations of safe havens for insurgents. I reported the comments of the Pashtun nationalists and others who accused the ISI of "financing and harbouring," but I also included the skepticism of those like the local JUI leader, who portrayed the Taliban as a spontaneous uprising. But sitting with the well-coiffed ISI colonel on the morning of Osama bin Laden's death, listening to him tell me that nothing had really happened in Abbottabad—that the helicopter assault was part of an elaborate drama—required a superhuman act of willpower not to accuse him of lying.

It also clarified a scene I had witnessed earlier the same week, as I walked to a restaurant with some local journalists, and we stumbled upon what appeared to be a group of Taliban in the darkened street.

They were rough-looking boys with large turbans, swarming over a big yellow piece of construction equipment, a front-end loader with the words *Government of Balochistan* stencilled on the side. Two of the young men stood in the scoop at the front of the machine, reaching up to hang banners from the streetlights on Quetta's main boulevard. The political flags and posters I had seen on my initial visit to the city in 2006 had given way to a more pro-Taliban mix. Up and down the streets, the black-and-white bars of the JUI were now interspersed with flags that did not merely allude to Taliban sympathies—these were the actual flags of the Taliban, adopted as the national symbol of Afghanistan during the years when it was known as an Islamic Emirate, a plain white background with a declaration of faith in Arabic script: "There is no god but God, and Mohammed is the messenger of God."

I turned to my colleagues: "Did those Taliban steal that construction vehicle?"

"No," one of them whispered. "Look closely."

In the shadows, I could see a few policemen standing nearby, sleepily guarding the young men while they used a Pakistani government vehicle to hang Taliban propaganda in the heart of a provincial capital. My friends steered me away, and when were out of earshot one of them said: "What else do you need to see? Now you understand the whole situation in Pakistan."

On the street in Kandahar city

CHAPTER 7

MASKED MEN FEBRUARY 2007

from: Graeme Smith <xxxx@gmail.com>

to: Stephen Northfield, Foreign Editor

        <xxxx@globeandmail.ca>, Philippe Devos, Deputy Foreign

        Editor <xxxx@globeandmail.ca>

date: Tue, Feb 13, 2007 at 8:09 AM

Hi guys,

As you know, we rent a small office in Kandahar city. It's a tiny,
modest affair on a dirt road in the south end of the downtown, and
we share the space with our fixer's brother, who runs a construction
company. Yesterday evening, around 6 p.m., my driver got a panicked
telephone call from a cook who works in the office. He reported
that three gunmen had burst through the metal doors and searched
the place. They wore cloths tied around their faces; two carried
Kalashnikov rifles, and the third was armed with a pistol. Without
saying anything, they beat the cook and rummaged through the office.
Nothing was stolen, despite the fact that valuable computers,
Internet routers and other equipment are stored there.

We don't know who did this, or why. My fixer in Quetta was
visited by the ISI today and questioned about my recent visit to

a notorious refugee camp near the Afghan border, but I'm skeptical about whether the two incidents are related.

I've decided to avoid returning to the office. I'll keep doing my work in Kandahar city, using the car as a temporary base, and with your permission I'll also devote some time to reviewing the way we do business in this city. I want to talk with trusted people about how we can maintain a presence in Kandahar without taking unnecessary risks. My working hypothesis is that we should rent an office in a more central, more secure part of the city and avoid taking roommates, but I want to check out the situation a little more carefully.

take care,
Graeme

I spent a week in early 2007 trying to figure out who raided my office in Kandahar. It had been an oasis in the city, a small nook sandwiched between two other businesses, with two storeys and an open courtyard where sunlight and hanging plants cascaded down from the sky. In the months that I rented the place, it had evolved from a simple meeting spot into a base of operations. We rigged up a satellite connection, installed two computers, and spent hours fixing the system as it endured the finicky power grid and my fixer's young relatives who sneaked onto the computers in search of pornography. There was a shabby kitchen where a cook made stewed okra and other delicious meals. I even slept there, sometimes, on the low cushions that lined the walls of the carpeted rooms. It was dangerous to step outside for a breath of air, but I could climb a stairway to the roof and peek out at the ramshackle skyline—at least, until the neighbours complained they had seen somebody up there and expressed concern about the privacy of the nearby yards where their women strolled without veils.

We never figured out why the place was attacked. A Taliban spokesman sounded genuinely confused when we described the incident by phone. He didn't think it was a Taliban operation, but he couldn't be sure because the insurgents had many factions. Several days later, he called back to confirm that the Taliban had not raided the office. As if to make up for his earlier uncertainty, he gave us a little display of Taliban surveillance, declaring that he knew exactly who I was and proudly describing the colour of a bag I'd been carrying as I walked out of the military base earlier that day. We consulted two other Taliban sources, and they both suggested the raiders might have been bandits, not insurgents, perhaps in search of a foreigner for a kidnapping. We never entirely ruled out the insurgents, however: a military officer said he considered them the most likely suspects, as capturing a journalist would grab headlines. But plenty of others had reason to take an unhealthy interest in me, or any Westerner. The criminal gangs in Kandahar included many of the notoriously corrupt police, and I would later hear first-hand accounts of police running informal prisons, holding people for ransom. Other friends suggested I might have been raided by agents from the National Directorate for Security, the secret police, perhaps because they were curious about the unexplained presence of a Westerner. There was also the possibility that we'd been searched by one of the militias loyal to Kandahar governor Asadullah Khalid, or provincial council chairman Ahmed Wali Karzai, but I detected no traces of animosity as I interviewed both of them later that month. Of the two politicians, Wali Karzai was more dangerous—a reputed drug dealer who lorded over the government-held zones of southern Afghanistan like a personal fiefdom—but I was always careful to treat him with respect.

There was also the possibility that I had attracted notice from the intelligence services of Pakistan and Iran during my fifteen-hundred-kilometre trip earlier that month to the three-way border junction those two countries share with Afghanistan. I had travelled by road from Kandahar, across the border into Pakistan, up through the mountain pass and into Balochistan. The rough scrub melted into waves of sand as we reached the south side of the Registan—literally "sand land"—a desert that divides the battlefields of Afghanistan from the lawless quarters of Iran and Pakistan where drug dealers and insurgents find their havens. Our journey ended in a market called Taftan, on the Iranian border. It looked like a recycling depot from hell, a jumble of scrap-metal, fuel containers, anything that could be smuggled. The border was closed at that moment because of a dispute between Iran and Pakistan, and I had just arrived at the office of a local commander to interview him about the problem when the telephone on his desk started ringing. He picked it up and gestured at me with a quizzical look. "Mr. Smith?" he said. I hadn't yet given him my name.

"Yes?"

"It's for you."

The voice on the phone sounded like a man who smoked too many cigarettes. Without introducing himself, he started asking questions about my movements in Pakistan's tribal areas. I identified myself as a journalist and said I was researching a story about the border. The man asked why I was poking around the Pakistan side instead of venturing into Iran. He sounded like a smart guy, and his English was good, so I tried some humour: "Because," I said, "Iran is not an open democracy like Pakistan."

The man laughed and coughed. I've often enjoyed conversations with intelligence officers because they seem to appreciate irony. On that trip, in fact, I was mostly interested in Iran's operations around the lawless three-way border junction. The research wasn't conclusive, but the story we published just before my office got raided contained some examples of insurgents getting weapons and medical treatment from inside Iran. (Later that spring, the United States started making open accusations about Iranian support for insurgent factions.) Despite the timing, however, I never really believed the Iranians had ransacked my office. They were clearly wondering about my presence in Kandahar, but I made a point of stopping for tea at their consulate in the city, and they invited me to their New Year's parties.

Regardless of who raided my office, however, the attack made it clear that I needed better security. I considered renting a compound in a more expensive, better-protected neighbourhood near the heart of the city. Rents were vastly higher in those areas, because anybody with a connection to the foreign presence wanted police checkpoints between their front doors and the Taliban villages outside the city. Shopping for real estate turned into a surreal experience, however, because the acquaintances who toured me around their empty compounds assumed that I'd be hiring a small army of guards, so their selling points usually came down to tactical considerations. I climbed onto the rooftop patio of one compound and the guy showing me around patted a low concrete wall and said, "Good construction, solid materials, could take an RPG hit. No problem." He paused to admire the view of nomads herding sheep in a nearby field, and suggested that the property would be especially comfortable in summer, when I could sleep on the roof. Presuming there weren't any rocket-propelled grenade attacks, of course. I didn't rent the place.

We also considered buying a gun for my translator, who was eager to get himself armed after the office raid. He even discussed handgun models with an Afghan security official who offered to sell him a Russian-made Makarov pistol. Kandahar's police chief took me aside and tried to persuade me about the importance of armed bodyguards, and for a fleeting moment it seemed like a good idea. I was frightened, and still inexperienced. Fortunately, my editor nixed the plan. He was right: journalists should avoid becoming part of the wars they cover, and a small pistol would not have provided much safety in a place where most thugs carry automatic rifles.

I went back to work cautiously. The incident had shaken me, and for the first time I sat down and typed out a security briefing for my boss in Canada. It's an absurd document, in some ways—my editor probably did not care about details such as my hair care routine—but it gave me comfort. It's also a picture of my daily life at the time, so I've edited some of the sections for publication here. They offer a sense of how I tried to blend in, how I travelled, and my struggle to find a safe place to sit down for interviews.

SECURITY BRIEFING

1. DISGUISE

Every day as I'm leaving the military base, I change into my Afghan outfit. This consists of a *shalwar kameez*, Kandahari cap, scarf and beat-up shoes with the heels mashed down. I also keep my beard and moustache very long, and I use moisturizing soap instead of shampoo in my hair to give myself a slightly unwashed appearance. I have a wardrobe of about seven *shalwar kameez*, and a few different scarves, so my appearance changes on a daily basis. My camera and notebooks are carried in a locally obtained plastic shopping bag. Sometimes I carry prayer beads, slinging them around my elbow in the customary way. My gait changes as I leave the base: I slouch, take smaller steps, walk more slowly and don't swing my arms. I've learned to greet passersby with a reasonable facsimile of a Pashtun greeting. Over time, I've had some indications that this does help me blend in. I'm most commonly mistaken for an Achakzai tribesman from the northern border areas. I once sat quietly in a Kandahar restaurant for half an hour without being noticed as a foreigner. Another time, I met a military translator who shook my hand, sat down next to me and talked for five minutes in Pashto before his amused friends pointed out that I didn't understand a word.

2. TRAVEL

We vary our timings for everything, partly because of security and partly because of the random nature of arrangements in this country. I leave the gates of Kandahar Air Field sometime between 6 a.m. and twelve noon, most days. Recently I've been varying my patterns further by basing myself at another military camp in the city for a few days at a time. The advantage of KAF is that our vehicle blends into the busy traffic of contractors, translators, and Afghan army soldiers and their families. The benefit of the other camp is that we avoid the twenty-five-minute run down Highway 4, which is notorious for roadside bombs. The other camp does have a nasty choke point a few hundred metres outside the gate, however, where the road and nearby walls are heavily scarred by bombs. Neither location is completely safe.

My driver usually watches for me through a piece of chain-link fence that he knows I'll pass as I'm walking to the gate at KAF. By the time I'm leaving the perimeter, he's already driving out of the parking lot and we meet just outside the gate. He served in the Afghan army before quitting to become a driver, and he's from the same village in Wardak province as one of my translators. We give him plenty of vacation time and a generous salary, on top of which I often give him small gifts of phone cards so he can call his new wife and family back home in Wardak. We've been working with him for more than a year, and he seems to have a strong sense of duty.

The car we're using for KAF runs at the moment is a dark blue Toyota Corolla, an entirely average vehicle on the roads around Kandahar. In town, we sometimes use a white Corolla. Both vehicles are shabby but not remarkably beat-up. Our deal with the vehicles' owner is that he must change them every three months, but he tends to be sluggish with that—it's more like every six months. In the car I'm usually sitting in front, not wearing a seatbelt. I'd rather buckle up, because the roads are insane and I've witnessed a dozen accidents myself, but wearing a seatbelt would mark me as a foreigner. We often encounter Afghan police and military checkpoints, where they ask for our driver's ID, search the car and look in the trunk. Sometimes they frisk us. During these encounters I usually try to avoid revealing that I'm a foreigner. Luckily, most Afghans treat these cops with surly disdain so I don't stick out by keeping my mouth shut. Sometimes, especially if we're stuck in a traffic jam downtown, I throw my scarf over my face and pretend to sleep. This hides my light-coloured eyes, the most un-Afghan part of my appearance.

We typically meet with one of my two translators at different locations in the city. Usually one of them will be walking down a road, and my driver will signal him with a phone call that we're approaching. The car pulls up, he hops inside and we head toward our interview. The translators take turns: whichever one is not working will stay at home and call me a couple of times a day to check in. The driver is told everything on a need-to-know basis, sometimes to the point where he gets instructions like, "turn right here," and "straight ahead one hundred metres." Interview subjects are usually given a vague idea about when we will arrive; fortunately, "I might see you tomorrow afternoon" is an ordinary way of setting up a business meeting in Kandahar.

We follow the same protocols going home. I usually arrive back at KAF between 5 p.m. and 9 p.m. The guards get nervous when they see a man with Afghan clothes carrying a bag at night, but yelling in English makes them lower their weapons. *(The guards relaxed most quickly, it seemed, when I hollered the names of fast-food outlets on the base: "BURGER KING!" "PIZZA HUT!")*

3. INTERVIEW LOCATIONS

This is a problem right now. If we're visiting somebody it's not a problem; that person has extended an invitation and we're his guests, which means the interview subject provides security. The person we're meeting will send an armed guard to watch for us as we're pulling into his road, or just get ready to open the gate when we arrive. Usually, the person we're visiting gets alerted by cellphone a few minutes before we arrive, which is especially important if the person has heavy security and needs to instruct his guards to relax.

The problems arise when we're inviting an interview subject to a meeting. A few months ago, we had a great system: people we trusted were invited for tea at our office. People we didn't trust were met at a popular guesthouse in a well-guarded compound downtown. People we really, really didn't trust were hosted at a more obscure guesthouse that is mostly empty except for the owner, an Afghan-Canadian, and his armed guards. Sadly, the Afghan-Canadian gave up his failed business and moved back to Canada. We also grew nervous about surveillance at the popular guesthouse. So recently we've been picking people up and interviewing them in the car, driving around Kandahar or parking in a huge field near a mosque.

Another reason for needing an office space is the uneven pace of work in the city. We often do an early interview and then we're forced to wait three or four hours until our next appointment. Not only is that interval unproductive without a workspace, it's dangerous—because, really, where do you go? Sometimes I nip over to a military base for lunch, but that exposes me to another pair of entry/exit passages near a military gate, which is the most risky part of my day. Sometimes I hang out at a guesthouse, but that's not safe either. Recently I've been resting at a friend's engineering office—but it's uncomfortable, because we're not exactly welcome (foreigner = trouble) and sometimes my fixer pokes his head through the gate and decides there are too many visitors, so we have to turn around and drive away. I would probably be welcome at some of the NGO compounds downtown, but my fixers feel less comfortable in those places and I certainly can't invite interview subjects. The NGOs are also a magnet for unwanted attention. Our solution, when the risks are so great, is to simply stack up as many back-to-back interviews as possible, and sometimes linger for an extra hour at the site of interview #1 before we're ready for #2.

4. COMMUNICATIONS

We try to make arrangements using a combination of phone calls and text messages, to foil intercepts. But frankly I'm a little skeptical about the insurgents' ability to pass a message to a bomber quickly enough to catch me if I'm making plans for the next morning, and the sheer inconvenience of the alternatives—using secret codes, for example—means we're sloppy about this. We do have "dirty" SIM chips installed in spare phones exclusively for sensitive calls, mostly to Taliban. I sometimes get phone calls from people speaking Pashto, but I always answer with a Pashtun greeting and then hang up. They're probably just wrong numbers, and not somebody testing to see whether the person on the other end speaks English. Some journalists travelling on rural highways will wipe any numbers from their phones that might get them into trouble at checkpoints, but I haven't bothered.

I spent fewer nights in the city after the raid. Despite the noise of aircraft, and the narrow canvas cots, I slept better at the military base. Evenings in Kandahar left me feeling exposed, always worried that the front gate of a guesthouse or friend's compound could be breached as easily as the metal door of my office. I also worried that my local friends behaved with too little regard for their own safety; one winter night, I sat with a group of Afghans around an oil heater, eyeing the rickety contraption as we bedded down. Flames danced near the sleeping pads we unrolled on the floor, fuelled by the regular drip, drip, drip from an antique brass valve that regulated the oil. We needed the warmth because the heavy concrete walls of my host's compounds in Kandahar city were damp and cool in winter, but I slept uneasily next to the flickering flame, worrying I would burn to death. I was also unsettled because one of my hosts put a Kalashnikov beside his pillow as we settled down for the night, and the barrel was aimed straight at me. Maybe I wouldn't have stayed awake worrying about this—he had been a fighter against the Soviets and handled weapons with confidence—if it weren't for a story he told us before we slept, about how one of his guards shot himself in the head. He ran a construction business, fixing roads and culverts, and like most people associated with the international mission he hired gunmen to protect his workers. A guard on the night shift had been sitting in a plastic lawn chair near the gate, struggling to stay awake. He propped the butt of his rifle on the ground and folded his palms over the barrel, leaning his forehead against the backs of his hands, and dozed off. His hands slid down the weapon so that his head rested directly against the muzzle. His fingers drifted lower, to the trigger. The safety wasn't latched, and the sound of the shot brought everybody running with guns in their hands. They found him bleeding from the head, and, after realizing that the compound wasn't under attack, they tried to revive him by splashing water on his face. A few bucketfuls failed to save him, so they threw him in the back of a pickup truck and drove to the morgue.

Kandahar's morgue consisted of a white trailer hidden in the trees behind Mirwais hospital, the largest medical facility in southern Afghanistan. Most people who died in the war were pulled from the battlefields by their own families and buried quickly, as required by custom, but thousands ended up at the morgue before relatives collected them. Many were never picked up, and attendants packed them into plain coffins and buried them in shallow graves near the northern slums. Wire shelves in the trailer had room for only twenty bodies, and the air conditioning often didn't work, so the place got crowded and reeked of death. It was the kind of smell that gets into your lungs and thickens, choking you. Nobody wanted to go inside and drop off the dead themselves: even in the middle of the night, they would search for a morgue worker to handle that unpleasant task. The handover itself required no paperwork, and people drove around the hospital and dumped bodies from their trucks, family sedans and donkey carts. Hospital staff tried to keep records of the dead, intercepting people on the way to the morgue and scribbling a few details into a battered notebook with the words *book of corpses* handwritten on the cover, but they documented only a minority of the incoming bodies.

Therefore it was a small miracle that a doctor was on duty that night and stopped the contractor's pickup truck before it reached the morgue. He pulled open the carpet that swaddled the body and checked for a pulse, astonishing the contractor and his men by announcing that their guard wasn't dead after all. They hauled him into the hospital, where a quick examination revealed that the man's injury was not even serious. The bullet had split his scalp and opened a gash on his forehead, but didn't break the skull. The doctor put smelling salts under the man's nose and he woke with a gasp. He went home that evening with a line of stitches and a good story. He could have regained consciousness among a pile of bodies in the morgue, or been buried alive in a plywood box—but death does not inspire the kind of seriousness in Kandahar that it does in rich countries. You're more likely to hear such stories told as jokes, not cautionary tales. I wanted to meet the guard and hear his version of the story, but his boss fired him for incompetence—you need guards who stay awake, especially in Kandahar.

I never worried about whether the guards stayed awake at Kandahar Air Field, in their high towers, and it wasn't a bad place to spend the evening if you learned to embrace its charms and eccentricities. Most of the nightlife was tame, considering the pressures that build with thousands of men and a small number of women sleeping inside a high-security perimeter. Some soldiers limited themselves to small indulgences like Cuban cigars, an embargo-flaunting pleasure for American troops. Shops on the base also carried a bewildering number of magazines devoted to guns, motorcycles and semi-naked girls. Kiosks sold shirts emblazoned with a red-and-blue image that resembled the Major League Baseball logo, except with a soldier aiming a rifle and the slogan "Major League Infidel." If those shirts suggested some kind of relationship between sport and killing, the impression was reinforced by the video games most popular among the soldiers. They preferred noisy shooting games, and sometimes I would pause near the rows of big-screen televisions, marvelling at the strangeness of men with automatic rifles at their sides, absorbed in computer simulations of their actual jobs. Perhaps it was relaxing to spend time in a virtual world where death was not permanent, and victory required only a certain number of kills.

The food at military bases was unspectacular, a basic calorie-delivery system, but one Thanksgiving the usual deep-fried stuff in the cafeteria was replaced with a spread of turkey, stuffing and other festive fare decorated with ice sculptures and fountains lit with coloured lamps. Soldiers shuffled into the cafeteria past a glowing replica of a bonfire, through the door of a fake wigwam, and sat down to dinner under the unsettling gaze of Native Americans made with paper mache. A huge Jesus stretched his arms in blessing over a gingerbread model of the airfield. It was a scene so rich with echoes of other invasions, other holy wars, that it seemed like a parody.

Many people on the base, including journalists, were required to sign a document promising to avoid what the military called "frater-nization," a rule the senior brass took seriously. They expelled several people for having sex—including, famously, a top Canadian general. But as the months stretched on, the war settling into a tailspin, the sense of purpose that once drove the soldiers faded into the back-ground and the personnel seemed to focus a little more on pleasure. One soldier told me that everybody wanted the keys to the armoured personnel carriers, because their air conditioning and soundproof-ing made them useful for trysts. A rumour circulated that some-body had smuggled a Filipina prostitute onto the camp, which would explain the leggy woman I had seen lounging in the sunshine with no apparent duties, wearing rhinestone sunglasses and reading pulp novels, but I could never confirm it. Nor could I ever confirm the widespread rumour that a soldier from one of the smaller countries, perhaps Estonia, had consumed too much moonshine and accepted a bet to swim across Emerald Lake, a large sewage pond filled with chemicals that turned the sludge a bright emerald colour. The sol-dier apparently made it across, but ended up in hospital with skin problems. I'm not sure about that story—especially the part about the moonshine, because bootleggers sold enough hard liquor that amateur brewing wasn't strictly necessary. One night I rode in a contractor's sport-utility vehicle as he made his rounds of the base to deliver bottles, his cellphone ringing constantly because a US military captain kept demanding to know when his illicit booze would arrive. Bottles clinked in the storage compartment and rolled under the seats as the smuggler crawled slowly along the gravel roads of the base, carefully observing the speed limit to avoid the military police.

Life settled into a new routine in the aftermath of the raid on my office. I spent most nights at the military base, often venturing into the city for research in the daytime. But passing between those two worlds on a regular basis sometimes felt jarring, as if crossing between parallel universes, and my sense of discomfort would only grow in the following months. I was about to investigate a dark side of the military presence in the south.

Inside Sarpoza prison

CHAPTER 8

DETAINEES APRIL 2007

I keep a souvenir that reminds me of my worst days in Afghanistan. It's a ballpoint pen, decorated with copper wire threaded into a pattern of beads. Somebody spent many hours making the cheap writing instrument into a work of art, and there's something pathetic about the scuffed plastic and its glittering enclosure. You cannot touch this object without feeling the poverty of the craftsman. A prisoner gave me this pen during our investigation of conditions in Afghan detention facilities in the spring of 2007. That was the season when I began to seriously doubt the nobility of the war.

My interest in the prisoners started a year earlier, as the fighting escalated. A translator for a Canadian television network brought a videotape to Kandahar Air Field, purported to show the confession of a Taliban commander. The video showed an exhausted man, with shackles on his bare feet, mumbling a brief description of a bombing. The translator had previously worked for US special forces, and he said the videotape came from his friends in Afghan intelligence. My colleagues weren't sure what to make of the video because it contained little information, and the prisoner appeared to be taking cues from somebody off-camera. We asked the translator, "Was he tortured?" Yes, he replied, the man was beaten.

That story never went public because we couldn't get enough details, but other troubling hints of prisoner mistreatment continued to emerge in the following months. Twice that spring, journalists travelling with troops in Kandahar heard about Afghan forces planning to kill a captive on the battlefield. After the second incident, a few reporters visited the Kandahar offices of the Afghanistan Independent Human Rights Commission (AIHRC) and asked the local director, a gentle old man, whether prisoners were mistreated in Afghan custody. The director answered yes, about 30 per cent of them are abused. He was probably understating the problem, but at the time the figure seemed shockingly large. It implied that NATO forces were capturing detainees and handing them over to local authorities who regularly abused them: a war crime, forbidden by the Geneva Conventions. A few days later, I sat down with the top NATO commander in the south, Brigadier-General Fraser, and asked him whether his soldiers respected the Conventions. The national forces under his command—British, Canadian, Dutch— had separate agreements with the Afghan government, but most of them stipulated that any prisoners taken by NATO soldiers should be quickly transferred to local custody. The Americans set up long-term detention facilities, but this merely delayed the problem until the US forces eventually transferred inmates to the Afghans down the line. Sooner or later, the NATO countries would rely on the Afghan government to accept prisoners and treat them humanely. The commander assured me the system was working. He hunched toward the voice recorder on the table between us, looked me in the eye, and spoke with deliberate slowness: "We respect the laws and the rights of individuals," he said. "We will make sure those rights are maintained and nothing bad happens to those people." The commander ignored a press officer who made nervous gestures. While in charge of all NATO forces in the region, Brigadier-General Fraser wore the uniform of the Canadian military, and the subject of detainees was politically radioactive in Canada—a country that prided itself as a champion of human rights—so the commander showed courage by speaking about the topic. But it's worth remembering what he told me that day, June 2, 2006, because it was a prelude to the scandal that erupted a year later. The general's denial—"Nothing bad happens to those people"—could not have been more emphatic. He reacted angrily to my suggestion that Canadian forces were handing over prisoners into a system that was infamous for torture, though earlier that spring, the US State Department had published reports that Afghan authorities routinely mistreat detainees, noting that "torture and abuse consisted of pulling out fingernails and toenails, burning with hot oil, beatings, sexual humiliation, and sodomy." But the brigadier-general told me those things were not happening in the south. When I asked how he could be certain, he replied curtly: "The ICRC [International Committee of the Red Cross] follows up on those issues."

A few days before the commander gave me those assurances, in fact, a Canadian diplomat wrote to his superiors about serious complaints from the International Committee of the Red Cross concerning a lack of co-operation from the military in Kandahar. An e-mail marked "secret," which leaked out years later, warned Ottawa that the local ICRC representative was having difficulty getting his phone calls answered.

Meanwhile, in my conversation with the brigadier-general, I kept trying to understand his personal feelings about the issue. "I'm just asking you about the morality of it," I said. "I mean, you're not ignorant of these things. You know where these guys end up. And you know that where these guys end up isn't up to international standards, by any means."

"Well, I guess I'd ask you, what would you do? You're asking me to say . . ." The commander trailed off. "I'm not sure what you're asking me."

"I'm asking, is it moral?"

"Is what moral? To hand Afghans over to Afghans?"

"Well, okay, maybe even better: Is it legal for Canadians to be putting Afghans in a system where we know they face a high percentage chance of abuse or torture?"

The military commander paused. My recording shows fourteen seconds of silence in the room. He continued: "We have procedures that are prepared to hand over potential detainees to legitimate authorities that we are comfortable with, that will do the right thing."

"That's the key," I said, snapping my fingers. "You're *comfortable* they're doing the right thing?"

"We have spent a lot of time developing that relationship, that we don't hand them over to anybody."

"Okay, I understand you don't hand them over to just anybody," I said, trying to steer him back toward the question, "but are you comfortable that the authorities you're handing them to are doing the right thing?"

The commander paused again, and sighed. "We follow the agreement we have between the two nations. We make sure that all the conditions within those agreements—"

I interjected, "That's different from being comfortable that you're doing the right thing. Right?"

He talked for awhile about the importance of the military intervention in Afghanistan. As he ran out of breath, he finally answered my question: "You can't say it's comfort," he admitted. A few seconds later, the press officer ended the interview.

Looking back at that conversation, I'm ashamed that the brigadier-general's answers didn't inspire more questions. I wrote a small article about detainee policy and ignored the subject for the rest of the year. Most other journalists did the same. Detainees fell into the same black hole of secrecy that swallowed intelligence operations and special forces. It was common knowledge that bad things happened to prisoners who were handed over to the Afghans, but nobody talked about it. Perhaps the soldiers refused to even think about it. Military life does not usually reward curiosity; personnel are encouraged to "stay in their lane" or "watch their arcs," and often refer to problems as being "above my pay grade." All of these phrases are shorthand for shutting up and doing your job.

When worrisome information did surface, journalists were usually inclined to give the military the benefit of the doubt; we were more apt to believe soldiers from our own country than accusers who did not speak our language. Two days after my interview with the commander, I showed a digital photograph to a Canadian military press officer. It was an image of an Afghan man in a hospital bed with his eyes closed, bleeding from the mouth. A human rights worker had taken the photo, and identified the man as Mullah Ibrahim, a suspected Taliban commander arrested southwest of Kandahar city in May 2006. Local sources indicated that the man was interrogated and beaten at the governor's palace. But the governor vehemently denied any role in questioning prisoners, suggesting he had more important business. The friendly press officer promised to look into the case of Mullah Ibrahim, and returned with a story about the old man suffering a liver disease. The mullah was sick—not tortured—the officer reassured us.

Years later, another Canadian officer laughed about journalists being so easily hoodwinked—"Of course he was tortured"—but I'm still not sure about Mullah Ibrahim, or several other detainees whose cases I did not fully investigate. Just asking questions about the issue drove a wedge between me and some of my military and diplomatic sources. Many friends who served as part of the mission still believe that I failed to understand the context around the torture debate. Afghanistan is a brutal country, they say, and it doesn't make sense to hold NATO forces or their local allies to absurd standards. Perhaps some part of me believed the same thing in 2006, as I struggled to understand the war. Now I feel guilty for failing to act earlier. The guilt also cuts in the opposite direction: I can imagine the faces of my military buddies, men who risked their lives for the sake of something they believed in. They're good people. They wanted to help

Afghanistan, and I feel awful knowing that some of them will read this chapter and throw down the book in disgust. But those faces aren't the ones that weigh most heavily on my conscience. What still bothers me are my memories of the people I met the following year: the detainees.

My search for the men who survived the Afghan interrogations started with a phone call from my editor in March 2007. I was visiting Moscow, and paused underneath a giant statue of Lenin as I listened to my boss telling me that his curiosity had been piqued by a series of recent articles from our Washington correspondent, Paul Koring. For more than a year, Mr. Koring had doggedly hunted down details of Canada's secret agreement for the transfer of prisoners to Afghan authorities, raising questions about legal safeguards. His reporting gained urgency as human rights watchdogs—including Ottawa law professor Amir Attaran, Amnesty International Canada and the British Columbia Civil Liberties Association—started digging into the file, questioning whether detainees were handled legally. At the same time, the Military Police Complaints Commission (MPCC) opened an investigation into the handling of prisoners. All of this caused a ruckus in Canada's parliament, prompting questions about whether the country was respecting international law. The refrain from Canada's politicians echoed the words of the military commander a year earlier: "Nothing bad happens to those people." The official version was that Afghanistan treated prisoners in accordance with the Geneva Conventions, and not a single one suffered abuse or torture. My editor asked me if that was plausible. "No," I told him, but I did not have details about the fate of transferred prisoners. He told me to drop everything and find them.

I spent the next month looking for first-person accounts from Kandahar's jails. Many former detainees were afraid to speak; I was a foreigner, and after being captured by foreigners they weren't willing to risk another interrogation. Others said they did not want to talk about the Afghan intelligence service, the NDS (National Directorate of Security), whose ranks still contained many officers trained by the Soviet KGB. If people whispered its name, they usually called it "KhAD," the acronym for the communist-era Ministry for State Security, infamous for torturing and executing prisoners. There was also the problem of travel: I was particularly interested in finding people who had been detained by Canadian troops, operating primarily west and north of Kandahar city, but those areas were too dangerous for me to visit. We offered lavish meals to anybody willing to risk the roads and drive into Kandahar, but few accepted the invitation. Some of my best local sources were tribal elders, but they weren't much help because most of them were allied with the government and had no interest in picking a fight with the regime. The elders arranged a few meetings with former detainees: stilted conversations with people who had spent a short time in custody before getting bailed out by their friends or relatives. Nonetheless, some of them described torture suffered by their cellmates. It was clear that we needed to keep searching.

The breakthrough came when we got inside Sarpoza prison, a crumbling old jail on the west side of the city. Journalists weren't allowed into the national-security wing, holding suspected Taliban prisoners. But after some negotiation, the warden named his price: three flashlights. I bought the Mag-Lites at a military store and donated them to the prison; shortly afterward, I found myself on a guided tour. The jailers tried to focus my attention on ways that the rich foreigners should assist the prison guards and improve their facilities. They watched carefully as I wrote down their requests: windows, doors, tables, chairs, beds and dozens of other necessities. Stepping through a series of barred gateways, we walked down hallways made of stone blocks, where prisoners cooked over gas canisters. The food supply was a problem; prisoners were given only a few pieces of bread each day, which they supplemented by purchasing their own meals. Pulling back the ragged curtains of the cells, he showed us that most prisoners slept on the floor, leaving them vulnerable to snakes, insects and other creatures that inhabited chinks in the masonry. Inmates had rigged up cloth shawls around the walls, jamming them in place with sticks, in an attempt to shield themselves from whatever crawled out. Similar cloths were pinned to the ceiling of some cells, for a different reason: "It's to keep the ceiling from falling on us," said a prisoner, who reached behind his sleeping mat and pulled out a handful of brick shards, tossing them at my feet. "These things fall on us while we sleep."

Despite its discomforts, weeks of visiting the prison taught me that the facility was actually pretty good by local standards. For many detainees, arrival at Sarpoza meant relief from harsher captivity in the holding cells operated by the local police and intelligence service. At Sarpoza, prisoners spent their days playing games in the courtyard shaded by trees, or whiled away the hours by crafting beaded trinkets (such as the pen that I've kept as a souvenir). The relaxed atmosphere inside the prison meant I could spend long afternoons drinking tea inside the national-security wing, slowly persuading detainees to tell me about themselves. One by one they related their stories, lifted their shirts, showed me their scars. An indulgent prison official supervised all the interviews, allowing the prisoners to speak freely, but forbidding me from photographing them. All of them had frightful accounts of how they ended up in the rambling prison, and the nastier jails and holding cells they experienced before arriving.

I interviewed thirty men who survived the detention system, some imprisoned at Sarpoza and others living free in Kandahar. A majority said they were captured by Canadian troops. The nationality of the forces was important because I was working for a Canadian newspaper, so we spent hours on detailed questions about the vehicles used by foreign soldiers; we could usually figure out that detainees were taken by Canadians from the description of their troop carriers. In other cases, the detainees' stories suggested they had been grabbed by US special forces or Afghan security services. Many prisoners did not know, or care, which particular type of foreign soldier was involved. No matter who captured them, however, there was a clear pattern of abuse by the Afghan authorities. Over and over, in separate conversations, the men described how the international troops tied their hands with plastic straps, covered their eyes and handed them over to torturers. They described beatings, whippings, starvation, choking and electrocution. When compiling the list of torture techniques, I was careful to leave out stories that didn't match the others. One prisoner, for instance, said he was shoved into a wooden box and tormented with boiling water; I didn't publish that anecdote in the newspaper because I couldn't cross-reference it. The stuff we *could* corroborate, of course, was bad enough. A majority of the people I interviewed had passed through the cramped cells in the basement of the Kandahar NDS office. Most of those held by the NDS for an extended time said they were whipped with electrical cables, usually a bundle of wires the length of an arm. Some said the whipping was so painful that they fell unconscious. Interrogators also electrocuted detainees, who described hearing the sound of a hand-crank generator and feeling the hot flush of electricity coursing through their muscles, seizing them with spasms. One man wiggled his hand in the air as he talked about it, making a limp gesture: "I was flopping like a fish on dry earth," he explained. Another man said the police hung him by his ankles for eight days of beating. Still another said he panicked as interrogators put a plastic bag over his head and squeezed his windpipe.

Some of the men who survived these ordeals looked like broken husks. With trembling hands, they whispered complaints of insomnia and chronic pain. Others lacked the physical capacity to complain, shuffling and mumbling through the stone hallways. One of these ruined men, a dark-haired prisoner wearing stained clothes, said he couldn't remember much except the beatings. He had forgotten his own hometown, his family, his tribal affiliation, almost everything except his reduced existence in the archipelago of jails. He knew that he sometimes had difficulty using the latrines, but he couldn't remember what kind of difficulty. One of his jailers explained that he could squat over the hole in the ground before defecating, but that he frequently forgot to pull down his pants. These cases upset the prison guards because they hated being surrogate parents. Some of the detainees were so badly impaired that somebody had to wash, dress and feed them. One guard confided that he felt the Afghan intelligence service was dumping human garbage into the prison.

Other inmates proved astonishingly sharp-minded, however. That turned out to be the case with a young man named Abdul Wali, whose memory was so good that I would eventually need two notebooks and two visits to record all of his details. At first, he was reluctant to talk. We found him in a cell of the national-security wing, a small man with curly dark hair, sweaty and matted. He played nervously with a broken wristwatch, kneading the metal bracelet through his fingers like a string of prayer beads. His situation was pretty much the same as everybody else's, he said: He was accused of involvement with the Taliban, and denied it. No judgment had been passed, so he wasn't sure how long he would stay imprisoned. Yes, he answered softly, he was tortured. He opened his shirt and showed scars on his chest. (He refused to show his naked back, although a human rights investigator—who later confirmed several aspects of his story—said the young man had more scarring on other parts of his torso.)

His ordeal started when he was detained by Canadian troops in the summer of 2006 in a grape field southwest of Kandahar city. He had no reason to hate the foreign soldiers, he said, although it's easy to understand why the Canadians thought he was a Taliban fighter. At age twenty-three, he fell into the category that the soldiers usually refer to as "fighting-age males." He belonged to one of the smaller Pushtun tribes that often felt disenfranchised under the new government. His hometown was located in Helmand province, a long way from the field where he encountered the Canadians—itself an unlikely place to be lingering because of battles in those fields earlier in the day.

None of those facts proved that he was an insurgent, Mr. Wali said. His alibi was that he needed to guard a farm that belonged to his brother-in-law. His relatives had abandoned their land as the fighting between Taliban and foreign soldiers grew more intense, but they assigned him to water the crops and prevent looting. Before the recent conflict, he said, he had been scratching out a living in a tailor shop with two of this brothers, mending garments for people forced by war and drought to live in a ramshackle camp in the desert. All the brothers lived with their wives and children in a mud house, fourteen people crowding into three rooms.

He was relaxing in the shade when the Canadian troops surrounded him. They took off his green pinstripe vest and tore open the lining, finding nothing except his wallet, which was decorated with cartoon characters and the words *Kiki & Coco*. Like other detainees, Mr. Wali described how the Canadian troops tied his hands with plastic cuffs and kept him in the back of their armoured vehicle for two or three hours. The foreigners didn't harm him, only asked questions through a translator and scribbled in a notepad. This was also typical of the stories I heard among the detainees; everybody praised the NATO troops for their good manners and gentle handling of prisoners. It was remarkable, because some of the detainees obviously had Taliban connections and they could, in theory, have scored propaganda points by claiming abuse at the hands of the so-called infidel armies. But like the others, Mr. Wali carefully specified that his torture started only *after* the Canadian troops handed him over to Afghan authorities. In fact, the beatings seemed to stop and start depending on whether the foreign troops happened to be nearby. Afghan forces and their international partners lived and worked closely together in forward bases, and it seems the Afghans had trouble keeping their interrogation methods secret. The captives noticed the uneasy relationship: "The foreign soldiers didn't like to see beating," Mr. Wali said.

Things got worse as he was transferred deeper into the Afghan system, away from foreign eyes. At a district headquarters, police officers took him to a room with bare concrete walls and cudgelled him with rifle butts, he said. They also jabbed him in the chest with the muzzles of their Kalashnikovs, which left him with the pattern of dark scars I saw on his chest. At one point, he said, about nine police officers pushed his face into the floor. One officer sat on the back of his head while the others pummelled him. A man in civilian clothes questioned him between beatings. He stayed in that cell for three days, with only two meals of tea and bread, then went onward to the dismal block of holding cells beside police headquarters in Kandahar city. Around midday, two officers took him upstairs to a room that overlooked a busy street—conveniently disused, as senior police officers preferred to work on the side of the building that faced the inner courtyard, so they would be less vulnerable to bombs. The officers shut the windows and closed the yellow curtains, and Mr. Wali had a moment to contemplate what was about to happen while the officers searched for a suitable whip. They wanted to find a length of chain, but settled on a bundle of electrical cables. Mr. Wali was rolled onto his stomach and thrashed on his back and legs.

They repeated the beatings on three consecutive days, then started asking for money. Stories of extortion and bribery were also common among the detainees; sometimes I got the impression that the only people remaining in Sarpoza were those who lacked the money or tribal connections to get released. Diplomats reached the same conclusion; in the same week that I was visiting the prison, a Dutch official told colleagues in Kabul that "any Talib could buy his freedom for ten dollars." In Mr. Wali's case, the police demanded payment to avoid transferring him to the feared Afghan intelligence service. He responded that he could not afford any bribes, and so they sent him to the NDS the same afternoon. There, the interrogators told him to pray and wash, then called him into an interview room. The man asking the questions had sickly greenish skin, Mr. Wali said. "He kicked me in the head, and I fell into a table. Blood came out my nose. He told me, 'Don't bleed on the carpet. Go wash your face.'" The NDS wanted his signature and thumbprint on a confession, admitting a role in the insurgency. Some interrogators also wanted money. He gave them neither. After a month of torture, they eventually dumped him in Sarpoza jail, where his wounds healed. When I met him, he had been waiting eight months for a formal sentence.

After thirty of these interviews, I felt exhausted but excited. We drove out through the tall black gates of the prison, and I swivelled around in the front seat to tell my translator that we were finally done with the investigation, and our work would change things. He gave me a condescending look, and said it didn't matter how many prisoners we interviewed or what kind of articles we published. I disagreed, and gave him an impassioned speech about the values of Western democracies. I predicted that people at home in NATO countries would not be pleased to hear that their Afghan allies were torturers. Diplomats had been predicting the same thing: in December 2006, a secret memo from the Canadian embassy reported concerns that detainee practices did not conform with international law, and that public outcry about abuse could "kill the whole mission."

When I published my findings, Canadians were especially upset about instances when troops may have known that Afghans were torturing their prisoners. In two cases, men had told me they were screaming loudly during torture by Afghan police at a small base where Canadian and local forces lived side by side. One of these men, an impoverished farmer with a thin face, described three days of interrogation without any meals at an outpost in western Kandahar. Between beatings, he said, Canadian soldiers visited him and offered advice about how to avoid mistreatment. "The Canadians told me, 'Give them real information, or they will do more bad things to you,'" the farmer said, smiling sadly, showing me where the interrogators had punched out his teeth.

Other detainees said they were confused about whether the Canadians knew about the torture, and I decided to finish my main article about detainees with that note of uncertainty. I described the puzzlement of a former detainee who said the Canadian troops had treated him gently as they tied his hands and loaded him into a troop carrier—a soldier carefully placing a hand over his head and preventing the detainee from bumping his skull on the metal sides of the vehicle as it bounced along a dirt road. The gesture made him wonder why the soldiers had bothered to protect him from minor bumps when the Afghan police would beat him viciously later the same day. That anecdote reinforced the most troubling question for the NATO forces: How much did the foreign troops know? Were they sending prisoners into the torture chambers for the purpose of having them violently interrogated, preferring their urgent need for intelligence over concerns for human rights? Or, as with other aspects of the mission, were they unwitting allies of an Afghan regime that preyed on its people?

I hoped it was the latter. As years passed and secret documents emerged, however, I started to think the NATO forces had turned a blind eye. I can't prove that any international forces knowingly colluded with torturers, but there was such a gap between public and private discussions that it made me suspicious. It made me angry, too, because I knew a lot of soldiers who never wanted to get involved with anything so nasty. These men and women get sent to faraway places and grind through their daily tasks in the belief that they're obeying leaders who think carefully about their orders. Most soldiers are not experts in international law: they trust their commanders. Reading the behind-the-scenes arguments about detainees, in the reams of documents that later emerged amid scandals and legal action, it's hard not to conclude that the commanders violated that trust.

Those troubling little gaps between public statements and the well-known but unspoken reality started to emerge in the aftermath of our stories. In public, the government dismissed the detainees' complaints as Taliban propaganda. Ministers claimed that if any torture existed in the Kandahar prisons, it would have been reported by the AIHRC, the country's own watchdog commission. The AIHRC gets millions of dollars from foreign donors such as Canada, and works with help from the United Nations to keep track of human rights issues. When my investigation was published, on April 23, 2007, Canada's defence minister stood up in parliament and declared that AIHRC monitoring was enough. "I have the personal assurance of the leader of the human rights commission in Kandahar," said the minister, Gordon O'Connor. The next day, I published another story revealing that the assurances were empty: the AIHRC was not allowed into the Kandahar intelligence prison. But the government stuck by its message that the AIHRC was the best safeguard against abuse in the system. On April 25, Canada's prime minister responded to questions about whether AIHRC monitoring was sufficient. Here is Stephen Harper's full answer, as noted in the parliamentary record:

> Mr. Speaker, military leaders in Afghanistan are constantly in contact with their counterparts and with the Afghanistan Independent Human Rights Commission. So far, they have not indicated to us that they have encountered these problems. Of course, we made it clear that we are there to help to any extent necessary.

I watched the prime minister speak those words, on live video streamed to my laptop at a military base in Kandahar, and shook my head in amazement. It was common knowledge that the AIHRC was well-intentioned but weak, with only three investigators who struggled to map the bewildering array of detainee issues in the southern region. I wasn't the only person who felt shocked by the government response; one of my sources, a Canadian official, said he wished the politicians would pay more attention to the e-mails coming from Afghanistan before opening their mouths. I never fully understood what he meant until, years later, investigators released a batch of government e-mails about detainees. Two days before the prime minister said he had no indications of problems, the Canadian embassy in Kabul filed a classified report that confirmed the AIHRC having "access problems" at facilities where Afghan intelligence held prisoners. "The commission is unable to monitor the condition of detainees," the document says.

In fact, the commission office in Kandahar faced much bigger problems than a lack of access. The staff themselves felt threatened in the aftermath of our stories. I had quoted the AIHRC's local director offering a frank description of what prisoners said they experienced in the custody of Afghan intelligence agents. "The NDS is torturing detainees," he told me. "I've heard stories of blood on the walls. It's a terrifying place: dark, dirty and bloody. When you hear about this place, no man feels comfortable with himself." But when my articles caused a scandal, he started giving interviews saying he had no knowledge of any torture. I visited him that week and asked him why he had reversed his position. His eyes watered and his voice quavered, but he continued saying he had no evidence that the NDS mistreated prisoners. The AIHRC's lead investigator at the time, Amir Mohammed Ansari, had been helping me for weeks but suddenly stopped answering his phone. We had some idea the AIHRC was feeling pressure; a source in the Kandahar governor's palace said he overheard a phone call from Hamid Karzai in which the Afghan president screamed at the Kandahar governor, upbraiding him for allowing the detainee issue to hurt relations with his foreign supporters. Immediately after that conversation, my source said, the governor in turn called the AIHRC director and screamed at him. Such anger must have been especially frightening for staff members at the human rights commission, who had first-hand knowledge of the unpleasant fates that awaited those who crossed the local authorities. But I didn't realize the extent to which Kabul spelled out its threats until I later saw a confidential government document outlining a phone call from the NDS director to the acting head of the AIHRC on April 25, 2007. The intelligence chief accused the human rights group of espionage and threatened to arrest the AIHRC's director in Kandahar "for being an Iranian spy."

After such threats, the Kandahar office of the AIHRC toned down its criticism of the government. The regional director was not arrested, although one of his assistants quit his job to escape the pressure. I've also wondered about the strange disappearance of his chief investigator, Mr. Ansari. A dignified man with a neatly trimmed grey beard, he frequently visited rural districts to investigate reports of civilian casualties. During one such trip into neighbouring Helmand province in 2007, he was kidnapped by unknown gunmen. His family paid a ransom several months later, but received nothing except his bloody identification card and directions to his grave. The corpse was beheaded, which fit the pattern of Taliban executions, but sources in Kandahar have speculated that his death may have been related to the fact that he helped me learn about the detainee system.

If Mr. Ansari died for the sake of protecting human rights in Kandahar, he probably did not take much comfort from the small victories that resulted from our work together. Still, I remember the expression on his face when I visited his office after our stories were published. Powerful people were angry that we had stirred up so much trouble, and he was receiving serious threats, but the look in his eye was triumphant. Here's how I described it to a friend:

```
from:  Graeme Smith <xxxxx@gmail.com>
to:    Kenny Yum <xxxxx@gmail.com>
date:  Fri, Apr 27, 2007 at 7:08 AM


I visited Kandahar city again yesterday and was astonished by how
creepy things got after word circulated that I had picked a fight
with the police, secret police and governor. Suddenly I had fewer
friends. . . . After months of threats, the raid on my office, the
kidnappings, it's all finally caught up with me. I'm scared.
```

. . . anyway, it's worth it. You should have seen the
expression on the face of the AIHRC investigator when I showed
up in his office. His boss was there, so he couldn't say much,
but he was basically like, "It's bloody, but we won. We can get
into the jail now." And that was really valuable to me, the idea
that maybe somewhere in the basement of the secret police
prison a torturer might ease up a little bit because he's afraid
of leaving bruises or scars that might get reported. Who knows
whether that will really happen, but it's a daydream that
keeps me going.

I still cling to the hope that we did a bit of good. The Canadian
government continued defending its practices, but Ottawa issued
an urgent demarche to several levels of the Afghan government on
the day we published our first story. The first point of the demarche
was that Canada took our allegations of torture "very seriously." A
flurry of meetings happened in Kabul, Kandahar and Ottawa, as
senior officials discussed how to react. One memo suggests that the
government initially considered a show of outrage without substan-
tial changes. The diplomat Richard Colvin, serving at the time as
second-in-command at the Canadian embassy in Kabul, wrote a dis-
senting view: "However much we demarche the National Directorate
of Security (NDS), phone Karzai . . . or issue press releases, in the
field, the same practices will continue as before." He recommended
Canada should start monitoring detainees for signs of abuse in
Afghan custody. He also reported to his superiors about meeting the
Afghan chief of intelligence, who claimed that his NDS agents could
not be blamed for any torture because "many of those beaten were
first beaten by the police." Colvin replied that Canadians did not care
which Afghan security force had abused detainees, and suggested the
spy agency should make a public declaration of its commitment to
human rights. Instead, the NDS published a statement calling our
reporting "baseless."

Canada's allies reacted to our reports with greater alarm. The US ambassador to Kabul expressed concern to the Canadians, as did the civilian head of NATO, who said the issue could have "enormous political implications." The Red Cross told the Canadians they should not be surprised by our investigation's results: ". . . the allegations of abuse made by those Afghans interviewed by Graeme Smith fit a common pattern," said an internal report. (Those comments were censored from the Canadians' final report with big diagonal pen strokes.)

Questions about detainees became an ongoing drama in Ottawa, where the affair was widely considered the first scandal faced by the minority Conservative government. The affair also fuelled an ongoing legal challenge to the detainee transfer system. A federal judge planned to hear arguments for an interim injunction banning the transfer of detainees on May 3, but adjourned the hearing when the government surprised the court with news that Canada had changed its policy. Earlier that day in Kabul, Canada had signed a new bilateral agreement with Afghanistan, providing more stringent safeguards on its detainee transfers. Most importantly, this included a promise that Canadian human rights inspectors would monitor detainees in Afghan custody—something the British and Dutch were already doing. It was an abrupt policy shift, and temporarily quelled debate about the issue in Canada.

In private, however, the NATO countries continued to argue about detainee policy. One telling example was an August meeting of representatives from countries with large contingents of soldiers in southern Afghanistan. They talked about better ways of monitoring prisoners, especially inside the secretive NDS facilities, with a computer database of inmates and improved access for human rights investigators. A diplomat from the European Union said those measures weren't enough to protect against torture, and suggested that transfers should be halted entirely. The diplomats considered avoiding the NDS by sending prisoners into the custody of other Afghan security forces, but concluded that none of the local authorities were trustworthy. "The general view was that GoA [Government of Afghanistan] as a whole is deeply problematic," a memo said. The meeting even heard that some Afghan elders preferred having their tribesmen captured by US special forces rather than NATO, because the Americans shipped their captives to their own detention centre instead of dumping them into the cruel Afghan system. That must have seemed ironic to the diplomats gathered in Kabul because several countries had taken pains to arrange their detainee transfers in a way that avoided American custody. In the age of Guantanamo, they had sensed political risk in participating in a US system they viewed as unaccountable and perhaps illegal. Unfortunately, the alternative proved worse.

The discussion eventually came around to a proposal that had already been considered: the idea that the NATO countries most heavily involved in the south—Britain, Canada and the Netherlands—should set up a prison under their own supervision. This concept seemed to get bogged down, however, because the Western countries did not want such a long-term commitment. That meeting, like many others, ended with no major proposals for action.

As other countries lamented the flaws in their detainee systems, Canada was still struggling to raise its own standards to the level of its counterparts. After the new transfer agreement was signed in May 2007, Canada started investigating what had happened to the roughly 130 detainees it had transferred by that point. Canadian officials knew what they would find—"we would note the likelihood if not inevitability that an impartial investigation will indeed confirm the allegations made in the *Globe & Mail*," a secret memo said—but they plodded ahead nonetheless. Because they had not previously attempted to track the detainees, it was hard to find individual men inside the dilapidated Afghan cellblocks. Dozens of names on their list remained question marks, lost somewhere in the system. Nor was it easy for the Canadians to set up a monitoring regime for fresh captives. It took five months to find a human rights investigator and send him to Kandahar, and when he finally started work in October 2007 the results were embarrassing. During one of his first visits to NDS headquarters in Kandahar, the Canadian government's investigator took aside a detainee for an interview and asked him about his interrogation by Afghan authorities. The man's answer was partially blacked out in government documents, but the uncensored parts show that the detainee complained he was beaten with electrical wires and rubber hoses. The questioning was so violent that he was knocked unconscious, the prisoner said. Most surprisingly, the detainee said the torture happened in the same room where he was meeting the Canadian investigator. In fact, he added, the interrogators usually left their torture implements under a chair in the room. "Under the chair, we found a large piece of braided electrical wire as well as a rubber hose," the investigator reported. Then the prisoner showed a bruise on his back, and asked the Canadians not to reveal to his captors that he had complained.

This kind of information put the Canadians in an awkward position. They stopped transferring prisoners to the NDS for a few months, but did not reveal the move publicly. This allowed Canada to make a gesture toward obeying international law without facing negative publicity or uncomfortable questions from NATO allies—who were still handing over detainees to the same Afghan authorities, and who had the same obligations under the Geneva Conventions. But the secrecy broke in January 2008, when the information emerged in a court hearing in Ottawa over the legality of the transfer system. Other NATO countries were upset by the news; by implication, Canada's actions suggested that its allies were committing war crimes. The Afghan government also expressed outrage, fearing that the insurgents could now make propaganda claims about the regime's brutality. As a practical matter, too, the holding cells at Kandahar Air Field were ill-equipped to keep prisoners for longer than a few days. The Canadians eventually resumed transfers, although in the following years they continued to secretly halt the handovers when they found evidence of problems in the Afghan system.

I drifted out of touch with detainee issues in Kandahar after finishing my assignment in the Afghanistan in early 2009, although I heard from human rights investigators that they remained worried that a two-tier system was emerging, as conditions somewhat improved for prisoners transferred from NATO custody but remained vicious for those captured by the Afghan forces. Local soldiers and police frequently worked side by side with foreign troops, so the international forces were also rumoured to be avoiding the hassle of taking prisoners by conducting "field transfers," or giving Afghan forces the job of collecting detainees. Despite all the flaws, however, it seemed the local authorities had started to understand that torture was a sensitive subject for their international allies. My friends in Kandahar said prisoners were still beaten in the local jails, but the kind of abuses we had discovered were becoming less common. Among all the things that got worse during my years in southern Afghanistan, at least we could assume that the detainee system got better, however minimally. As I was getting ready to leave Kandahar for the last time, throwing away old junk in the media tent, I found the ballpoint pen that the prisoner had given me two years earlier— the copper wire still shiny, and the object retaining its strange beauty. I stowed the pen at the bottom of my suitcase, and when I returned home to Canada the pen got buried in a pile of spare change I kept in an upturned hat.

I had almost forgotten about that souvenir when a friend called me on November 18, 2009. "Turn on your television," he said. Canadian news channels were going live with coverage of a parliamentary hearing on Afghan detainees. Richard Colvin, the diplomat who had struggled to fix the detainee system during his time in Afghanistan, had been summoned before a committee. By that point he had been promoted to an intelligence liaison job in Washington, but the committee asked him to delve into his archives and talk about what the Canadian embassy in Kabul knew about detainees in the earlier years of the war. Colvin said the torture went even beyond the methods I had reported, and described the transferred detainees being burned, knifed and raped. More importantly, he maintained that senior military and diplomatic officials decided to ignore warnings about the system in 2006 and 2007. "As I learned more about our detainee practices," Colvin said, "I came to the conclusion that they were contrary to Canada's values, contrary to Canada's interests, contrary to Canada's official policies, and also contrary to international law; that is, they were un-Canadian, counterproductive and probably illegal."

Colvin's testimony implied that Canada had knowingly broken international law, and it caused another firestorm of debate in Ottawa about detainee policy. The arguments focused on the big question that I had failed to resolve in my earlier investigation: How much did the foreign troops know? I decided to invite an old friend for dinner. I cooked him a steak, poured drinks, and afterward I brought out the pen. He admired its meticulous decoration, and then, with a thoughtful expression on his face, he removed the cap and started sketching on a piece of paper. He drew a map of the Kandahar governor's palace, and marked the location of a small outpost where Canadian liaison officers lived. I nodded my head; I knew the place. He indicated a small office across a grassy courtyard, not far from the Canadians. "This was a torture chamber," he said. I had never visited that part of the palace, but I had heard the stories about the governor's bodyguards. I had even interviewed a detainee in Sarpoza prison who claimed the governor supervised his torture over a period of eighteen days at the palace, but we had never published that story. Part of the problem was that we lacked corroboration for the prisoner's claims, and partly we were afraid of retribution by the governor against our local staff. Years later, holding my souvenir pen, my friend listened to my audio recording of that interview and confirmed my suspicions. Yes, he said, the governor held prisoners in his palace. Yes, he said, those inmates were tortured. He had personally seen one hapless prisoner hanging from the ceiling, "trussed like a chicken." I pressed him on the question that still bothered me: Did any of the foreign troops know about the torture? My friend said he wasn't sure. He suggested that I ask the Canadian soldiers themselves.

Over the next few weeks, I looked up several of my buddies from Kandahar. The liaison officers who worked near the palace were often smart guys, given the delicate task of managing relationships with the governor and Afghan security forces. With detainee issues making front-page news across the country, they knew why I was getting in touch. All of them said they did not see or hear any indications of torture by Afghan authorities, but that such tactics would be unsurprising. It was a violent country, they said; it was unreasonable to expect the Afghan forces to maintain high standards of conduct when they faced insurgents who regularly beheaded their captives. I was particularly curious about the soldiers' relationships with the governor and his men. Other sources had confirmed that the palace guards were rounding up and violently interrogating suspected insurgents, and I wanted to know if the soldiers who worked near the palace, just a few minutes' walk from the front door, knew anything about such activity. After all, they were so friendly with the governor that they played Xbox video games with him, and offered him breakfast cereals that would improve his daily intake of dietary fibre. The officers also cultivated close relationships with Afghan security officials, including the local intelligence chief. They needed information to save lives on the battlefield, so they avoided asking questions about how the Afghans conducted their interrogations.

In each of these conversations, I pulled out the prisoner's pen and explained its history. I talked about what I learned from the detainees in Sarpoza prison, and the scars on inmates' bodies. Every time, I got something like a shrug from the Canadian soldiers. They had varying degrees of understanding about what happened inside the governor's palace—one of them told me that the governor's men had borrowed extra plastic ties for their captives' wrists—but all of them maintained that NATO was only supporting the sovereign government of Afghanistan. They couldn't understand why the media were "freaking out" over the detainees. "I made a point of never asking how they got the information," an officer said. "If they had told me about torture, it would have impeded my ability to get the intelligence we needed about the Taliban."

These officers seemed like reasonable men. They exuded the kind of trustworthiness that you find in the best soldiers. If you need to give somebody a gun and ask him to protect your life, that's the kind of person you want. But I came away from these conversations weighed down with sadness. Somebody high up the ranks put these soldiers in that little outpost in the governor's front garden. Somebody told them to make friends with the Afghan authorities. Those orders came down from a military leadership that should have known how distasteful such arrangements were, how closely these troops were co-operating with torturers. The Canadians clandestinely listened to the governor's cellphone conversations: recording, transcribing, and translating, analyzing. That intelligence was passed up the chain of command. My great fear is that somewhere in the buzz of information, there was a terrible calculation, a decision to avoid fighting by the rules. These days, when I look at my souvenir pen, I'm not reminded of how our journalism resulted in minor improvements in the detention system. I feel grief and rage. I imagine the man who sat in a Kandahar prison and looped copper wire through all those little beads. I think about how we failed him.

Unlike scars, these things don't fade. Torture will remain a troubling mark on NATO's history in Afghanistan. Fresh horrors continue to be revealed, followed by a shameful pattern of hand-wringing and uproar—and then a return to the routines of abuse. A british court ruled in June 2010 that it's illegal for troops from the United Kingdom to transfer detainees into NDS custody in Kabul because of the high risk of torture, but allowed transfers in the southern provinces on condition of improved monitoring in local jails. Those detention facilities in the south showed no sign of improvement, however, when the United Nations conducted a landmark study of torture in Afghan custody in 2010 and 2011, sending interviewers to private meetings with 379 detainees at forty-seven detention centres across the country. The notorious NDS facility in Kandahar merited its own section in the final report, with two-thirds of respondents describing torture at the hands of interrogators. The abuses were similar to what I'd recorded in my investigation three years earlier, and most of the methods for inflicting pain remained consistent. As word leaked about the UN's findings in September 2011, the NATO command suspended all transfers of prisoners into Afghan custody. Nobody could reasonably expect the freeze to last, however. Kate Clark, a well-known analyst, observed that "the scandal needs to be repeated, which makes it seem as if the amnesia over NDS torture is willful."

This cycle of outrage and convenient forgetting seems likely to continue as the United States transfers prisoners as part of the handover to Afghan security forces in 2014. Even some human rights specialists throw up their hands when asked about this looming collision between principles and expediency. In theory, the foreign troops should never give detainees to authorities who practise torture; in practice, there is no obvious destination available for hundreds of prisoners as the international forces shut down their detention facilities. Apologists will point out that the new Afghan state is considerably less brutal than previous regimes; in the late 1800s, for example, petty thieves were punished by having their hands chopped off and their bloody stumps plunged into boiling oil. The Taliban continued using amputation as a punishment into the 1990s, and also revived the old tradition of burying people alive. In that context, perhaps an Afghan system that flays captives with electrical cables could be viewed as a minor improvement. But that misses the essential distinction that the iron-fisted rulers of bygone eras did not have thousands of Western advisors looking over their shoulders. Afghans think about the current government, with some justification, as a creation of the international community and a living representation of modern ideas about democracy. The excesses of the NDS could be blamed, in the early years, on habits inherited from Soviet KGB trainers in the 1980s. But more than a decade of Western presence in the country means that some responsibility for the NDS actions must fall on its new partners. The United Nations noted that the NDS gets "technical assistance" and training from Germany, Britain and the United States, and pointedly referred to the fact that UN investigators tried and failed to get inside the notorious NDS Department 124, a holding facility located near the US embassy in Kabul and a building reputedly used as a base by the US Central Intelligence Agency. If the harsh practices of Afghan interrogators were only a matter of ancient customs, it would be reasonable to expect the nastiest reports to emerge from rural provinces that lack foreign supervision. But the opposite is true: among the detainees who had passed through Department 124, in the centre of Kabul, twenty-six of twenty-eight interviewed by the United Nations said they suffered torture—making such complaints more common than in Kandahar. One detainee said that Department 124 is commonly referred to as "Hell," and another said that the torture included wrenching and twisting of genitals. This apparently happened within convenient walking distance of the nicely decorated apartments where US embassy officials sat behind their concrete blast walls. That proximity lies at the heart of the legacy problem in Afghanistan. The Westerners became intimately embroiled with a dirty war, and the filthy awfulness of it will remain a stain on their reputation.

Canadian artillery unit in Helmand province

CHAPTER 9

FIGHTING SEASON MAY 2007

The fighting season arrived in spring. Violence climbed slowly as the weather got warmer, then stagnated for a few weeks as everything paused for the opium harvest. Taliban fighters put down their guns and picked up farm tools. Then, at some point in April or May, the harvest finished and the young labourers turned into an insurgent army. You could almost pinpoint that moment—the end of harvest, the start of the fighting—to a particular week, depending on the maturity of the poppies. I couldn't read anything in the rolling expanses of pink, purple and red flowers, but my local friends said the blooming fields in the spring of 2007 indicated that the violence would spike in the middle of May.

Military officials disagreed. The relative calm of the winter season had renewed their optimism, leading them to think that the Taliban were still reeling from their losses during Operation Medusa the previous year. The smart money inside the diplomatic compounds in Kabul and the military bases in Kandahar was betting that the insurgents had lost their momentum. Senior officials predicted the 2007 fighting season would bring less violence than the previous year, or at least nothing worse. I decided to spend a couple of weeks on the battlefield, testing that theory. My motivation wasn't purely rational; researching local jails and the moral ambiguities of the

NATO mission had left me yearning for the simplicity of battle. I had once joked with my colleagues that firefights don't impress writers because there's a limit to the narrative possibilities of "bang, bang, bang," but at that point I wanted to immerse myself in the military's narrow world. I wanted to forget about torture, wanted to leave behind those hard questions. I craved front lines, good guys and bad guys. I hopped a convoy and headed west.

At first, everything was peaceful. I spent a few days with an artillery unit on a hill known as Sperwan Ghar, southwest of Kandahar city. A road spiralled up the summit, which rose out of the surrounding farmland like a fairy-tale fortress, topped with US and Afghan flags. Everything you could see from the pinnacle of the hill had been a hot zone in the previous fighting season, when bodies littered a nearby road. Now the artillery was silent. Some of the platoons had not fired a single shot in months. The soldiers squatted on their mud parapets, peering down at villagers who wandered the fields with herds of goats, or collected the last of the poppy crop. The troops knew that the harvest would finish in the next week, and there wasn't much they could do except watch the slow progress of days. The outpost baked in the sun.

The only enemies that showed up at first were the small creatures living in the crevices of the sandbag fortifications. One soldier forgot to shake out his sleeping bag before settling down at night and was bitten by a yellow scorpion. The sting numbed the right side of his body, and he was evacuated for medical treatment. A commander reassured the troops that he would return to duty soon, but the incident did nothing to ease the fear of pests. One night I was sitting with a few men on a makeshift porch, camouflage netting stretched across pine boards and plywood, leaning back against a wall of sandbags, when I heard a scurrying sound over my shoulder. A camel spider scuttled out of its burrow and paused a few centimetres from the trimmed line between a sergeant's brush cut and his sunburned neck. I nudged him, and he jumped to his feet. Furry and brownish, the camel spider was legendary among foreign troops in Afghanistan. Many soldiers believed the arachnid was deadly, but this was just another of the false rumours about Afghanistan and its inhabitants. The sergeant jabbed at it with a pair of pliers, unsuccessfully, and the nimble thing slipped back into the sandbag wall. Another soldier brought a spray can of lubricant, flipped open a lighter, and scorched the whole area with his improvised flame-thrower. For a moment, a cluster of men watched smoke rise from the blackened fabric of the sandbags, inspecting for signs of life. I was sure the thing was dead, but the camel spider soon tumbled out of the sandbags and wriggled on the plywood, burnt and steaming. A soldier attacked it with a combat knife, cutting it into a dozen pieces. The corpse was tiny, barely enough charred legs and body to fill a matchbox. That night, the troops sprayed double the usual dose of repellants in their sleeping quarters. A chemical mist pervaded the bunker, curdling with the smells of sweat and foot fungus. I lay on my bunk, breathing the odours, reviewing the evening's excitement in my mind and thinking about how the military sometimes fails to identify its real enemies. The camel spider had not posed any danger; while capable of painful bites, it wasn't venomous. In fact, the arachnid was useful against genuine threats because it hunted poisonous insects and scorpions. But the troops were afraid and irritated, their skin covered with red bites from things that chewed on them while they slept. The camel spider was a convenient target. Its obliteration seemed in keeping with all of NATO's misplaced fury.

Then again, Afghanistan breeds toughness. The following afternoon I joined a group of soldiers as they cheered two ants in a tug-of-war over a corn chip. The men were absorbed in this contest of insect strength; when somebody commented that the bugs seemed stronger in Afghanistan, everybody agreed. There was something urgent about the way the flies climbed on your face, worming their way into your eyes and nostrils, hunting for moisture. The flies were less skittish than the houseflies back home. You swatted at them and they circled back to buzz in your hair or sip the spittle from the corner of your mouth. If you wanted to get rid of them, killing was the only way.

The cigarette smoke also helped with the swarming flies. Soldiers played poker for cigarettes, the crumpled paper tubes trading hands so many times that they had to twist the tips to keep the tobacco from falling out. Sometimes they continued these games into the night, playing with headlamps under the stars, using red filters on their lights to make them less visible to Taliban in the fields beyond the perimeter. After months of deployment, they had exhausted most options for entertainment. Their stashes of men's magazines were rumpled and used. I brought them fresh copies of *Maxim* from a store at the airfield, but this was disappointingly tame for soldiers who had developed a taste for serious pornography. The troops had watched all the DVDs in their collections. They shared a laptop with intermittent access to a satellite modem, but there's a limit to the number of times you can send your girlfriend e-mails about the weather during an unyielding series of sunny days. So the soldiers dealt another hand of cards, swatted flies, exhaled streams of tobacco smoke and waited for battle.

Just before it began, I caught a helicopter ride further west to an outpost in Sangin district of Helmand province. The base stood on a plateau overlooking a fertile valley, near a town that served as a hub for opium trafficking. There had recently been so few attacks that British troops boasted of their brigade commander feeling safe enough to casually shop in the bazaar. That spring they installed a new Afghan district leader and set up a few smaller patrol bases around the town. They hoped to start reconstruction work in the district and extend their security zone all the way up the valley to the Kajaki Dam so they could increase the supply of hydroelectricity to the south. As the harvest drew to a close, however, the troops saw signs that the fleeting peace was ending. Hundreds of young men appeared on the roads, crowded into trucks and cars. They were unarmed and got through NATO checkpoints by calling themselves farm labourers. Many of them obviously *had* been working the fields, because they had scarred hands and stained shirts, but the soldiers wondered where they were going next.

The trouble started with a single bullet in the night. In the second week of May, a group of US special forces known as Task Force Scorpion was driving along the river north of Sangin when they hit an insurgent ambush. The Taliban fired rocket-propelled grenades and automatic rifles, and one of them got a lucky shot over the chest plate in an American's body armour. The bullet ricocheted off the man's collarbone and down into his torso, killing him. His comrades pulled back and called for air support, including attack helicopters, fighter jets and a gunship. They guessed a few dozen insurgents were killed that evening. I heard about the incident the next morning from an American major. He had promised to take me on a patrol north of Sangin, but he cut it short and circled back to base as it became clear that this was going to be a bad day. The dirt roads were jammed with vehicles carrying the human wreckage from the previous night. Many of the victims arrived at the gates of the military base, as villagers tried to get medical treatment for the survivors and compensation for the deceased. Rusty vehicles jolted up the steep laneway to the main gates, so full of human bodies that it was hard to tell the dead from the injured. Soldiers scrambled into disaster response mode, snapping on rubber gloves and grabbing stretchers. They heaved the injured out of trucks and set up field clinics, giving the victims oxygen and intravenous drips. One man was pulled from a hatchback sedan on a folded blanket and set down on a stretcher in the shade of a metal shipping container. He was covered with blood—hands, feet, shirt—the red stains turning dark and crusty. Bewildered by the medical exams, he moaned and struggled.

"Relax, just relax. It's fine," a medic barked, as an interpreter murmured in Pashto.

"Hey, hey, listen to me," the medic continued. "Can you feel your fingers? I need to know. Can you feel your fingers? Nah, he can't feel his fingers. Probably has nerve damage. I need to know about his arm. Does this hurt? Does this hurt? Does this hurt? Is he having any problems breathing?"

The patient lolled his head and whimpered.

"Don't move your arm, okay? Keep your arm right there," the medic said.

"We've got more inbound right now," somebody said, and all eyes turned to the stream of vehicles bringing more casualties. The governor would later estimate twenty-one civilians were killed, but nobody could know for sure. As the injured washed up at the gates of the military base I counted at least fifteen children among them. They were strangely quiet, gazing at the alien features of the base: helicopters, razor wire, medical apparatus. The boys stared hard at the female medics, who must have seemed like erotic angels in tight shirts and running shorts, a different species from the local women in burkas. A thirteen-year-old boy stood mesmerized under the shade of a hospital tent as a medical team worked on his injured uncle. Maybe he was still mildly in shock, cradling a bandaged hand with a shrapnel wound, or perhaps he was stunned by the sight of his uncle, who was missing a chunk of his back the size of a large dinner plate. A soldier peeled a dressing off the wound and the uncle winced, the skinless muscle of his shoulder glistening. The boy turned away, and I asked him what happened. A bomb collapsed his house, he said. Four of his relatives were killed, and he could hear two of his younger brothers crying under the rubble. He told them to shut up because he wasn't sure what other dangers waited in the darkness. Scrabbling through the ruined building, he found them in a corner and dragged them out by their shoulders. At daybreak he saw a dozen of his fellow villagers lying dead. Some survivors remained on the ground, too, because people were afraid to emerge from their hiding spots and collect them. He remembered a girl flailing in the dirt with her foot blown off. "She was crying, and there was nobody to help her," he said.

Most of the victims were members of tribes that did not usually support the Taliban in that valley. When I asked him how he felt about the insurgents after the bombing, the boy looked at me seriously. His school had been closed for a year because the Taliban had beheaded four students. Nobody in the village liked the Taliban. But even as he watched the foreign troops trying to save his uncle's life, he couldn't find anything nice to say about the international forces.

My notes end with this scribble: "1:53 p.m. Order to stay in CA [Canadian] area." That's the exact time in the afternoon when the US special forces commander tried to stop me from reporting the story about civilian casualties. He instructed that I should be confined to a remote corner of the base—and that if I wandered out of that zone, he would evict me from the base. This was a death threat, in effect. I didn't really think the soldiers would push me outside the gates; although the special forces never had a sophisticated grasp of public relations, they probably understood how bad it would look if villagers lynched a journalist. Still, I couldn't ignore the order. American counter-terrorism worked outside the usual rules. The special forces were pissed off and exhausted after losing one of their comrades the night before. One of them had already tried to confiscate my camera. The hapless officer assigned to drag me away was apologetic, but ultimately he was carrying a pistol and I was not. I retreated to a shady bunker.

The base was returning to normal, anyway. The flow of civilian casualties had finally dried up, and a couple of American soldiers resumed their usual banter. They saw that I was visibly shaken by the incident, so they tried some military-grade humour to smooth things over. The small guy pointed to his well-muscled friend and tried to persuade me that he served as a body double in *Lord of the Rings*. Then, more seriously, he asked if I had seen the porn version of the film.

"The *Porn of the Rings*?" I said.

"*Porn of the Rings*," the big guy said, nodding and smiling. We contemplated silently, watching the afternoon heat waves. Somewhere on the other side of the camp, medics were sewing up children blasted by air strikes. Soldiers learn to avoid dwelling on such things. It was more pleasant to think about naked elves.

The next morning I was woken with a shake on the shoulder by a British officer. News had spread to his section of the camp that I had angered the US special forces on the previous day, and it turned out that I wasn't the only person who didn't get along with them. There was no love between the British soldiers and Task Force Scorpion, especially after the Americans mistakenly killed civilians during the ambush and sent the whole valley into an uproar. This kind of tension was remarkably common between the US forces and their NATO allies in Afghanistan. All too often, the Europeans viewed the Americans as trigger-happy cowboys, while the US soldiers saw their counterparts as weak and useless. The American counter-terrorism forces had a different mission and separate chain of command from the NATO troops; while the elite commandos hunted for threats to global security, the rest of the international forces were struggling to put down a local insurgency. Translated into action, this meant that bearded Americans ran around at night kicking down doors, while clean-shaven regular troops went on day patrols and held meetings to foster goodwill and set up the basics of government. These differences made for an uneasy dynamic among the international allies, but it helped me on that particular morning in 2007. I'd been trying for days to get permission to join a British patrol, with no success until the American commander threatened to kick me off the base. Being hated by the Americans somehow made me loved by the British. The world's greatest military alliance was clearly dysfunctional, but its problems got me a ride into the valley.

The Taliban had enjoyed remarkable control in parts of the Sangin valley in recent months. British troops established an outpost in the middle of town in spring 2006, as part of NATO's surge into southern Afghanistan, but what followed was a humiliating siege. The insurgents cut off the roads, forcing the troops to get supplies by helicopter. Taliban patrolled the area; I had obtained video footage of them conducting leisurely searches of cars on the highway, apparently unafraid of the British troops penned up in their base nearby. A major offensive in the spring of 2007 finally broke the siege, but insurgents still roamed the hills north of town. With the onset of fighting season, it seemed the Taliban were moving back toward the half-ruined settlement.

The insurgents' new offensive brought them to the doorstep of Captain James Shaw of the 1st Battalion Grenadier Guards. He commanded one of several British teams working with Afghan forces in Sangin, sleeping alongside the local troops in a crumbling mud building near the town market. Like other outposts, this one lacked a toilet. Showers consisted of a plastic bag of water dribbled over your head. Somehow the captain had scrounged a few cans of gin-and-tonic, a rare pleasure in a country where alcohol is usually restricted, but otherwise the soldiers were living rough. Such outposts were part of a counter-insurgency strategy that called for making the troops part of the community. The thinking was that locals would start to trust the foreign soldiers if they cemented themselves in the neighbourhood, which would lead to better intelligence. In practice, many Afghans seemed to have abandoned the town. This was a pattern that repeated itself across the country, as villagers correctly saw the soldiers as magnets for trouble. Still, an old woman who visited the outpost for afternoon tea raised the captain's hopes. She described a cache of Taliban weapons just north of the town, and gave details about how to find it. This was exactly the sort of information the foreign troops craved. Some of the soldiers were skeptical, but Captain Shaw radiated enthusiasm. His boyish face, under a brush of blonde hair, went pink with excitement as he rounded up his men. The rumoured cache was only five kilometres away, which he guessed wasn't so far north that he risked encountering Taliban. Captain Shaw's small unit had only three jeeps and a few pickup trucks, so he hoped to find the weapons and return without a fight.

As we bumped up the road, I leaned out of a jeep and enjoyed the breeze on my face. You can't get that kind of experience in most of the NATO vehicles; the Dutch, Canadians and Americans had armoured carriers with layers of steel or ceramic protection between passengers and the world outside. But the British, in a fit of hubris, deployed their troops in modified Land Rovers, with improvised armour that seemed jerry-built. Somebody had lashed bullet-resistant blankets along the sides with plastic straps, a baleful attempt to make them safer, but the soldiers couldn't do anything about the open-topped roof. Their best defence was to stay observant, swivelling their guns at every passing car as we rolled through the blasted outskirts of town. We passed empty buildings, shuttered stores and a mosque with a missing wall. Breaking into the countryside, our convoy churned past farmland that sloped away to the left. Children hauled bundles of dry poppy stalks through the fallow fields.

A few minutes outside of town, a craggy hill on our right side exploded in a shower of grey smoke streaked with dirt. Rocket-propelled grenades whistled toward us from a stand of trees on our left. I threw myself to the floor of the jeep while the soldier above me yelled and started firing. The clatter of weapons came from all around, the sound of Taliban rifles mingling with the fire from Afghan and British soldiers. The loudest bangs came from the weapon of a British soldier standing beside me, his rifle spewing brass that bounced off my helmet as I ducked and cowered. The young soldier squinted through his scope and jolted out more rounds, then swore heartily as another vehicle slammed into ours, throwing him off balance. In the first moments of the ambush, the British were jamming their vehicles into reverse and pulling back. For them, it was standard procedure: get out of the Taliban's sights and return fire. The Afghans did the opposite, bailing out of their pickup trucks and charging forward. Two of the Afghan soldiers had been wounded, and many others had miraculously avoided injury when an anti-tank mortar slammed into their tailgate—the mortar was a dud, fortunately, and the impact only shattered a rear window. This narrow escape seemed to embolden the local troops, who advanced to a ditch and looked back at the retreating British with scorn.

Despite the Afghans' bravery, it was the British who answered with the most firepower. After pulling a short distance away, they started hammering the tree line and a compound with machine guns. The soldier beside me jumped out of our jeep, leaving the back hatch open. For a few minutes I crouched in the open hatchway, taking photos of the firefight, until I realized the dark square doorway was framing me as an easy target. I didn't want to give up my clear view, but fear prompted me to shut the hatch and continue watching from a small window, narrating my observations into an audio recorder. My voice sounds weirdly calm in the digital recording, as if I was stupefied by adrenaline. "I'm watching through what I *hope* is a bulletproof plate of glass, a tiny grilled window at the back of the troop carrier," I said. Moments later, the microphone captured a series of high-pitched singing notes as Taliban bullets rang off the metal door and the window in front of my face. Closing the hatch had been a good decision, it turned out. The volley also confirmed that the yellow glass was, in fact, resistant to gunfire. I pressed my face against the pane to watch.

A sergeant scurried out from the cover of his vehicle to set up a mortar tube. He tried to steady the weapon while finding the range, tilting the tube until a bubble in greenish liquid indicated that he had the correct angle. Taliban bullets punched the air around him, hitting the vehicles with more of those awful high-pitched notes. The sergeant's legs wouldn't stop shaking. He dropped a mortar into the tube and sent it thudding into the tree line, smoke and dust rising a storey above the foliage. After a few more successful shots, as they felt themselves gaining the upper hand, a sense of euphoria seemed to overtake the sergeant and a few of his comrades. He pulled out a silver pocket camera, pressed record, and laughed wildly into the lens, setting the device on the front bumper of his jeep to capture footage of himself in action. "This is great!" a soldier shouted, above the concussive din.

Captain Shaw looked grim, however, crouching behind a vehicle with a spindly communications device. The radio told him no aircraft or artillery were ready to hit the Taliban positions; the airspace was blocked by incoming medical helicopters, ferrying wounded from another battle. Nor did the British captain have any way of talking to the Afghan troops, who seemed intent on facing the enemy despite having suffered casualties. He needed to pull them back, but they could not hear his shouts. Finally, the captain charged forward with another soldier, ducking low through the Taliban's arcs of fire. A red flash with a loud bang kicked up smoke as something exploded in the middle of the road, perhaps a dozen metres from the British vehicles. Soldiers manning the machine guns ran out of bullets, fumbling with fresh boxes of ammunition. One screamed in pain as he inadvertently touched the hot barrel of his gun. Another gunner shouted and waved at a small girl wearing a purple dress, trying to get her to move away as she led a donkey through the crossfire between the British and the Taliban. She was too distant to hear him, just a waifish figure ambling through a dry field. At one point she appeared to stop, as if unsure which direction led to safety, and a moment later she disappeared amid the brown stalks.

Finally the young captain succeeded in hauling the Afghan troops back to their vehicles for a retreat. Another group of British soldiers arrived to cover our withdrawal, and our convoy started to return south along the gravel road. As we got moving, however, a soldier beside me noticed two men in black turbans and waistcoats cresting the hill about one hundred metres away, on the opposite side from the original ambush. They looked like civilians at first glance; then they pulled out Kalashnikov rifles and sprayed the convoy. There was a moment of surprise that we'd been outflanked, and a split second of even greater surprise that nobody was hurt by the wild shooting at nearly point-blank range. Then the attackers went down in a cloud of dust as the troops retaliated with much better aim. We sped away at full speed. "Go, go, go, go, go!" a soldier shouted. "Get us out of here."

But it was difficult to escape the Taliban. That evening, after a medical helicopter took away the injured Afghans, shots cracked over barricades of our outpost. The night filled with sounds of men shouting and running. Somebody sent up flares, casting a ghostly light over a confused scene. The phosphorescence revealed British and Afghan soldiers watching nervously over the walls, toward an empty graveyard where Taliban fighters were sneaking toward us. It was only a probing attack, intended to gauge the strength of our defences. But the truth was that our defences weren't very strong. The British troops didn't trust the Afghan guards to stay awake, or hold their positions in the face of an attack, so Captain Shaw ordered two-man rotations of British troops to keep watch through the night, which meant little sleep for his six men. As the flares winked out and darkness returned, Captain Shaw turned to me and offered a handgun. I refused, explaining that journalists don't carry weapons. The young captain was insistent. "You might need it," he said, holding out the firearm, its black polish gleaming under his headlamp. "We don't know what will happen tonight." His face had lost its boyishness. We had a short conversation about the fact that I was utterly incompetent with guns, but agreed that he should leave the pistol and several ammunition clips on the floor beside my sleeping mat. We spent a restless night, with the thudding noises of fighting in the distance, but the insurgents never made a serious attempt to take the outpost. Thankfully, I never had to touch the gun.

Morning brought a sleepy review of the previous day. Soldiers counted the ammunition spent, including a thousand machine-gun bullets and fifty mortar rounds. Captain Shaw held a meeting with his counterpart in the Afghan army, a platoon commander with a thick beard. The local commander was anxious to reassure his foreign friends that he had correctly judged the old woman's intelligence about a weapons cache.

"Well, I think we did find the weapons," Captain Shaw said. "They were fired at us."

The Afghan estimated that the ambush included more than thirty insurgents, judging by their boldness. The British captain was skeptical of the number, guessing the Taliban group was smaller, but in any case he concluded that many more troops would be required next time he ventured north of town. The onset of the fighting season had ignited a wave of violence to Sangin; a roadside bomb exploded near our outpost that morning, the second in as many days. At another small British checkpoint nearby, tribal elders had brought the bodies of three children killed in recent battles, but they had no information about the girl in the purple dress.

The old woman whose information led to the ill-fated patrol showed up in the afternoon. She wore a black scarf that framed her leathery face, and carried herself with rigid poise. She was unapologetic about the ambush, and scolded the troops for failing to call ahead so she could guide them safely. She urged the soldiers to try again with a bigger force, because her village north of Sangin had been overrun with insurgents who demanded food and shelter at gunpoint. The Taliban had exiled her family and many others to a nearby desert, she said. The Afghan commander assured her that his men had killed at least one Taliban fighter during the ambush, but the old woman looked at the floor and cocked her head sadly. No, she said, all of the insurgents escaped. She did bring a bit of good news, however: the girl in the purple dress arrived home safely. The woman's face crinkled into a smile. "Her injury was a small wound on her finger."

Captain Shaw later admitted that he misjudged the situation, saying it was a poor idea to drive north of Sangin with such a small patrol. The official predictions about the fighting season also proved incorrect; that summer's violence was the worst since the beginning of the insurgency. Every time the soldiers suffered a setback, such as Captain Shaw's disastrous patrol, the prescription was "more troops." The officers were schooled in counter-insurgency theories that claimed restive zones could be pacified with a saturation of forces. Whatever magic number of troops would have settled down places such as Sangin, however, the actual strength of the units on the ground never seemed like enough. On the day when we drove into an ambush, slightly more than ten thousand international forces were deployed in southern Afghanistan. That number peaked around seventy thousand soldiers in the following years, and the small British squads in open-topped jeeps were replaced with double-sized patrols of US Marines, equipped with armoured vehicles that weigh fourteen tons each. The influx of firepower did not bring peace, however; it's now well known that every increase in troop numbers in southern Afghanistan brought a corresponding increase in violence.

When military officials talk about their legacy, when they try to explain why the bloodletting was necessary, they usually point to a small number of infrastructure projects—but most importantly, they argue, NATO is leaving behind a strengthened Afghan administration. They describe this as a key indicator of progress, but I sometimes wondered what was so great about spreading Kabul's influence into the remote districts. Terrified of both sides, civilians were caught in the crossfire, like the little girl in the purple dress. Why, precisely, was it important to push the Afghan government's reach into such valleys? I asked that question of everybody I met—including, eventually, President Karzai himself.

Afghan police in training, reluctantly

CHAPTER 10

THE KARZAI REGIME SEPTEMBER 2007

The government in southern Afghanistan resembled the dust devils that flitted into empty quarters, appearing and disappearing, taking form only long enough to make you wonder if they had shape. The illusion of governance was stronger in Kabul, where you might encounter young Afghan officials wearing the latest fashion—hair slicked back, a polyester suit, fake alligator-skin shoes—who slipped enough acronyms into their carefully enunciated English that they could almost pass for technocrats. Such young men were eager to sell foreigners the dream of government. In the rest of the country, the influence of Kabul was a gust of wind that stormed into town and vanished. One day the police showed up at a checkpoint, stopping cars and peering into their backseats in a half-hearted search for suicide bombers, but the next day their post sat empty, nothing left of their presence but a bullet-riddled shipping container once used as a guard house. Had the Taliban chased them away? Or were they lounging in the fields, smoking hashish? Nobody asked, because you did not want to get involved. The regime was something that inflicted itself upon you. All the better if you could escape its reach.

Western commentators often lamented this as "weak government," but if you asked somebody in Kandahar whether the government was too weak, he might tell you, "Not weak enough." Tribesmen fondly remembered the royal family, which ruled until the 1970s in a style that now seems cunningly feeble. The former king, Zahir Shah, did not have many police in the rural areas, but this wasn't a problem because he did not make many demands. When a policeman had some reason to visit a remote village, the officer could travel by himself with only a pistol for protection. Villagers understood that the government posed little threat, so they did not threaten the government's envoys. A tribal elder described one officer's journey from Kandahar city to a distant spot in the mountains; during the return trip, he realized he had lost his hat. A delegation of villagers showed up the next morning at police headquarters, having carefully transported the policeman's cap back to the city. That was a golden age in the memory of local residents, a time of respect between the villagers who ruled themselves, and the central government that pretended to control the territory.

President Hamid Karzai painted himself as a successor to the royals, with murals and billboards juxtaposing his face against images of former kings. It was an unflattering comparison for the president, however. Unlike the previous monarchs, Karzai could not send his officials into distant villages by themselves. Law enforcement required, at minimum, convoys of pickup trucks brimming with men and weapons. These patrols frequently ran into trouble and found themselves calling for help. The international troops mistook this for weakness; they assumed that the Afghans needed more combat training and equipment, but this was a side issue. The bigger problem was how the Afghans misused their modest strength.

Many of the abuses of government power cannot be discussed openly, even now. But consider one example from the summer of 2007, when two police factions were squabbling over a highway west of Kandahar city. Both sides wanted to control the road, which meant a share in the drug trade. Many checkpoints on that route were manned by a militia loyal to Habibullah Jan, a chain-smoking old warlord who had become an elected parliamentarian. His rival was Ahmed Wali Karzai, the provincial council chairman and younger half-brother of the president. These men were theoretically on the same side, working with the US and NATO forces against the Taliban, but they fought each other fiercely. So it wasn't clear who to blame for the bomb that exploded in the road one summer day, killing five of Ahmed Wali's men in a pickup truck. Most people in the vicinity of the blast ran away in fear, except for two farm labourers tending grapevines. Police arrested them on suspicion of triggering the bomb—possibly because they belonged to the tribe of Ahmed Wali's rival. Rather than taking the captives to jail, the officers drove them to a slum and dumped them in the basement of a mud house. It seems they were imprisoned in a family residence that also served as a private jail: the prisoners occasionally saw men in police uniforms, but also had visits from children who wandered into their makeshift cell and looked at them curiously. One of the captives had well-connected relatives who managed to get him free, although he was tortured for weeks beforehand. The other prisoner's mutilated body was discovered later, floating in a canal on the north side of Kandahar city. A man who saw the corpse told me the skin dangled from the body in narrow strips, as if he'd been sliced with knives before he was executed with a cut throat. His relatives complained to the authorities, but always got the same answer: It was Ahmed Wali's men. There's nothing you can do. Nor was there anything I could do, as a journalist who did not want to run afoul of Kandahar's rulers. I never did prove that the younger Karzai brother had any connection to that death, and perhaps he did not. He was so influential that his name got tangled up in many stories, good and bad, until he was assassinated in 2011. Even his death was a mystery: one of his henchmen shot him at point-blank range in his house, but nobody got a chance to interrogate the assassin about his motives. Ahmed Wali's supporters killed the attacker, dragged the body through the streets, and strung it up in a central square as a warning about the consequences of betrayal.

The NATO forces tried to curb the excesses of local authorities. Foreign troops had enjoyed some modest success with programs euphemistically called "mentoring" or "training" for the Afghan military, which involved international forces supervising the daily work of local soldiers, often herding their trainees across the battlefield like errant children. As problems with the Kandahar police became more embarrassing in the summer of 2007, the Canadians hastily decided to extend their mentorship to the local force. Troops preparing for deployment were told at the last minute that they would be teaching skills to law enforcement officers, not soldiers.

I happened to be visiting an outpost west of Kandahar city when the police mentorship concept was first tested. A young Canadian officer had been assigned to teach ten Afghan policemen how to defend their new checkpoint, recently constructed with wooden beams that still smelled of fresh lumber. The night before the program officially launched, the Canadian captain picked his way through the darkness toward his students. Burning remnants of a recent mortar attack smoldered nearby, the orange embers casting the only light in the surrounding farmland. The captain brushed open the curtain in the doorway of the Afghan police station, which consisted of only a metal shipping container crowded with men and rifles, silhouetted in the glow from a penlight. The Afghans ushered him to a place of honour, on a cushion beside the police commander, and poured him a cup of tea. The captain sipped hesitantly. He struggled to cross his legs like the other men in the room, his combat boots making him clumsy.

"We will start tomorrow morning," the captain said. "What do you want to learn?"

He had to repeat the question a couple of times because the translator had trouble with the soldier's French-Canadian accent. Even after the police commander understood the question, there was a long silence as he paused to think. Finally, the hard-faced policeman declared that he had more battlefield experience than any of the Canadians. He served in a militia for a tribal warlord who ruled part of the district before the Taliban rose to power, and for a short period after their defeat. The international community poured millions of dollars into disarming such warlords, then re-armed many of the same gunmen during the rushed creation of new police units. "I don't know what you could teach us," the policeman said.

The Canadian tried to persuade his reluctant pupil that the foreign troops could help him stay alive by drilling his men in basic infantry techniques.

"Will this program involve running?" the policeman asked, skeptically. He reminded the Canadian that his officers were observing fasts for the holy month of Ramadan, which meant they lacked energy. Eventually he agreed that the training could be limited to two hours, starting at 6 a.m., when the soldiers were still digesting their pre-dawn meals. The Canadian captain did his best to encourage the Afghans, suggesting they could learn how to ration their bullets, how to move under covering fire and how to pin down their enemies with machine guns.

The policeman was nonplussed by the offer. He launched into a tirade about how his men had not received their salary in months, a common problem as superior officers embezzled money from the pay system. In this case, the policeman specifically accused his district police chief, who had been fired under mysterious circumstances earlier in the day. (I found the chief preparing to leave his headquarters a few days later: filthy, unshaven, looting his own office and stealing gasoline from government trucks.)

The next morning, at six o'clock, the Canadian captain stood in a field near the outpost and waited for his students. They straggled in half an hour late, and showed little enthusiasm for his description of hand signals they could use to communicate in battle. The Canadian gamely tried to continue with the lessons, until his interpreter decided it was silly to continue playing along.

"Sir, I don't think they care about these things," said the interpreter, a skinny kid in a blue baseball cap.

"It will come," the Canadian said.

The interpreter gamely made another pitch to the policemen, but only started a babble of argument.

"They're saying we've been doing this for years," the interpreter said. "I try to tell them, you suffer so many casualties, you must learn so you do not die."

"Good, good," the captain said. "Did they understand?"

"I think so," the interpreter said. But he looked uncertain.

Afghan politicians could only imagine those absurd scenes. The men fighting, and dying in large numbers, almost never saw their leaders. It was different for the NATO forces, whose generals made a point of travelling to the battlefields, often picking up rifles and replacing sentries on armoured vehicles, proud to face the same perils as infantrymen. By contrast, risk-taking was not fashionable in the Afghan government. If you wanted to find an Afghan police chief or brigade commander, you usually had to make an appointment to visit a heavily guarded office. You could expect to find hospitality in their offices, perhaps a tasty snack, but you did not usually expect to get much insight into the world beyond their walls.

That was a main reason why I never bothered to request an interview with President Karzai. If the problem of insulated officials was bad in Kandahar city, I figured it could only be worse in the presidential palace in Kabul. Others weren't so skeptical of him; a United Nations official who spoke with him on a weekly basis told me that he considered Karzai a "flawed jewel" whose failures could be blamed on those who surrounded him.

In any case, Karzai was not too insulated to make a canny move in the summer of 2007, as the war became increasingly controversial in NATO countries, and Canada faced a politically sensitive decision about whether to withdraw troops. Karzai took the unusual step of summoning every Canadian journalist in the country to see him. We had only half a day's warning before climbing onto a transport plane in Kandahar and roaring north to Kabul, where a convoy of armoured luxury vehicles took us to the finest hotel in the capital. The Serena Hotel did not serve alcohol, but a Canadian embassy staffer smuggled cans of Heineken into each of our rooms. By the time of our appointment with the president, the media pack was relaxed and smelled faintly of beer and herbal soap. Another convoy whisked us through the darkened city, the streets empty because of curfew. The president's security men stripped us of our gear, searched us and made us stand in the road while guard dogs sniffed for explosives. These checks were repeated several times with rigour that seemed almost theatrical. Presidential bodyguards with black suits and black shirts muttered into their walkie-talkies as they ushered us through the palace gates, into a courtyard of tall evergreens and up the stone steps into the royal offices. Formally dressed waiters served tea on silver trays. Finally we arrived in a ballroom lined with pink marble and wood panels, decorated with garish gold-painted furniture that resembled leftovers from a Bollywood movie set. After all the pomp leading up to our meeting, Karzai made his entrance with a show of modesty. He clutched his wool cap to his chest while shaking hands with everybody in the room, greeting them warmly and joking with the cameramen as they clipped a microphone to his lapel. Then he turned serious, launching into a sales pitch for war.

Canada should not withdraw its soldiers as scheduled in 2009, he told us, because his government was not yet capable of defending itself. Famous for his dramatic flourishes, the president made his arguments in stark terms. "Afghanistan will fall back into anarchy, anarchy will bring back safe havens to terrorists, among other things, and terrorists will then hurt you back there in Canada and the United States," Karzai said. "Simple as that." He avoided the word *insurgents*, and railed against *terrorists*. He was, in effect, portraying his country as a bulwark against evil.

Karzai's plea for extra troop commitments would reverse itself in the following years, as he started to argue that the Afghan security forces were ready to assume responsibility for the country when foreign troops depart. But one part of his speech remained consistent: the president did not significantly change his position on negotiations. Then, as now, he says that he's willing to negotiate with the Taliban, but only if the insurgents accept the existing constitution and rules of the political game. When asked if he would consider sharing power with insurgent factions, he scowled:

No, nothing like that. This country belongs to all. There is a constitution; there is a way of life. Let's come and participate and win [elections]. It's a country for all of us. The Taliban and everybody else should remember President Kennedy's words, when he said to the American people, "Ask not what America can give you, ask what you can give to America." That's our position. We're telling all Afghans, who are for one reason or another carrying out attacks against their own country, that they should not ask what Afghanistan can do for them, but ask what is it they can do for their country and their people. Simple.

Simple. Why did he keep using that word? Because he wanted the foreigners to see a polarized conflict: democracy versus terrorism, good versus evil. It smelled wrong. Karzai's stand in favour of the constitution sounded noble, except that the constitution concentrated power in the hands of the president. His invitation to his enemies to join elections rang hollow, given the allegations of massive fraud in the electoral process. His claim that Afghanistan "belongs to all" overlooked the fact that his relatively modern views often rankled the conservative villagers. Most people in the country lived outside the cities, and many village men did not allow their wives and daughters to show their faces outside the house, which made the 2004 constitution that enshrined the female right to vote a radically progressive document. That same constitution also mandated a higher percentage of female parliamentarians in Kabul than existed in the equivalent assemblies of Britain, Canada and the United States. It's hard to imagine that the villagers saw the government as something that "belongs to us all." It's also difficult to see how this model of government could be imposed on Afghanistan with anything less than crushing force.

Karzai's opponents were not so inflexible. Shortly before our interview with the president, a Pakistani journalist who worked with me as a translator had submitted a list of questions to Gulbuddin Hekmatyar, leader of an insurgent faction in eastern Afghanistan. Three days after receiving the questions, the warlord sent back a computer disc with his video-recorded answers. His staff showed off their technical capabilities by offering the video in low- and high-resolution formats, even including a transcript for easy reference. The old militia commander wore a neatly pressed suit jacket, looking rather professional for a leader whose gunmen beheaded their enemies. The substance of his reply was also surprisingly nuanced, as he offered his suggestion for ending the war:

> *The current situation has a solution in the following way. All foreign troops must leave Afghanistan. Also, the Afghan people must sit together and make a decision that the foreign troops should leave. The Americans must accept this, and they must leave. We will never participate in the meetings in which they don't discuss this issue. Therefore we take up weapons for the independence of Afghanistan. There is no other way. Also, we want peace and security in Afghanistan like everybody else, but for that to happen the foreign troops should leave and foreigners should stop meddling in Afghanistan: Moscow, Washington or our neighbouring countries. Power should be handed over to other temporary government, and they will have a shura, a new constitution, and they must work in Islamic rule and we should have real and fair elections, which follow Islamic rules. In this case, I am ready for negotiations.*

There were plenty of reasons to be skeptical about Hekmatyar. He did not speak for the Taliban leadership, as he ran his own insurgent group, and he was probably toning down his language for the sake of appealing to a foreign audience. But his statement fit with the general trend of Taliban demands, which usually focused on political aims inside Afghanistan, without straying into the realm of global jihad. Their central demand, a troop withdrawal, could have plunged the country into civil war if implemented too abruptly, but in the long term it was a goal shared by the international forces. Perhaps most importantly, the insurgents seemed ready to talk about everything, including the basic rules of political engagement in Kabul. By refusing to discuss the constitution, Karzai was taking a strong position on negotiations. This did not help to quell the conflict, however; it was another case of the government being "too strong."

Not that it mattered, at the time. Neither the insurgents nor Kabul seemed genuinely enthusiastic about peace talks, and sometimes it was hard to tell which side was being more stubborn about the process. Cynicism pervaded the talk about negotiations: on a flight from Kandahar to Kabul I sat beside an officer from Afghanistan's intelligence service, and from the moment we buckled up to the time we stepped off the plane, he grilled me about the foreigners' true intentions. He wondered if the US–NATO strategy was to prolong the war as a means of cementing positions at Afghan airfields within range of Iran and China. The insurgents had similar conspiracy theories, worrying that the international troops wanted to stay forever.

Even the smallest efforts at détente ran into problems. In December 2006, a delegation of elders from villages southwest of Kandahar city visited the palace of the provincial governor. They were a group of serious men with an offer that seemed sincere: withdraw the military outpost from Sperwan Ghar, the hill overlooking their houses, and they would keep the Taliban away themselves. They felt capable of delivering on this promise because they had already raised the idea with Mullah Mohammed Mansoor, a former minister in the Taliban regime who had since become a major insurgent commander. It's easy to see why the NATO forces would have been reluctant to give up their hilltop outpost, a commanding piece of high ground from which an artillery gun could hit almost any part of the rebellious Panjwai valley. But the foreign troops might also have been tempted by the idea of bringing some calm to a district that has suffered so much. As it turned out, NATO never got a chance to talk with the elders about their proposal: Kandahar's provincial council rejected the idea, in another misplaced show of strength.

One wet morning in January 2008, I drove to the one village in southern Afghanistan where the government's strength should have been most appreciated. It was a short trip, five kilometres south of Kandahar, but the situation had grown so bad that it was a considerable risk. In better times, after the fall of the Taliban regime in 2001 and 2002, many journalists had visited this particular village. It was only a cluster of mud huts, but the name on the map indicated its importance in the new regime: Karz. The president's hometown is where correspondents stopped, in the early years, for a quick story about ordinary people cheering the new leader. In those initial stories, Karzai's tribesmen crowded around the television cameras and described their wish lists for their village: a school, paved roads, maybe a soccer team. In fact, some of those things had been achieved by the time I arrived. The new regime had paved the main road and re-opened a school that had been closed by the Taliban. Children scrambled over new playground equipment as workers carried bricks for classrooms under construction. It was a hopeful scene, nothing like the neglected places I had visited in the rest of the province. But the people themselves did not speak optimistically about their country. The school's deputy director decorated his office wall with two large portraits of Karzai, whom he described fondly as a former classmate. Despite that personal connection, he couldn't bring himself to say anything nice about the president. The economy had improved in recent years, he said, "but the economy is mostly for rich people."

His biggest concern, though, was security. The fighting that ripped through the south rarely touched Karz directly, but the villagers were now outnumbered by families that had fled the violence west of the city and sought refuge in relatives' homes and temporary camps. Many of the displaced people had lived in makeshift shelters for more than a year, refusing to go home as the bombing and artillery strikes increased. "The fighting gets worse and worse," the schoolmaster said. "Under the Taliban we had better security, no corruption, no stealing, no murders." He tried to make apologies for the president he knew in boyhood, saying these failures were not all the fault of Karzai, but a teacher who had been listening to our conversation interjected with a sharp contradiction. The schoolmaster's bare office echoed with their argument; my translator whispered that the teacher was asking his boss to tell the truth. Finally the school director slumped back in his chair, defeated, and allowed his teacher the last word. The white-haired instructor faced me and picked a few words to summarize the Karzai regime.

"It's corrupt," he said. "Morally and economically."

On rare occasions, the foreign troops managed to protect people in the south from their own government. In the Panjwai valley, the gunner of an armoured vehicle became a local hero for using cannon fire to scare off a group of police who had been harassing villagers. For the most part, however, people took affairs into their own hands. The assassination of Ahmed Wali Karzai was the most prominent example of a trend that grew every year during my time in the south, a rising tide of killings among prominent citizens. Sometimes the deaths were private matters, old feuds settled violently. More often, the killings fit a pattern. The Taliban's enemies, and potential enemies, were being eliminated one at a time. We were about to feel the heavy significance of those assassinations.

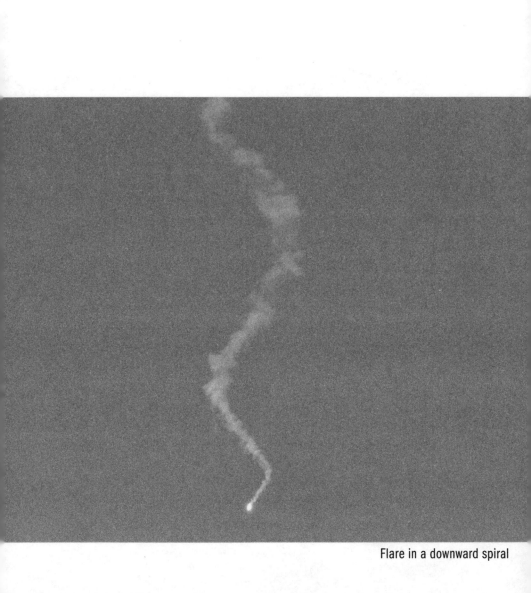

Flare in a downward spiral

CHAPTER 11

DEATH OF A WARLORD OCTOBER 2007

A Canadian battle group commander walked into the media tent at Kandahar Air Field one morning. It was unusual for a high-ranking officer to step into our den, which stank of unwashed flak jackets. I tried to get up and shake his hand, but it turned into a clumsy spectacle as I struggled out of my canvas recliner and got tangled in a headphone cord. The grey-haired commander waited until I composed myself, then asked: "Do you have a phone number for Habibullah Jan?" Of course I had his number, and numbers for two of his sons; staying in touch with the old warlord was essential for any journalist covering the districts west of Kandahar city. Habibullah Jan was part of a generation of hard-bitten former mujahedeen commanders, men who rose to power as brave warriors against the Soviet occupation in the 1980s and then squandered their reputations in a civil war amongst themselves. The Taliban drove them away in 1994, but they returned and flourished under the new regime, reincarnated as police chiefs, security contractors or implementing partners for development aid. In the case of Habibullah Jan, he had gotten himself elected to parliament in Kabul, a job he subsequently ignored in favour of supervising his private army in Kandahar. He also assisted foreign troops with the planning of Operation Medusa, and collected tokens of appreciation like certificates and plaques from senior military leaders. I was a little surprised that the Canadian commander didn't already have his contact details. The officer noticed my confusion as he was scribbling down the numbers, and explained: "This guy is a pain in the ass. I'm thinking about killing him." He snapped shut his notebook and walked out, leaving me wondering if he was joking or if I'd just inadvertently put the old warlord's life in danger.

As it turned out, international forces did not kill Habibullah Jan. He died much later in a Taliban-style ambush. The uncertainty over his allegiances, however, as well as the larger ambiguity about who qualified as NATO's friend or enemy, reflected the strange relationship between the foreigners and the warlords. The military labelled many of them as "white": a third category on the battlefield, neither "red" enemies nor "blue" allies. One intelligence officer told me this category was often ignored by his colleagues, who did not see the relevance of studying figures who weren't directly taking sides. Foreign diplomats also tended to dismiss the ex-mujahedeen as a bunch of rogues who needed to be shepherded into the new government system. Fear of their local fiefdoms had encouraged the post-2001 planners to give Afghanistan one of the most centralized systems of government in the world. You were either "with us, or against us." Politics was not so binary in the south, however, making it hard to define who was "with us." A thug who executes contracts for the military in the daytime and executes prisoners at night: Is he an ally? What about the drug dealer who keeps the peace in his district, but quietly does business with the Taliban?

These questions became even more difficult to answer when applied to the biggest warlords, the leaders of powerful tribes. Much of the previous generation of tribal leaders had died or fled during the three decades of war, and the men who replaced them often clawed their way to prominence on the battlefield. Maybe they were simple gunmen in the 1980s when they faced Soviet tanks, but by now they were dignified elders who sat on tribal councils and represented thousands of kinsmen. Tribes traditionally served as the main political forces in southern Afghanistan, especially when the government has been weak. In the uncertainty of life in Kandahar, tribalism had again emerged as an important way of deciding whom to trust. The major tribes had no official power in the government, but seemed capable of reaching decision with broad authority. The United Nations spent millions of dollars on successive programs to disarm the warlords and tribal chiefs, but in Kandahar these programs had little practical effect on the tribal strongmen. Everybody assumed they could mobilize thousands of armed men if necessary.

I didn't realize quite how much authority rested with these unofficial chiefs until I looked into the death of a diplomat. Glyn Berry, fifty-nine, political director of Canada's reconstruction team, died in January 2006 when a suicide bomber drove a silver minivan packed with explosives into a military convoy. The Canadians evacuated their injured and dead, and left the lead investigation to the Afghan police. Officers poked through the wreckage until they found the identification numbers on the chassis and engine block of the attacker's vehicle, a four-cylinder diesel Toyota Town Ace. They also deciphered the licence plate number, and went looking for its owner. This kind of police investigation did not usually work in Kandahar, where people make deals in cash with no records. Hundreds of nearly identical Toyotas stand in huge lots on the edge of the city, a waypoint for car smugglers. But the investigators got lucky in the hours that followed the diplomat's death: the traffic department pointed them to the vehicle's last registered owner. He showed them letters certifying that he sold the vehicle to a second man, who in turn could document the fact that he sold the minivan to another pair of men. One of the buyers was missing a leg, he said, and the other was named Pir Mohammed. Police arrested Mr. Mohammed the next morning, when he couldn't come up with a good explanation for what he did with the vehicle. They searched his house and reported finding a rocket-propelled grenade launcher, a Kalashnikov rifle, ammunition, documents in Arabic and a photograph of a reputed Taliban leader.

His home also had car parts strewn around the courtyard, which relatives explained as the detritus of a second-hand car business, but which the police saw as evidence that he ran a chop shop for turning vehicles into bombs. The officers threw him into the cramped holding cells at police headquarters. In his mug shot, he looks like any other local resident, perhaps thirty years old, wearing a suit vest over his traditional clothes, with a mop of curly black hair sticking out from his turban. The police report called Mr. Mohammed a "terrorist" and a "mastermind." The document offers little to support the idea that he was any sort of ringleader, but under the circumstances it did seem reasonable to hold him.

However, the investigation did not seem reasonable to Kandahar's most powerful tribal warlord, Mullah Naqib. He was sometimes called by his full name, Naqibullah, and sometimes people used labels other than "warlord" to describe him because that word didn't seem big enough for his hulking presence. Looking back through my newspaper stories, it's interesting to see how my shorthand for him started out cold and analytical—I described him as a "powerbroker" in 2006—but later became warmer, and by 2007 I was calling him a "jovial, grey-bearded strongman." Among all the old warriors who fought the Soviets and later became leaders in southern Afghanistan, he was easily the most prominent. His forces turned the Arghandab valley north of Kandahar city into a killing ground in the 1980s, repelling wave after wave of Soviet troops from the pomegranate orchards and grape fields. After the Russians finally retreated, the communist administration reached an understanding with Mullah Naqib that recognized his authority in the valley—a truce that likely saved the local government from being overrun by mujahedeen rebels. The communist regime eventually collapsed in 1992, and Mullah Naqib's tribesmen joined the rush to divide the spoils among the former resistance fighters, but he played peacemaker again in 1994 when the Taliban started sweeping away the squabbling mujahedeen factions. Mullah Naqib's faction was the largest, and he represented a tribe, the Alokozai, whose fighting strength had been noted by every commander in the region since Alexander the Great. Mullah Naqib avoided a bloodbath with his decision to pull his men back into their strongholds north of the city, handing over power to the Taliban. He later served as kingmaker for a third time after 2001, when he helped broker the Taliban's surrender and threw his support behind the new regime of Hamid Karzai. Despite his lack of official status in the government, he continued his role as adjudicator of disputes, holding court in his comfortable house on the north side of Kandahar city, so it was natural that his tribesmen would ask him for help with the case of the slain diplomat.

The man arrested for the bombing, Pir Mohammed, belonged to a family of Islamic teachers, respected members of the Alokozai tribe. In the hours after his arrest, they visited Mullah Naqib and pleaded their case, arguing that it wasn't possible for him to have assisted the insurgency. Their family had feuded with the Taliban in previous years, they claimed, over a disagreement about a holiday on the lunar calendar. The warlord considered their case, and what happened next became a study in the way power worked in Kandahar. This was the moment of transaction, when a family trades its status within the tribe for a favour. Mullah Naqib led a delegation of elders to the home of Ahmed Wali Karzai, the president's half-brother, who made a phone call to the governor. The governor called the police chief, and the suspect went free. All of this happened in less than two days. It illustrated whom ordinary people trusted to solve their problems—a tribal leader, not the government—and showed the hierarchy within the local administration, ostensibly run by the governor but supervised by Ahmed Wali Karzai, a member of the ruling family.

My newspaper articles about this incident suggested that Mullah Naqib was an anachronism, following ancient rules of tribal leadership that did not belong in modern Afghanistan. I wrote at length about interference in the courts, and international efforts to build a new system of justice. Canadian officials were not pleased about Mullah Naqib's meddling with the investigation, and responded to my articles by raising the issue with Afghanistan's intelligence chief in Kabul. One of my stories was accompanied by a photo of Mullah Naqib shaking hands with Canadian prime minister Stephen Harper, and the affair got picked up by blogs under the headline, "Harper shakes hands with terrorist warlord." I had not intended to portray the warlord as a villain, but the tone of the coverage rankled Sarah Chayes, an American author who was then living in Kandahar city. She scolded me via e-mail, complaining that I painted the warlord as a "monster" and suggesting that the international community should try to improve its relations with respected figures such as Naqib.

She was right; the warlord deserved better. Mullah Naqib's influence may not have been welcomed by the Canadians in that particular episode, but in reality the government's justice system was far less trustworthy, overall, than he was. He may have gained fame and power by shooting rockets at Soviet aircraft, but in his middle years he had played a stabilizing role in Kandahar that few people fully appreciated—until his death.

The warlord's territory had been fairly calm as the rest of the south erupted into insurgency in 2006, which led to rumours that Naqib must have cut a deal of some kind with the Taliban. The insurgents themselves spread those whispers: one Taliban operative tried to persuade me that Mullah Naqib had endorsed an insurgent attack because he was disappointed with the government. Any doubts about his loyalty to Kabul were erased in March 2007, however, when a bomb exploded near his armoured sport-utility vehicle, injuring him badly. The Taliban wanted him out of the way, but the bearish old man did not give up. He returned to Kandahar after several months of treatment in India, limping and leaning on a crutch. He looked tired, with white streaks in his beard. His long-time friend Sarah Chayes said he seemed disconsolate about the worsening situation. When he finally died of a heart attack in October 2007, she claimed that his death was not related to the bombing. She sat with him on the veranda of his home the night before he died, looking at his gardens and talking about the Taliban's growing strength. "He died of a broken heart," she said.

Insurgents had been trickling into Arghandab district in the previous months, but the warlord's death unleashed a flood of trouble in his home territory. At the time of Mullah Naqib's funeral, no regular troops were posted in his district. Military bases had been unnecessary in the valley, even though the terrain offered plenty of hiding places for insurgents and could have served as a pathway to the edge of Kandahar city from the Taliban enclaves in the north. In the days after Mullah Naqib's death, however, many people wondered if the Alokozai tribe would continue serving as guardians of those northern approaches. Feuds emerged among tribal figures who wanted to succeed him as leader, and President Hamid Karzai, who rarely risked a trip to Kandahar, arrived by helicopter to resolve the leadership question. As hundreds of tribesmen gathered in Mullah Naqib's front garden to mourn his passing, the president stood before them and placed a silver turban on the head of Kalimullah Naqibi, a chubby twenty-six-year-old whose main qualification for the job was being Mullah Naqib's son. The president obviously hoped that the young man would maintain his father's loyalty to the government, although some in attendance grumbled that the Karzai might also have wanted an inexperienced leader for the tribe as a way of ensuring the Karzai family's dominance of Kandahar city politics. The official line was that the president's gesture merely recognized a selection already made by Alokozai tribal elders, but most people in the city understood the central government had interfered with tribal traditions. I felt sorry for the new leader, sitting in his father's house, carrying his father's cellphone, trying to live up to his father's legend. He claimed to be happy about his new role, but then he paused, and his face clouded. Speaking more quietly, he invoked a Pashto saying—"When the turban falls from the head, it lands on the shoulders"—meaning that the burdens of the father are passed to the sons.

The weight of those burdens soon became clear. Arghandab's police chief received threatening phone calls a week after Mullah Naqib's death, warning him to allow safe passage through the district for Taliban fighters. He refused, and two weeks later hundreds of insurgents poured into the valley in a coordinated assault from three sides. They swarmed the north bank of the river, seizing about half the district and storming into Mullah Naqib's hometown. They danced on the roof of the warlord's house and dug holes around his property in an apparent search for a weapons stash. Mullah Naqib had surrendered many of the arms he used during his fight against the Soviets, but he had been rumoured to keep a supply of leftovers, perhaps even shoulder-mounted missiles capable of shooting down NATO aircraft. It wasn't clear whether the Taliban found anything on their treasure hunt, but the raid sent a message about the insurgents' power. Foreign troops scrambled to muster a counterattack, and soon pushed the Taliban away.

This marked a change in the military landscape. For years, the primary threats to Kandahar city had come from the southwest, the same places where Operation Medusa had been fought. Now the international troops found themselves opening a new front, defending from the north. Arghandab grew steadily more violent after Naqib's death, eventually requiring entire battalions of US troops to keep the insurgents at bay. The valley became notorious as one of the most dangerous places in the country.

Mullah Naqib was the biggest of the fallen warlords, but not the last. The Taliban's assassination campaign gathered pace after his loss. One of the failed candidates to replace him, and a powerful warlord in his own right, was Abdul Hakim Jan, an uneducated fighter whose trademark was a habit of wearing blue clothes. He had been fighting the Taliban since the movement's birth, and according to legend even armed his wives with automatic rifles. He reinvented himself as a police commander under the new government, becoming a fierce opponent of the insurgents. That probably explains why the Taliban went after him with such spectacular blood lust, sending a suicide bomber who caught him as he was sitting down to watch a dogfight and enjoy a picnic with tea and oranges. The blast killed him, along with perhaps a hundred fellow spectators who had gathered in a field to see the match. In the aftermath of that assassination, one of the first people I called for information was Malim Akbar Khan Khakrezwal, a former intelligence chief and an ex-mujahedeen leader himself, who said the warlord had been receiving threats from the Taliban but refused to stay away from public gatherings. Such advice didn't help Mr. Khakrezwal himself, as gunmen found him outside his house four months later and shot him dead. His brother, a former police chief, had already been assassinated in another bombing. The next month it was Habibullah Jan, the chain-smoking warlord whose cellphone numbers I had given to the Canadian commander, who was gunned down near his house. Men on motorcycles sprayed him with bullets as he was taking a short evening walk from his office to his wife's quarters.

It went on and on, like a panicked pulse. The assassination squads behaved with terrible efficiency, and usually without attracting much notice. We never heard of any arrests. The killers often struck in daylight with plenty of witnesses, and they usually followed a routine: two insurgents on a small Honda motorbike drive up, the man on the back of the bike pulls a Kalashnikov from under his shawl and unleashes a short burst. The hits that gained attention were the big warlords or major government officials, but more often the targets were petty. The death of an aid worker, or a translator, or just the unlucky relative of somebody suspected of collaborating with the foreigners, did little to help the insurgents on the battlefield. But the killings communicated the Taliban's power, and sapped the will of those trying to help the government. When my acquaintances started dying, at first I posted short obituaries like this on Facebook:

My former landlord
by Graeme Smith on Friday, September 12, 2008, at 3:46 p.m.

I set up an office in Kandahar city in late 2006, a lovely compound on the south side of the city shared with my translator's brother. My landlord was Nazar Mohammed Aga, a tall, big-bearded man who lived nearby. He had worked for a long time at Kandahar's electricity department. The Taliban hired him into the department during their regime, and when they fled the city in 2001 he stayed to work for the new government, eventually becoming the department's deputy chief. His office was a stone building near the main road through the city, where the stone stairs were dangerously smoothed by the years. The furniture looked as though it had been purchased at a second-hand store and given a rigorous beating. Even in the electricity office, there was no electricity. Mohammed Aga and his staff had no computers. They scribbled their notes in old books that looked like ancient tomes. Not that the deputy chief could read any of it—he was illiterate. Still, he was respected. His department's fortunes have been looking up recently, as NATO has finally transported a new turbine to a hydro-electric dam in the mountains north of Kandahar, meaning that within a couple of years the electricity department might have some electricity to administer.

I'd almost forgotten about Mohammed Aga, until today. We closed up the office in February 2007, after three gunmen kicked in the metal doors and searched the compound. Nobody was seriously hurt, but it scared us and I never went back to the office. That location, on a dirt road beside the city's main Roshan cell phone office, near the soccer stadium where the Taliban government once staged executions, had once been considered close enough to the city centre that it would be relatively safe. Apparently the bearded old office administrator had never stopped feeling relatively safe on that road, because he didn't stop his habit of walking down the street to pray at a nearby mosque and returning home on foot by the same route every evening. He didn't have any bodyguards, didn't carry any weapons. The Taliban ambushed him as he was walking home tonight, around 8:15 p.m., shooting him dead.

I stopped writing these laments after a while. The deaths were small tragedies in the midst of a much bigger sadness, the unravelling of an entire region. But the sheer comprehensiveness of the assassinations eventually made them a major factor. The Taliban were systematically removing any powerful figures in the south that had any connection with the government. Unlike the foreign troops, who struggled to distinguish friends from enemies, the Taliban knew precisely who qualified for their target lists. Two of the best news outlets in southern Afghanistan, the newspaper *Surgar Daily* and the website Benawa.com, counted more than five hundred major assassinations from 2002 to mid-2010 in the province of Kandahar. Their lists of the dead are missing many names, however, and the true numbers will never be known.

The victims we did track closely were the old warlords. For a journalist, they were often the people you called when you wanted to find a specific person, or confirm a fact, or when you needed an armed escort into the districts. They knew the gossip, and never missed a chance to badmouth rivals. Slowly, however, my contact list became riddled with annotations beside their names: "DEAD." I'd still call those numbers sometimes, because former mujahedeen commanders would often bequeath their fiefdoms—and their cellphones   to relatives, but the replacements were disappointing. The young Naqibi never led his tribe the way his father did; the sons of Habibullah Jan showed little enthusiasm for the family business of controlling a stretch of territory west of the city. Foreign observers of the war had spent years trying to decide if these characters were helpful or not, wrestling with questions about how to neutralize or exploit their influence, but perhaps we only learned to appreciate them after they had disappeared. Most of them had blood on their hands and still posed a serious danger to anybody who crossed them—but they stood as an alternative to the Taliban. Without them, the south belonged to the insurgents.

The last of these big mujahedeen figures was Ustad Abdul Halim. He had been a minor character during the war against the communists, but emerged as a player during the factional warfare after the Soviet withdrawal. By the time I met him in 2007, he was serving as a security advisor to the governor. It was always a relief to dig my toes into the thick grass in his courtyard after plodding through the city's dirty lanes. His power had faded since the days when his militias controlled a broad swath of farmland southwest of Kandahar city, but he kept himself well informed about the progress of the war. His bodyguards' new M-16 rifles, a status symbol in a place where everybody else carried Kalashnikovs, also suggested that he retained some stake in the business of violence. One day we sat in canvas chairs among his rose bushes as he worked his way through a pack of Marlboros and lectured me about how the NATO countries should have anticipated the scale of the problem that awaited them in the south. "It was a trap," he said, with a chuckle. "You stepped on a landmine." He had a trick of saying these things in a way that seemed amusing, delivering the worst news with a twinkle in his eyes. One of my colleagues called him "a campy version of Saddam Hussein."

Once, on vacation in Toronto, I went gift shopping for the old warrior. I wandered for hours, wondering what I could give a guy who already has his own personal army. I found myself in a store that sells wristwatches, trying to explain to the woman behind the counter that I needed something huge that could belong to a gangster. "Your friend is like a rapper?" she asked. "Well no, he's a warlord," I said. "Close enough. Almost the same thing." As it turned out, the warlord was delighted by the gift. I didn't expect him to enjoy it for very long, however. His house was located on the west side of Kandahar city, an area increasingly permeated by insurgents, and the Taliban threatened him on a regular basis. I figured he was next on the assassination list, but he endured a few more years in Kandahar before finally declaring his retirement in 2010 and moving north to Kabul. As of this writing, the leathery warrior remains alive. When Ustad Halim moved away from the south, my friend Alex Strick van Linschoten, a well-respected academic who lived in Kandahar, marked the occasion with an e-mail to a few journalists. He reported that the influence of former anti-Soviet commanders had all but disappeared, leaving the local government more vulnerable. "I think this is the last of the giant dinosaur mujahedeen commanders to leave the city," he wrote. "There is nobody else left. If the beginning of the end needed a starting date, I'd plant it somewhere in this week."

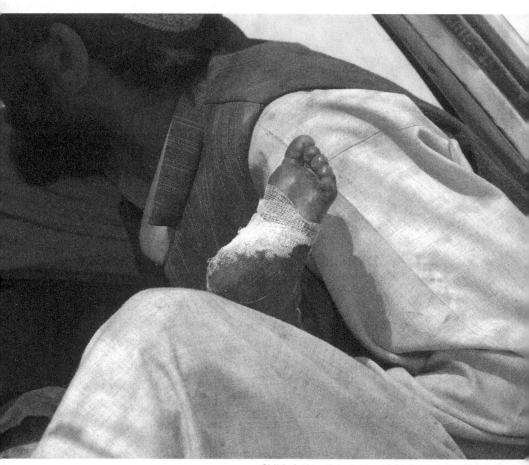

Child victim of a night raid by international forces

CHAPTER 12

LESSONS FROM THE TALIBAN SURVEY MARCH 2008

ndless prattle about the war filled the media. Square-jawed international troops stood on sandbag parapets at sunset so that television crews could record their thoughts as they squinted at the badlands. Soldiers attached cameras to their helmets and released the footage. Their daily lives became whole seasons of reality television. Even the insurgent leaders had their say, in grainy videos and audio statements. Local journalists lived with the regular chime of text messages sent to their phones from the Taliban's official spokesmen. The only participants in the conflict who rarely spoke to the world were the Taliban foot soldiers. Despite all the chatter about them, the fighters themselves were mostly silent.

On the rare occasions when a journalist made contact with insurgent fighters, the story usually turned into a tale of adventure for the journalist. I was guilty of this myself. My frightening brushes with the Taliban had not given me profound insights into the insurgency, but had instead supplied anecdotes that I could repeat with breathless drama: the car chase through Kandahar's slums in 2006, or the journey across the border to Quetta's back alleys in 2007. Some of my colleagues were kidnapped or even killed doing this work. Those who survived got away with amazing stories, book deals or footage that earned good prices from television networks. At its best, this material gave glimpses of everyday life in Taliban camps, but more often we saw shaky images of men brandishing Kalashnikovs and predicting the demise of America. It was usually the same story, that of a brave reporter who goes into Taliban territory, witnesses scary things and emerges with vague conclusions about the warrior spirit.

Frustrated by this formula, I decided to try something else: a Taliban survey. My editor approved a budget, and we hired a free-lance researcher in 2007. I had known "Hafiz" for almost a year, but I avoided learning his real name because I didn't want to make his life more dangerous. I did not write down his cellphone number on the assumption that US forces would find it tempting to track my calls and hunt down my Taliban contacts. When I wanted to meet him, I drove to the western outskirts of Kandahar city and climbed the steps of a half-empty apartment block. He lived in a tiny room, furnished with only a bedroll. His window gave him a view of a vacant lot and a ruined grain elevator. Hafiz worked as a policeman for the Taliban regime; after 2001 he helped out at a relative's cell-phone shop, but did not make enough money and fell into debt. One of the people who loaned him money was my translator in Kandahar, which gave us an advantage when it came to persuading him to make risky trips into the villages. Month by month, he proved himself a more capable journalist. His formal education consisted mostly of memorizing the Koran (which gave him the honorific "Hafiz"), but he quickly learned new skills: finding interview subjects, asking questions from a list, recording the answers and, most challengingly, thinking of follow-up questions.

We offered Hafiz the equivalent of about twenty-five dollars per interview and sent him into five districts outside of Kandahar city to meet insurgent fighters. At first I equipped him with pocket-sized cameras, but these kept disappearing—sometimes he blamed police checkpoints, other times the Taliban—and eventually we settled on cellphones that recorded video. The phone contained a memory chip half the size of his thumbnail, making it easy to slip into folds of his clothing. In total, he smuggled back forty-two interviews with Taliban fighters. The recordings were short and almost useless at first, but their quality improved as he learned the art of prodding his subjects and grew more comfortable asking hard questions. Eight months later, after we double- and triple-checked the material, we ended up with 512 pages of transcript. You can still watch all of the interviews at www.globeandmail.com/talkingtothetaliban, and decide for yourself what to make of them. Others churned through the mountain of stuff and found their own insights; some academics have footnoted our survey to support their claim that the Taliban are a bunch of crazy extremists who won't negotiate, while other experts cited the material to make exactly the opposite argument. Teachers have used the survey as part of their lessons for classes ranging from grade seven to graduate seminars. An artist captured still images from the Taliban videos and used them as the inspiration for a series of drawings, and a curator displayed snippets of them in a gallery installation.

It was an interesting chunk of data, but in some ways it did not prove much; short statements by masked men do not lend themselves to firm conclusions. The Taliban cheated a little as we asked them questions, too, because they eavesdropped on each other's answers. This made the exercise more like a series of focus groups and not a scientific survey. By the time we published the results in March 2008, I worried that the few strong points to emerge from the project would seem too obvious. Some of my colleagues said the same thing; a leading expert on the Taliban listened to the interviews in their original Pashto and told me that it gave him nothing but a headache and a reminder that the insurgents are, in his words, "village idiots." What still surprises me, however, is how many of these basic truths about the Taliban are not widely understood. Things that seemed obvious to my friends and acquaintances in Kandahar took years to reach the desks of generals and politicians, and some never did at all. Even now, years later, these four lessons remain important.

1. THE WAR IS A FAMILY FEUD.

Intelligence analysts spend years learning the Pashtun tribal structures, and locals will tell you a whole lifetime isn't enough to master all the branches and sub-branches, the family trees whose fingers reach into every corner of local politics. But anybody can watch our Taliban videos and notice a pattern in the way the fighters introduce themselves. After the customary throat-clearing ("In the name of God, the most merciful, the most compassionate . . .") they identify their tribal affiliation. Most of the tribes' names end with the suffix "-*zai*," meaning "son," tracing bloodlines that go back centuries. Walking the streets of Kandahar city, you would bump into a lot of people who identified with the big tribes that hold power in the government: Popalzai, Alokozai and Barakzai. Out in the villages, however, our researcher found very few of those tribesmen in the insurgent ranks. Only five of forty-two named themselves as members of those three tribes. (Among those, the two who belonged to the president's tribe, Popalzai, appeared to have bitter personal reasons for joining the armed opposition: one said his family was bombed by foreign aircraft, and the other said the government repeatedly eradicated his opium fields.) The rest of the Taliban in our survey belonged to tribes that weren't handsomely profiting from the foreign presence, and felt a sense of victimhood. Those connected to the rich foreigners showered patronage on their own clans, while the excluded groups jealously fought for their share. It wasn't so different from *The Sopranos*, or any other stories of a family squabble that turns violent.

Shortly after we published our survey, a secret US intelligence report on tribes reached a similar conclusion. Taliban are not primarily driven by external forces, the report said; outside help from Pakistani territory is important, but not so important as local rivalries. The report described the Karzai government using instruments of official power to support his own Popalzai tribe and selected allies within his tribal confederacy. Taliban exploit the resulting anger among the other tribes, many of whom find themselves on the losing side of arguments over money, opium, land or water. The US assessment concluded that the Taliban do not support any particular tribes wholeheartedly, but the conflict is increasingly coloured by those ancient rivalries.

Nobody wanted to talk about this. Foreign governments needed to rally their electorates by labelling their enemies in Afghanistan as global terrorists, and their Kabul proxies as the founders of a new democracy—not tribal factions, grabbing wealth and punishing their enemies. Nor did the Taliban themselves want to talk about the tribal aspect of the war. On a trip to Quetta to visit his family, our researcher had a frightening encounter with politically sophisticated Taliban who criticized him for collecting data on the insurgency's tribal makeup. The insurgency's leaders wanted to emphasize religion, not tribe or ethnicity, as the binding thread of their movement. It sounded much better, declaring war in defence of Islam rather than making self-serving appeals to enrich your own tribe. War in the name of all Muslims was also a more inclusive slogan than invoking tribal politics, which are mostly confined to the Pashtun south and east. I also wondered if even the most bloodthirsty Taliban understood the terrible dangers of tribal war: one of my Afghan acquaintances looked at the results of our survey and concluded that the conflict isn't yet a genuine tribal conflict. In such cases, he said, neighbours kill neighbours on a much greater scale than the current war.

This remains one of the most frightening risks for Afghanistan in the years after most foreign troops pull out: the nightmare of anarchy. If clear battle lines do not emerge between government forces in the north and Taliban-allied groups in the south, a power vacuum may grow in places where neither Karzai nor his opponents have enough armed men to assert themselves. Afghans may turn to their own tribes for security, reducing the country to scattered fiefdoms. Fatalists will be tempted to see this kind of warfare as a natural state among the tribes, but Afghans say this is a misreading of history. The tribes lived at peace with each other for centuries and could do it again. The Afghans are not savages who fight endlessly. Tribalism remains a dangerous fault line that runs though the conflict, however, threatening to make a bad situation much worse.

2. AIR STRIKES PUSHED PEOPLE TO JOIN THE INSURGENCY.

It seems obvious that dropping bombs on people will make them fight back, but this is especially true of people who live according to traditions of honour and revenge. Foreigners often have a hard time deciphering how the ancient rules of Pashtunwali, a code much older than Islam, apply to modern Afghanistan. Centuries have worn down the traditions, blurring away sharp definitions, but the old rules thrust themselves into everyday life. One day, on a highway near Kandahar city, my driver lost his usual game of chicken with oncoming traffic. Our car screeched and swerved, clipping the front bumper of an oncoming taxi. Both vehicles spun to a stop on the paved road. Traffic diverted into the flat desert around us, engulfing the scene in dust. My driver jumped out and rushed toward the taxi driver, waving his arms and berating the guy for a crash that was likely his own fault. Men gathered, and I slouched low in my seat, pulling up my Afghan scarf to hide my face. My driver eventually realized it was risky to leave a foreigner sitting in an unfriendly crowd—but instead of giving up, he rushed over to the taxi and snatched the keys from the ignition. Then he sprinted back to our car, drove away, and left the taxi driver stranded and screaming in the middle of the highway. My driver wasn't angry, just impelled to settle the score. Our vehicle limped back to the office of the contractor who owned the car. The driver's boss seemed dismayed when he saw the crumpled grille, but listened to the story and smiled when the driver reached into his pocket and slammed the taxi keys on his boss's desk. He got revenge; everything was okay.

The same logic applied to air strikes. Afghans saw the international forces as cowardly when they called firepower from the sky. When a civilian died, whole families felt a need for revenge. Even well-aimed bombs, killing only armed insurgents, triggered a social system of call-ups, pushing the younger brothers or cousins of men slain in battle to replace them. Blood repaid blood. This stood out in our survey: even before we asked questions about bombings or civilian deaths, some Taliban raised the issue as a reason for war. Asked specifically about the air strikes, almost a third of them claimed their family members died in such incidents during the current war. That's a lot of carnage: if true, it suggests that insurgents either joined the Taliban because their families were bombed, or the most rebellious villages suffered heavy losses in air strikes. Either way, insurgents used the bombings as a rallying cry, a reason for hitting back at the foreigners. In the same breath, some Taliban fighters complained about Russian air strikes in the 1980s, suggesting that memories of the Soviet invasion still fuelled the current insurgency. Horror stories of the Russian occupation must have sprung to life every time young Afghans heard the roar of jets. In other responses, however, it was clear that their anger stemmed from more recent events. A twenty-five-year-old man said he joined the Taliban after two of his uncles died under air strikes in Pashmul, a village about fifteen kilometres west of Kandahar city that saw heavy combat, especially during Operation Medusa in 2006. He used civilian deaths as a justification for war: "The foreign troops came to Afghanistan, killed many innocent people and elders and bombed them, so I started jihad," he said. In interview after interview, the armed fighters set out the logic of the war in the same way my driver talked about his car crash: they were wronged, and were fighting to make it right.

It's worth remembering that we did those interviews in 2007. Hundreds of civilians died that year as the war escalated and the tonnage of air strikes doubled. Afghanistan got bombed far more than Iraq, partly because its open terrain made for easier targeting. But the tonnages stopped rising in the following years, even as the conflict intensified, because military leaders realized they couldn't make friends—couldn't win the war, in other words—if they blasted villages flat. General Stanley McChrystal became especially strict about reducing air strikes during his year in command of the international forces. After General David Petraeus replaced him in the summer of 2010, however, the bombings intensified again. As troops withdraw in 2014, they will find themselves tempted to rely on air strikes to make up for their reduced numbers. A smaller contingent of US forces may stay behind in the years after the main withdrawal, and they will almost certainly need to call for air support to keep themselves safe. The risk will be that increased bombings could, in fact, undermine the overall security of the stay-behind forces as air strikes inspire more hatred.

3. DESTROYING POPPY FIELDS MAKES THINGS WORSE.

The Taliban not only summoned young men to fight for the sake of defending lives, but also livelihoods. Illegal opium stood far above any other source of cash flowing into the south, and millions of people depended on the industry to feed their families. Poppy fields stretched to the horizon, bursting with colour every spring: satellites spotted those fields easily, so the United Nations could accurately read the landscape and predict which provinces would yield the biggest crop. Across the south, in general, the places that blossomed with the most poppies also broke into the greatest violence. Our survey found the same overlap on the ground, too: a majority of the Taliban admitted a personal role in the drug industry, with more than 80 per cent of respondents saying they farmed opium themselves, and a similar percentage saying their family or friends make their living the same way.

Those numbers supported the idea that opium and the insurgency grew in tandem, in the same places. Illegal activity flourished in lawless territory, not surprisingly. For several years, the international community applied a blunt logic to this problem: If the Taliban thrive amid the poppy fields, then why not burn the fields? This idea became popular as a way of both cutting a supply of ill-gotten cash to the insurgency and stemming the flow of drugs reaching world markets. The theory sounded appealing, but it proved to be horribly flawed. The foreigners paid for eradication teams to drive out into the countryside, hacking and burning the farmers' only means of survival. Losing fields often meant crippling debts. Dealers killed men who couldn't pay, or took their daughters as so-called "opium brides," sometimes toddlers barely old enough to talk. This escalated as the foreign donors pushed for bigger eradication campaigns in 2005, 2006 and 2007. At its peak, the teams destroyed almost twenty thousand hectares in a single year, or roughly a tenth of the country's crop. The United States wanted more, offering aircraft to spray the fields with herbicide, but other countries argued against it. They worried that eradicators were stirring up too much violence.

Our survey supported the idea that destroying fields inspired people to fight: half of the Taliban respondents said they had been targeted by government eradication efforts, sometimes more than once. The Taliban could have been exaggerating the reach of the eradication, but their detailed accounts of the corrupt officials who ran these programs suggested they were speaking from bitter personal experience. Fighters also praised their Taliban comrades for success in driving away counter-narcotics programs, proudly describing how the eradicators could not touch insurgent strongholds. A twenty-five-year-old former driver, wearing dark sunglasses and a white turban, admitted he farmed poppy and claimed that the government destroyed his field.

"So what was your reaction to the government then?" our researcher asked.

"We are fighting against them," he replied.

"Okay, so you mean to say that you are fighting for poppies?"

"No, no. We are only fighting for the approval of God. But as I said, they attacked us and it is our responsibility to fight against them."

It took years of bloody uprisings in the south before the international community started to understand that their war on drugs worsened the conflict. Eradication fell to a quarter its previous levels in 2008 and 2009, and dropped again in 2010 as counter-narcotics officials shifted their focus away from poppy growers. All sides of the war seemed to understand that the country would someday need a legal economy—that Afghanistan could not sustain itself forever as the world's biggest opium supplier—but that impoverishing farmers wasn't going to work. Interestingly, even the insurgent fighters viewed opium as a short-term solution. "We are forced to grow it. We don't have a car or a road or anything, so what should we eat if we don't grow it? Tell me. If we had factories, we would not grow the poppies," said a twenty-eight-year-old tribesman. He cradled an assault rifle, with a bigger machine gun propped against the wall behind him, chatting knowledgeably about the cost of fuel for the water pumps that nourish his fields. Poppy remains the only profitable crop, he said, even though it's morally distasteful. "Everyone knows that it is not good," he said.

Poppy eradication continues in Afghanistan. Countries that suffer the worst effects of cheap Afghan drugs, especially Russia, continue to push for stronger action against opium growers in the south, and some counter-narcotics officials still dream of razing the fields. That solution has not entirely lost its allure, and remains a potential disaster for the south.

4. TALIBAN NATIONALISM LEAVES ROOM TO NEGOTIATE.

Here is the most important thing I learned from surveying the Taliban: no matter how stupid, or stubborn, or ignorant, or xenophobic, or religiously misguided these men are—they are nonetheless nationalists. You could even call them patriots, in the ugliest sense of the word. During the interviews they didn't seem to know much about the outside world, except that they wanted to keep many aspects of modernity out of their beloved Afghanistan. They showed no fondness for Pakistan, despite the support from that country for the insurgency, and every fighter in our survey rejected the legitimacy of the border, saying that the Pakistani cities of Quetta and Peshawar belong inside Afghanistan. If the conversation moved beyond the troubled relationship between Afghanistan and Pakistan, however, their grasp of international affairs became hazy. They did not know how many countries joined the NATO alliance against them, knew nothing about those distant lands, and expressed disdain for such useless information. Faced with a multiple-choice question about Canada's location, only one of forty-two fighters correctly guessed the country's location north of the United States. Some of them did not even realize that the word *Canada* signifies a country: "It might be an old and destroyed city," one of them said. They fared better with questions about the United States, but appeared to understand the Americans as mainly a direct equivalent of past empires that sent crusaders to the Middle East.

The fighters' political views seemed like a relic of bygone centuries, and the same applied to their social attitudes. Some of the most revealing moments in our interviews happened in the quiet interludes between questions, when the insurgents volunteered their own unprompted thoughts. Spontaneously, two of them started complaining about modern life in Kabul. They probably had never seen the capital, but the villagers loved trading stories about the sins and excesses of the city. "There are some things forbidden by Islam and the Koran, like alcohol, adultery and cinemas," said a twenty-seven-year-old farmer, with a belt of machine-gun bullets draped around his neck. Another insurgent talked about the corrupting power of foreign movies, possibly referring to the brisk trade in illegal pornography that flourished under the new regime. "They are enthusiastic about the dollar and cinemas," the gunman said. "That's why we are fighting them."

I had noticed the same kind of deep suspicion about Western social codes during my face-to-face conversations with insurgents. At the end of a meeting with a Taliban organizer at a guesthouse in Kabul, the insurgent patted my pillow and gave me a knowing look:

"You have girls in your guesthouses, yes?" he said. The Taliban were convinced that foreigners spread moral rot.

Still, the insurgents seemed willing to back any leader who would cleanse the capital of corrupting influences—whether that purification happened under Mullah Omar or some other figure. Their lack of personal loyalty became one of the biggest headlines of our project. It seemed amazing that twenty-four insurgents, more than half those surveyed, would be willing to look into a video recorder and declare their so-called "Commander of the Faithful" not essential to their war, and not necessarily the best leader for Afghanistan. Those responses were especially surprising from fighters whose other answers suggested total commitment to the cause. Some even suggested it needn't be a Taliban government in Kabul at all, only that they wanted to influence the selection of a new leader. "We are not saying that it should be our government," a fighter said. "But we want only a Muslim king." They kept circling back to this idea, that the leadership of Afghanistan should depend only on a man's willingness to implement their version of Islamic rules. They did not express any plans for influencing the world beyond the rugged lands of their ancestors. They had only the foggiest notion of the West, and primarily wanted to escape its reach. These did not seem like men who necessarily wanted to crash planes into distant cities, and most of them would never see a skyscraper in their lives.

Many observers picked up on this parochialism when reading the transcripts of our videos. "Key among these observations and messages is the general Taliban lack of interest in global jihad," wrote Richard H. Smyth, a professor of international relations at the US Army War College. This lesson proved unpalatable for others, however, because it undermined the whole argument for war. If the troops were not fighting global terrorists, if they were battling rural bumpkins with no greater ambition than shutting down the cinemas of Kabul, what exactly was at stake? Would killing these farmers really make the world safer? The oft-repeated phrase "If we don't fight them over there, we'll fight them over here" sounded hollow in this light.

Politicians did not stop repeating that idea, however. It gave a sense of purpose to every gunfight, this notion that the troops confronted evil men who wanted to bring down the entire structure of Western civilization. In 2010, the military historian Max Boot wrote in a column: ". . . [I]t's silly to disassociate the fight against the Taliban in Afghanistan, as so many critics of the war effort do, from the broader struggle against jihadist groups bent on inflicting serious harm on America and on our allies." My hunch is that Boot is wrong, but he's not the only one who thinks this way. I've had long arguments with Afghan officials who tell me the insurgents are using their avowed nationalism as a Trojan Horse to hide their sinister global ambitions. They fear the Taliban will grab power and become more extreme, making the country into a cesspool of terrorism. They remind me that the desire for revenge will not stop when the troops withdraw, that the men whose families died in air strikes or ground offensives will continue trying to hit back at the foreigners in their home countries.

One certainty is that either way, we will find out. Troop withdrawals will probably leave zones of the country without a significant presence of security forces. Will these enclaves turn into training camps for the next big attack on the West? I'm skeptical. Insurgents have already carved out sanctuaries in rural Afghanistan, and no reports have emerged since 9/11 of major international terrorism traced back to those hideouts. I doubt that waves of Taliban attacking foreign cities will become the stuff of future headlines. Some analysts will think I'm crazy, but maybe we should listen to the twenty-five-year-old former driver who took up arms against the government but promised to lay down his weapons when the foreigners leave.

"Why are you fighting against this government?" our researcher asked him. "Because they are with the non-Muslims," he replied. "If there were no non-Muslims we would not fight with them, because one Muslim does not fight with another Muslim. But when we are fighting an Afghan soldier, it is because they are in an American convoy."

There was an almost childish naïveté to the idea that Muslims would never fight each other, given the history of conflict across the region, but the insurgent was making an important point: he labelled his enemies in the Afghan government as "Muslim." Official statements from the Taliban often refused to recognize the Kabul regime as an Islamic government, saying the regime had betrayed the religion, but this front-line insurgent seemed to disagree. He expressed reluctance to battle with fellow Afghans.

"If they weren't in a convoy with Americans, you wouldn't fight with them?"

"No," he said. "Then we wouldn't fight."

Sleepy guards at Sarpoza prison

CHAPTER 13

JAILBREAK JUNE 2008

In the middle of the night I walked onto the Dubai tarmac, its surfaces radiating summer heat, and met the rusting old lady who would return me to war. Her name was Ludmilla, or at least that's what somebody had stencilled on her fuselage. I would not normally climb into an aircraft that looked so hazardous, but the old cargo plane was my only option for getting back to Kandahar. I needed to fly quickly, because the Taliban were pulling off the biggest coup they had ever achieved, a massive jailbreak. It was a story that couldn't wait for the next regular flight. A colleague had passed me the name of an airline official who could get me on board a cargo run, and somebody who spoke poor English directed me to bring cash to a nondescript building near the airport. I had kept the taxi waiting, wary of the bleak industrial zone, and climbed the stairs to an office where I got a handwritten receipt and a promise that my name would be placed on a manifest as a "cargo handler." A clerk reassured me that no actual handling of cargo would be necessary, except my own. Later that night I was heaving my bags up through the nose hatch of the old Antonov and shaking hands with a crew of tipsy Russians. It seemed like a reasonable travel option at the time, although when I later tried to recommend this route to the renowned magazine writer Elizabeth Rubin she replied with an incredulous e-mail: "i have three words for you. you are crazy!!!!!!!"

It *was* crazy. Ludmilla seemed like such an antique model that she lacked electronics in the cockpit, just dials and knobs, like something from a black-and-white film. Exhausted, I curled into a fetal ball and tried to catch some rest before tackling the major work that awaited when I landed in Kandahar. On the previous Friday, June 13, the Taliban had broken into Sarpoza prison, the main jail for southern Afghanistan, and set free a huge number of inmates. I ended up using the phrase "at least eight hundred," a cautious guess that ranked the incident among the biggest jailbreaks in modern history. Nobody had explained how a band of ragged gunmen managed to pull it off in a city protected by two foreign military bases and thousands of local and international security forces. Immediately after the escape, the Taliban also invaded the Arghandab valley north of Kandahar city, sending waves of villagers fleeing south. When I jumped out of Ludmilla's nose and walked into the darkened military base in Kandahar, I found it throbbing with activity. Everybody was wide awake, wondering what the hell had happened.

Most attention initially focused on the insurgents' attack in Arghandab, and the counter-offensive against them. The Taliban had repeated the ground sweep they conducted the previous autumn after the death of Mullah Naqib, rampaging into the district from three sides and capturing most of the territory north of the river. The allies—French, American, Canadian and Afghan—flew in reinforcements and massed a large army on the river's south bank. It looked like it would be another Medusa-style confrontation. The insurgents disappeared a few days later, however, just as the battle was getting underway. By the time I arrived, I found Canadian and French commanders looking at a map together, puzzling through the logic of their opponents' retreat.

"They're gone," the Canadian general said.

"But why did they come?" asked the French officer, sitting in the shade.

The Canadian estimated that the attack consisted of perhaps a hundred to 150 fighters, a display of insurgent force but not a serious effort to hold terrain. His Afghan allies disagreed, putting the number at something like six hundred, claiming they had thwarted a major Taliban offensive. Kandahar governor Asadullah Khalid confronted the Canadian general at a meeting in a small outpost, pointing to a sweat-drenched Afghan army officer and declaring that he had reported killing two hundred insurgents in recent days.

"So, why is NATO saying only a few Taliban were there?" Mr. Khalid said.

Hearing no answer, the governor took a mobile phone from an assistant and flashed pictures of dead bodies on the tiny screen: "Look, we have photos," he said.

The Canadian general laughed. "One, two," he said, pointing at the images. "That's not two hundred."

The governor seemed intent on proving his point. He invited me to join his entourage and see the bodies myself. It was typical of the governor's almost disconcerting bravery that he would lead a convoy of sport-utility vehicles into a maze of dirt roads where the international forces refused to go without an armoured company. A monitor in the dashboard showed the outside temperature at forty-one degrees Celsius, but the governor seemed relaxed in the air-conditioned interior. He enjoyed warfare, and gave his enemies credit for the recent jailbreak with the same good humour of a sportsman talking about the opposing team.

"It was a great victory for the Taliban," the governor said as the vehicle bucked and jolted. He added that the local insurgents must have invited outside help to accomplish such a big operation. "I know the Taliban in this province, and they are not so smart."

Our convoy halted outside a village on the north bank; we could not drive further because bombs remained buried in the road. A sapper had removed the trigger mechanism from one of them, leaving the green plastic tub of explosives barely visible in the dust, marked with red spray paint. Mr. Khalid gestured at the hazard casually, the way somebody might warn a friend to avoid dog poop on a sidewalk, and walked toward a shady grove of trees along an irrigation ditch. The governor explained that a wounded Taliban commander had retreated to this spot during the recent battle, and a large group of insurgent fighters rushed to help him. Aerial surveillance tracked their movements and summoned an air strike.

We smelled the blast crater before seeing it. Bodies sprawled together in heaps, crawling with flies, hard to distinguish from each other. Some of the corpses looked small and fragile; the insurgents were known for employing young fighters, perhaps even children. Several leaked blood from every orifice, making them look as if they were crying red tears. The stench overwhelmed us. Hardened members of the governor's elite bodyguard turned away, covering their faces with cloth. Mr. Khalid, however, did not flinch, staring at the bodies with mild disappointment. He had clearly expected to see more carnage, and halved his earlier casualty estimate. Then he sighed and clapped his hands: "Lunchtime!"

There was no way to explain to him that heaps of charred human flesh putrefying under the blazing sun had not inspired my appetite. Nor was there any chance to wash my hands before we sat down in a thatch hut that served as a guest dining room for a warlord who lived nearby. Politeness demanded that I scoop up the rice and beans with my dirty fingers and shovel down at least a few mouthfuls.

Diarrhea slowed me down for a few days, and then I went into the city to check out the jail. The Taliban offensive north of town had been smaller than advertised, and in fact seemed like a diversion to help their comrades get away from the scene of the jailbreak. It still boggled my mind: the idea that the Taliban could just smash their way into the huge stone-walled institution. My translator and I drove over to the west side of town, hoping that our contacts at the jail had survived—and if they had, that they might welcome us inside.

As we pulled up, I wasn't sure we had arrived at the right place. The front entrance of the prison was almost unrecognizable, like a junkyard strewn with broken masonry. The remains of two vehicles stood beside the road, their metal skins crumpled and melted. The black gates that had once seemed so imposing were simply missing, blown away by an explosion. The only remnant of those gates, a chunk of steel the size of a picnic table, had landed in a courtyard 125 metres away. The deputy warden greeted us warmly, taking us into an office with jagged remnants of glass in the window frames. I knew this man from our detainee investigation a year earlier; he knew that I trusted him, but he still seemed anxious to show me evidence that his men had not colluded with the escapers. He pulled a padlock from his desk drawer and handed it to me. The heavy lock remained closed, still attached to a broken hasp, and felt roughened up. The jailer made a gesture with his hands to indicate a machine gun firing at the lock. He was trying to show me that the guards on duty had not surrendered the keys to the Taliban; the insurgents broke inside with sheer force. His own son, a guard, had died during the assault, he said, pointing to the shallow ditch under a water tower where an insurgent's rocket-propelled grenade had blasted the young man to pieces.

Although the deputy warden defended the honour of the men who stood guard that day, he harboured suspicions about his own boss. He had warned the warden several times about strange activity in the jail beforehand, he said, but his superior showed a curious lack of interest about his reports. In fairness, we had all heard rumours of a possible jailbreak; the story circulating two years earlier had been that the Taliban planned to slip through the gates with an ambulance full of gunmen. That was the summer of 2006, before Operation Medusa, when the Taliban dug trenches in the fields near the western outskirts of the city and such rumours seemed plausible.

Now, in 2008, the insurgents had again established strongholds near the city—this time just south of the prison. The international forces knew about those Taliban hideouts but lacked the numbers to solve the problem. Nor did the prison staff seem ready to deal with the growing unrest inside their walls; as the deputy warden toured me around the ghostly halls, and we met the few staff and prisoners who remained, their stories made it sound like the inmates had been running the place in the weeks before the jailbreak.

It started with a mysterious committee of seven prisoners, in the wing that held people accused of murder, kidnapping and terrorism. This cabal somehow seized control of the best rooms, the more comfortable cells on the north side of the wing. Those cells looked untouched when I arrived: half-eaten plates of food and forgotten sandals remained strewn across the straw mats on the floor, suggesting a hasty exit. Somebody had posted a sign on the door of the biggest room: "No interruptions from 4 p.m. to 6 p.m." The committee apparently met during those hours every afternoon. After emerging from their conclave in the evenings, they preached to their fellow prisoners, scolding anybody who insulted the Taliban or its leadership, and again when they failed to wake up for morning prayers. Somebody painted an Arabic slogan on the wall of their meeting room: "Jihad is mandatory." The committee also enjoyed an unusual degree of luxury: their rooms had televisions, weightlifting equipment, even an improvised knife with a handle fashioned from masking tape, darkened with opium tar, suggesting that the Taliban prisoners were getting high. An empty gin bottle contained fragrant spices. Smuggled cellphones were apparently common in the cells, and these prisoners had obtained a more dangerous kind of contraband, too; near a window with a view of the central guard tower, small brass casings lay scattered on the floor, showing that somebody fired a handgun during the escape. This explained the false reports, initially, that the insurgents broke through the jail perimeter in two places. No guards had died in the central tower that night, but the shots coming from an unexpected direction likely added to the confusion among prison staff.

It seemed notable that the guards had taken no action as the most dangerous captives in the prison sat around, smoked drugs, chatted on their phones, enforced religious rules—and prepared an escape. It's possible, however, that they felt cowed by the insurgents. Prison guards ranked among the lowest-paid Afghan security forces, below even the police, and the Taliban had been growing stronger in the rural areas within view of the prison watchtowers. The inmates had appeared docile on my other visits, but they had grown restless before the jailbreak. They had organized a hunger strike in the previous month, refusing to eat solid food. Many of them had languished for months or years without a conviction from the special judge who heard political cases, and the prisoners claimed this lack of due process meant they could be jailed indefinitely. The protest ended when local authorities promised to send a judge to the prison to rule on their cases, but that never happened. Instead, the problems escalated. A week before the jailbreak, guards sat down together for their evening meal of stewed mutton and some of them noticed a bitter taste in the food, like tobacco. Dozens started vomiting, bleeding from the nose and mouth, falling unconscious. Several went to hospital, where doctors said they were victims of poisoning. None of them died, and no prisoners escaped during the confusion, but it was a sign of trouble ahead.

The director, a colonel in the prison service, responded to the rising tensions by holding regular meetings with three members of the prisoners' committee. He described these meetings to the rest of the staff as a way of mediating problems, but he conducted them in secret. I never did find out what happened during those sessions; one of the prison officials who helped arrange the meetings was shot in the head, execution-style, during the jailbreak, and the colonel himself was jailed soon afterward. A female officer who oversaw the women's section of the prison said she happened to see the colonel in front of his office on the day of the attack. He smiled at her and said: "Something might happen tonight. If any of the prisoners owes you money, collect it. If you owe them money, pay it." She wasn't sure if he was joking, because he seemed untroubled by his warning. When mayhem erupted later that evening, the colonel was safely at home; he got a flurry of calls from security officials when the truck bomb blew open the prison gates, but he apparently told them that the tanker exploded by accident and didn't affect the prison. This could have been an innocent mistake, but probably wasn't. My translator later spoke with an insurgent who escaped, a twenty-eight-year-old fighter who bragged about how the escapees got help from insiders. "Important officials from the jail helped us bring in pistols and mobile phones, and we also bought some explosives for the bombing," the fugitive said. I heard something similar from a nineteen-year-old inmate who escaped but then returned to jail because he had only a short time remaining on his sentence and didn't want to live as a fugitive. The Taliban fighters who broke him free and shepherded his group of prisoners into the darkness had explained that jail staff had assisted with the operation. "The Taliban had a secret meeting with the prison director, one week before the attack," the prisoner said. "Maybe they paid him money, I don't know." (The colonel eventually got out of jail; in 2011, he was serving as a police commander for a small neighbourhood in the city.)

Either way, it's hard to see how the Afghan forces could have done anything about the well-coordinated assault. In the hours beforehand, Taliban messengers circulated a warning in the neighbourhood, telling residents to evacuate, and the stretch of highway leading west from the city grew quiet as people slipped away. Nobody told the eight policemen who lived in a bunker only six hundred metres east of the prison, and nobody passed word to the large police barracks about twenty-two hundred metres to the west. Officers at both of those positions said they were caught by surprise when insurgents started shooting bullets and rocket-propelled grenades at their outposts around 9:10 p.m. Policemen initially considered it a routine, if unusually intense, bit of harassment; the insurgents often hit government outposts at night, killing or wounding a few officers and disappearing. The officers nearest to Sarpoza prison responded with sensible caution, hunkering behind their sandbags and firing back. With the local security forces pinned down, the insurgents drove a fuel tanker up to the prison gates. The driver hopped down from the cab and ran away: insurgents later suggested that a suicide switch in the truck had failed, so the tanker did not immediately detonate, but it was more likely that the driver just wanted to save himself. The Taliban quickly improvised a solution, firing rocket-propelled grenades at the tanker. The first shot whistled high and missed, but the second ignited a huge explosion. Windows and mirrors shattered a kilometre away, and a ball of white light rose over the prison. One of my acquaintances, a Western security official, felt the tremor running through the city and looked at his watch; he later climbed to a spot overlooking the scene and noted the timeline:

9:10 p.m.:	Small explosions near the prison. Small-arms fire.
9:18 or 9:19 p.m.:	Large explosion. Shooting heard from at least six different directions around the downtown core.
10 p.m.:	Fighting slows.
10:50 p.m.:	Relatively quiet.
11 p.m.:	Canadian vehicles arrive at the scene.

The aftermath of the blast was a time for prayers in the rattled city. At a business across the street from the jail, damaged by the explosion, a seventy-year-old watchman with a long grey beard and a shaved head took up his green plastic prayer beads and started reciting holy words as he listened to the gunfire. Inside the jail, a guard climbed into a cupboard and silently appealed to Allah. A short scuffle in the Taliban wing ended as the prisoners overwhelmed a few guards and waited for their comrades to save them, calling friends on their cellphones and holding the handsets into the air as they shouted to the sky, "*Allahu Akbar*!" Their rescuers arrived a few minutes later, shooting their way down the central corridor that runs toward the national-security wing and blasting the locks with belt-fed machine guns. They timed the raid with unnerving precision, arriving before the prisoners returned to their cells for the evening, but late enough to enjoy the advantage of darkness. They seemed anxious to get away quickly, yelling at prisoners to hurry.

Hundreds of inmates streamed across the smoking rubble where the front gate once stood. Most escaped gleefully, but a few lingered behind—including a beautiful twenty-year-old woman named Rukiya. She had served two months in prison for running away from her husband, a crime under Afghanistan's version of *sharia* law. Her husband was jailed in a separate wing on charges of beating her, and during the chaos of the jailbreak he ran through the smoke calling her name. A witness said he forced Rukiya to run barefoot across the jagged rubble of the gateway and into the street. She struggled, trying to escape, and her husband appealed for help from a nearby Taliban commander. The insurgent leader, his identity concealed by a scarf wrapped around his head, instructed the woman to obey her husband. She refused. The insurgent gave her husband his Kalashnikov rifle and permission to execute the unruly woman. "He put many bullets in her; I watched her die," a witness told me. "She lay on the road until the next morning. I don't know what happened to the body."

The murdering husband escaped with the rest of the mob, which broke into smaller groups under Taliban guard and scattered among the houses to the south of the prison. They ran down alleys, through vineyards and wheat fields. Their Taliban guides told them to hit the ground when they heard aircraft overhead, but this precaution was futile because it was impossible to hide the teeming mass of escapees from NATO surveillance. Some prisoners kept running all night, but many flopped down in the fields one or two kilometres from the jailbreak, half-expecting to get rounded up again. To their surprise, security forces captured almost none of the fugitives. Hundreds of Afghan police, reserve units and intelligence officers approached from the east, but they moved slowly toward the insurgents who continued covering the retreat. When they did reach the jail, some Afghan security forces contented themselves with looting instead of searching for escapees; guards told me that the worst ransacking of Sarpoza was not committed by insurgents, but rather by the police who first arrived at the scene. Stepping over the bodies of their colleagues, Afghan policemen spirited away whatever valuables remained in the jail: money, clothes and weapons. The police stopped thieving when the foreign troops arrived, the so-called Quick Reaction Force, stationed only six kilometres away but so late to reach the scene that the shooting had already died down when the troop carriers rolled up. The Canadian commander responsible for the province, a thoughtful officer named Brigadier-General Denis Thompson, later explained why he did not send his soldiers there more quickly.

You can't go charging around, especially if you think you're about to enter a situation where it's a well-orchestrated attack. You can't be rash; you've got to be, I won't use the word cautious, I guess the word is prudent. . . . You can ask yourself the rhetorical question, what if we find one hundred fugitives in the fields? What is ISAF's [International Security Assistance Force's] duty in that circumstance? Is it to go arrest people who are a combination of people, who are criminals and potential insurgents?

More to the point, the Canadian commander expressed doubts about whether it would have done any good to send NATO soldiers into dense terrain in the middle of the night. He worried that a bad situation could have become far bloodier.

How would you determine who to zap strap? They're not wearing orange jumpsuits. That's what people need to appreciate: we don't do civil order, because we can't tell Frank from Joe. . . . Why aren't you out there rounding up fugitives? Because, remember, they're not insurgents, they're fugitives. It's a whole different ballgame—they're unarmed. You're not going to sweep down there. It's not a legitimate military target.

He was right: the tools at his disposal, soldiers trained to kill, were not the correct implements for the task. What would have happened if a platoon of US or Canadian soldiers had chased down a bunch of dirty men in a field? How would they have figured out the difference between fugitives, insurgents and villagers? It could have gotten messy, especially because international forces later disarmed five bombs planted as traps for pursuers. That didn't prevent Afghan officials from complaining about the lack of backup from their foreign allies, however. Two days after the attack, the provincial council held a private session that criticized the international troops, saying the jailbreak had revealed their weakness. Kabul fired the three top security officials in Kandahar afterward; I later ate dinner with one of them, the former police chief, who expressed amazement that blame for the incident fell on the Afghan forces. Between bites of lamb and chicken, the stubble-bearded veteran said NATO soldiers should have unleashed their firepower on the jail-breakers. "Who came to release the prisoners?" he said. "It was the Taliban. What is NATO doing here in Afghanistan? They are fighting the Taliban." He paused to look at me, as if waiting for an explanation. Afghan forces don't have the foreign troops' night-vision goggles and modern weapons, he said, so how could the international forces expect his men to charge into the fray that night?

The simple answer, the answer that usually came up during such moments, when the fragility of the whole effort in Afghanistan became obvious, was that the international community needed to work harder, to build a better system of government and local security. This usually fell under the heading of "capacity-building," the idea that if only the Afghans were better equipped, then maybe all problems could be solved. Afghan officials encouraged this kind of maximalist thinking because they profited from it. A review of the jailbreak by the local intelligence service focused on the prison's physical defences. An official from the National Directorate for Security presented his agency's findings this way, according to an internal report:

Col. ——— stated that the problems at the prison were the result of too few and incapable guards and too few weapons. Furthermore the walls of the prison were not adequate; they required concertina wire and towers on all four corners. The delegation provided a list of items they feel are required to improve the security of the prison. Which are: a sufficient amount of weapons and ammunition, a new CP [command post] at each of the outside corners of the prison, radio equipment, vehicles for prisoners' transport, repairs of electricity and plumbing and roadblocks to restrict entry to the prison.

That's the entire analysis. It does not mention how a raiding party of insurgents sneaked into the city without anybody noticing, or how the signs of unrest—the hunger strike, the poisoning, the radical committee of inmates—failed to arouse suspicion. Nor does it mention the breakdown of trust that allowed the Taliban to warn people in the neighbourhood of an impending attack, confident that nobody would tip off the authorities. A more scholarly review of the incident, published in the *Canadian Army Journal*, did examine some of those contextual factors but still reached the same conclusion: spend more money. It blamed a "shortage of resources" and called for new funding to "improve the security of such facilities through more competent manning and increased funding for construction and maintenance," among other things.

This preference for a narrow interpretation of events became almost pathological at Kandahar Air Field. A media staffer for the

Canadian government visited the journalists' tent to suggest that we should write about how the attack was, in fact, a "blessing in disguise" because it opened an opportunity to refurbish the facility and install new front gates. Canada's top diplomat in Kandahar repeated this message in an on-the-record briefing. I assumed that the officials understood this was industrial-grade propaganda, but sometimes their statements raised a more frightening possibility: maybe they inhabited a different mental universe. Maybe their devotion to the mission made it hard to contemplate the broader implications.

The jailbreak should have raised the question of whether the sum total of the screw-ups might be greater than the individual failures. Corruption, poor intelligence and the weakness of Afghan forces were well-known problems, and each could theoretically get fixed. None of those improvements would matter, however, if the ideas behind the mission proved incorrect. The foreigners assumed that the Taliban were unpopular, that most ordinary Afghans wanted to live in a country allied with Western powers. Over and over, military leaders repeated some version of the mantra "clear, hold, build," implying that money spent to improve a community should earn its loyalty. By that measure, Sarpoza prison should have been a roaring success. The institution fell squarely into the zone around the city where international donors concentrated most of their efforts; even within that zone, few places had enjoyed such largesse. In the year before the prison break, the Canadian government spent millions overhauling the facility with new septic systems, solar-powered lighting, a staff training room, metal doors for the cells, bars on the windows, concertina wire, an infirmary, landscaping, new guard towers and upgraded washroom facilities. Painted walls replaced the rough stone surfaces; where chunks of masonry used to fall on prisoners as they slept, the ceiling now arched smoothly overhead. Piles of garbage and scrap metal, previously alive with the scurrying sounds of rats, were cleared out and replaced with expanses of fresh gravel. Workers filled in a creek running through the compound. New buildings were constructed: a place for conjugal visits, a separate room for security checks of female visitors, an armoury and a carpentry workshop. The foreigners paid for truckloads of new mattresses, and gave the guards new uniforms and new vehicles. They supplied medicine and hygiene kits. More projects were underway at the time of the attack, as well, requiring frequent visits by Canadian officials, but they failed to smell the trouble brewing under their noses.

It's hard to fault the foreigners for this: they cleared, they held, they built—but it fell apart in an instant. None of the international community's efforts at Sarpoza were inadequate in themselves, but they didn't add up to something useful. This point would get proven over and over, across Afghanistan. There would be an illusion of progress, a new institution or outpost, but everything could crumble in a few minutes.

For those who interpreted the Sarpoza incident in a narrow way, seeing only the technical challenge of improving prison security, the following years offered another chance to test their ideas. Sarpoza was rebuilt, and the Canadian government donated cash for the repair of houses and shops damaged by the truck bomb. More foreign money paid for the tripling of the guards' meagre salaries. The new version of the prison was better guarded, with higher walls and more professional staff. Female guards received a twelve-day "security self-awareness" training program, and Canadian foreign affairs minister Lawrence Cannon visited in 2009 to showcase the model facility. New front gates were installed with impressive blast walls, designed to resist truck bombs—and the new fortifications did, in fact, withstand a similar blast the following year, in 2009, when the Taliban reportedly detonated a truck packed with explosives near the front entrance. An American officer boasted that the prison gates were now so strong that insurgents would need a nuclear bomb to breach the perimeter.

The problem was not the strength of the walls, however, but the fact that they stood on shaky foundations—figuratively and literally.

The Taliban had taken advantage of this weakness in 2003 by tunnelling into the soft dirt under the walls and rescuing dozens of their comrades. Despite the upgrades to the prison defences, this subterranean problem remained unsolved in the fall of 2010, when a Taliban supporter rented a small building across the road from the prison. The insurgents pretended to set up a workshop, manufacturing concrete building supplies in the daytime while at night the place served as a headquarters for another rescue operation. Painstakingly, over several months, a man with a pickaxe dug a tunnel under the road and beneath the political section in the northeast corner of the jail. Taliban statements later claimed that his tunnelling was guided by his own memory of incarceration at Sarpoza, where he once served three months, with help from Google Maps. Prison guards said they did not notice the sound of digging underfoot, and nobody reported the loads of dirt trucked away from the workshop across from the prison. None of the guards reported hearing a hydraulic jack breaking the concrete floor of the prison. Perhaps the riskiest moment for the diggers happened a couple of weeks before the jailbreak, and was later revealed by the writer Luke Mogelson in an article for *GQ* magazine: a neighbour, the owner of an electronics store next door, got suspicious and tried to sneak a look inside the fake workshop. Witnesses told Mr. Mogelson that a man emerged and hit the shop owner on the head with a metal pipe, leaving him with injuries that would later kill him. Such a brazen murder next door to a security facility naturally brought some attention, and staff from the Afghan police, intelligence, and prison services all visited the scene to ask questions. Their inquiries apparently did not reveal the fact that the incident took place in front of a sham business, which concealed the mouth of an escape tunnel.

So, for a second time, in April 2011, hundreds of men captured as insurgents walked free from the biggest jail in southern Afghanistan. "We had good weapons, and many police, and foreign troops were nearby every night," a senior prison official told me on the morning after the second jailbreak. "Last night all these things were present, all our forces, we had enough preparation for fighting. But we did not fight. Why? That is a big question." He was paraphrasing what I had concluded about the previous jailbreak—that the sum total of the foreign assistance did not add up to security. His simple phrase, "We had enough preparation for fighting," pointed to the fact that the Afghans' challenges went beyond military prowess. The international community and its local allies had learned how to fix the technical problems with the prison facility—shoddy gates, poor lighting, insufficient guards—but there was nothing they could do about the bigger problem, that few people in the south seemed enthusiastic about resisting the Taliban. When insurgents feel comfortable setting up shop across the street from your prison, it doesn't matter if your walls are thick. You will always be undermined.

Attack helicopter in Uruzgan province

CHAPTER 14

AT THE GATES OF KABUL SEPTEMBER 2008

No matter what happened in the rest of the country, we always had Kabul. Foreigners returned there after long months in the provinces, after lonely nights on military bases or isolated compounds, sleeping in the metal hulls of modified shipping containers or guesthouses without guests. Men straggled into the city with dirty beards and a craving for beer. Women shrugged off their burkas, the blue veils that kept them anonymous, and went back to their standard expat outfits: jeans, headscarves, hiking shoes and long shirts. They continued stripping their layers after arriving inside the high-walled compounds that served as the foreigners' private world. Past the heavy doors of a restaurant, past the identity checks and metal-detecting wands of the guards, through the secure bombproof passageways, I would step into a poolside garden where uniformed waiters served chilled drinks. Sitting with my laptop and a gin and tonic one afternoon, I saw a blonde woman stagger out of the security gate with an expression of profound gratitude to be back in the relative luxury of the capital. She removed her headscarf like she was casting off a yoke, and later changed into a bikini. After a swim, she reclined on a lounger and explained the basics of Kabul's party circuit. Festivities kicked off on Thursday nights, before the traditional day of rest on Friday, and continued into the weekend. Often they were tame affairs, just friends sitting on carpets spread out on the grass of a back garden, but sometimes they assumed a frenzied energy. The expat community always seemed to be toasting somebody's arrival or departure, she said. The war attracted young professionals who saw themselves in a heroic role, saving locals from misery, or fighting the evil darkness of terrorism, or perhaps both at the same time. Somehow, those glamorous pursuits also required lots of alcohol: I've seen more drunk people cram into a house in Kabul than in any other city in the world. There was often a grimness to the drinking, a deliberate grinding down of consciousness, but occasionally women would show up in something shimmery, or sparkly, or wearing a tiara. This added a frisson to the dancing, and gave momentum to the evenings beyond the need to blur awareness. By the end of the night you could see disappointment on the faces of people who realized they could not drink themselves out of Afghanistan.

After a few of those parties, I stumbled back through the streets of Kabul toward my hotel. The streets looked peaceful in darkness, not crowded with cars and beggars. Stray dogs ran in packs. Guards slept in tiny huts, or stayed awake smoking with automatic rifles resting across their knees. The only shops still open were bakeries, with boys kneading lumps of dough and the fragrance of bread pushing away the gutter stench. The guards at my hotel would be surprised to see a foreigner walking at night, undisguised in jeans and a T-shirt, but they didn't seem to mind in the early years. That changed during my visit in September 2008. A manager knocked at my door after a late evening and reminded me that things were getting worse. He recommended against evening strolls, and suggested one of the car services that catered to foreigners. At least three companies ran fleets of sedans day and night; their rates had climbed, but five or six dollars would still get you across the downtown. Spotting these cars used to be easy, as they printed company logos on their doors, but then security concerns forced them to peel off the decals and hide among the traffic. They also removed the radio dispatch system from the vehicles' interiors, making them and their drivers less conspicuous. By 2008, the dispatchers had started giving security numbers to every customer, something you could mutter to the driver to ensure you were climbing into the right vehicle. Even those precautions did not meet the standards of the United Nations, which preferred to keep drivers sitting outside in armoured UN vehicles—which, perversely, made the parties more conspicuous.

Guards often barred Afghans from such gatherings, partly because alcohol is illegal in Afghanistan and police tolerance for boozing usually extended only to expats. Unfortunately, this had the effect of keeping Afghans away from some of the most important conversations about the future of their country. An ambassador once told me that his best work happened at social gatherings in Kabul, not during his official duties, and journalists would say the same thing: you needed to drink with the right people to understand the capital. I sometimes forgot those unwritten rules forbidding Afghans from certain parts of their own city; during one visit in 2008, when I tried to walk into a hotel with my translator, the manager hesitated before allowing my colleague into the establishment. I'd known the manager for a long time, but it was hard for him to accept the fact that my friend was wearing traditional clothes and a sparkly cap that marked him as a resident of Kandahar, the heartland of the Taliban. The hotel had recently purchased barbed wire, mesh screens to prevent hand grenades from landing on the tennis courts, and a cage-like structure for the main entrance. We stepped into the cage, and a guard bolted the door behind us before another unlocked the door ahead. Like most guards in Kabul, the security men were Tajiks, from the northern ethnic group, veterans of wars against the Taliban in the 1990s. They harboured deep suspicions of Pashtuns—and especially southern Pashtuns, like my translator. The guards stared hard at him, and word spread about the unusual visitor. An elderly security officer visited him for a long conversation; the officer turned out to be the local informant for the National Directorate for Security (the secret police) and a former member of the feared communist intelligence service. But my translator got along with him, surprisingly, and became so comfortable in the hotel that he eventually decided it was the safest place for a meeting with a Taliban operative.

I had not intended to meet any more Taliban because it seemed unnecessarily risky, but my translator described this man as a close friend he had known for years—and besides, he explained, this guy wasn't actually a fighter. He worked a respectable job in Kabul, and his relatives included drivers for the United Nations. He just happened to have friends in the mountains who fought against the foreign troops, and he might be able to explain the situation around Kabul. I could not resist the offer, because my initial impressions of the capital that September left me with a sense of paranoia. Each year brought more locks, thicker blast walls and higher barricades. I wanted to know why the city residents were digging in.

We waited for our friend outside the walls of the guesthouse, because the guards wouldn't have allowed him near the gates by himself. They gave him a rigorous frisking and scrutinized his identity card, but eventually let him inside, scowling at his enormous beard and the loop of prayer beads on his forearm. We went up to my fixer's room and laid out bedding and pillows on the floor to make traditional seating; we looked like boys on a sleepover. We chatted casually for the next four hours. At times, our new friend pulled out a cellphone and called up Taliban commanders, putting them on speakerphone so we could interview them. It soon became clear that he had stronger connections to the insurgency than we had assumed, and that he profited from those links. He offered, for a fee, to take us outside the city and introduce us to a prominent insurgent leader. ("Nooo," my translator said, with a frightened laugh.) He tried to sell us US military equipment and weaponry seized by the Taliban from raided convoys. For a price, he offered training pamphlets for Hizb-e-Islami, an insurgent group linked with the Taliban. However, none of these propositions could match the revenues from his usual line of business: serving as a middleman for Taliban who controlled patches of terrain outside of Kabul.

I knew the insurgents were strengthening their positions around the capital, but did not understand what that meant in practical terms. The middleman spelled it out: the real money, he said, came from kidnappings and extortion. He had expertise in both. Recently, he said, he held a Chinese engineer hostage for almost two weeks. The kidnap victim served as local director of a Chinese construction firm with a major road contract in the nearby province of Wardak. The company had not purchased any protection from the insurgents, he said, so the foreigner became fair game for kidnapping. Taliban grabbed him, received a ransom of $500,000, and set him free. The Chinese firm arranged to pay a monthly protection fee to the local Taliban in that district, and an identical amount to the Hizb-e-Islami militia operating nearby. This insurance proved useful two days later, when bandits kidnapped the same Chinese engineer. Hizb-e-Islami gunmen tracked down the kidnappers and forced them to hand over the hostage, unharmed, and set him free a second time. At that point, he said, the Kabul government issued public statements crowing about how Afghan security forces had pressured the insurgents into giving up the kidnap victim. "This offended the Taliban," he said. "So they captured him again, and told the government, 'Do what you can. We will keep this engineer.'" The Chinese man spent another month in captivity, including thirteen days with the man sitting in front of me. The kidnapper seemed proud of his hospitality, describing how he gave the hostage proper food and exercise. Eventually they released the captive for a third and final time, and the construction work continued. Insurgents took a substantial fee.

I'd heard similar stories. At parties in Kabul, you could hear contractors cursing about the percentage they were forced to pay the Taliban. I told my new Taliban friend about widespread rumours that $10 million in US government funding for a road in eastern

Afghanistan had been siphoned off by America's arch-enemy, a Taliban ally named Jalaluddin Haqqani, who granted protection for the workers.

"Yes, I heard this also," he said, and named the agent who brokered the deal.

"That ten million covers one year? Two years?"

"It's until the completion of the project."

I described another story from an acquaintance, about an engineer who worked for the insurgents in Kabul, offering professional assessments of bid documents to make sure their extortion targets weren't lying to the Taliban about the value of their work. The whole concept of a "Taliban engineer" working in the capital seemed incredible to me, but I'd heard that he was a qualified professional who would show up at contractors' offices to examine their plans and assess the Taliban's cut. My new friend nodded with a matter-of-fact expression, confirming that this was routine. Sometimes it's a percentage of the project's value, he said, and sometimes the insurgents demand a fixed amount of cash per kilometre of road construction. But these negotiations are fraught with uncertainty, he added, because some Taliban commanders disliked corruption, or were mercurial in their business deals. He described problems he was encountering with a project in the southeastern province of Paktika, where local insurgents had refused a bribe of $500,000 for a road survey.

"I wanted to get part of this project, so I went to the Taliban commander in that area to discuss it with him. The Taliban commander there was my friend, he had good behaviour with me. When I mentioned the project, told him I want to bring two engineers to survey for the road, he said, 'No, I will not allow the road. When they make a road, every day they will come, investigate our homes, see our women, kill our children, kill our young people. Nowadays we are quiet. In these five years, no Americans came to our village because we don't have a road. If they make this project, they will build it for themselves, not for us.' He rejected it, even the survey."

"But maybe if they pay him $10 million?" I suggested.

"He is very tough. I think he will not accept it. He was detained twice by the Americans. The first time, he said to the people of the bazaar, do not tell the Americans I am a big commander. Tell them I'm a shepherd. So the first time he was arrested by the Americans, he called to the people: 'Am I a Taliban commander? Or am I a shepherd?' And the people said no, he's a shepherd. The military translators told this to the Americans, and they released him. He told a translator, give me your phone number. When I see the Taliban commander, I will call you. When he got back to his home, he called them. He said, I am the commander, and you didn't recognize me."

The bearded man laughed, and continued: "Later he was arrested again. He told the Americans, 'I'm a shepherd, I have a lot of sheep in the desert. You can go with me and see them.' He called again to the people in the bazaar. Again, they said he's a shepherd. And they released him again."

"Do they need permission from this commander to make the road?" I asked, steering him back to the question of how the Taliban profit from construction projects. "Maybe they can get permission from other Taliban."

"No, he's very powerful because the road goes through his area. There are no schools, no hospitals in his area. Only madrassas [religious schools]. It's a very poor area. When there is any sick man, they bring him to a hospital in Ghazni on a donkey or a motorbike, because there is no good road."

We paused our conversation, cracking open cans of soda. Outside in the tennis courts, we could hear the squeak of shoes and the rhythms of serve and volley. I never did amass enough confirmed detail to write about the Taliban extortion rackets and the recycling of international aid money into the insurgency, although the journalist Jean MacKenzie later published an excellent investigation in *GlobalPost*. For the moment, I was concerned mostly about what this implied about the situation in the rural areas. An intelligence source had recently given me a look at the CIA's classified district assessments that showed a worrying degree of insurgent control in the countryside. At the beginning of 2008, the agency used labels such as "insurgent controlled" or "insurgent contested" to describe Taliban presence in over 130 of the 398 districts assessed, mostly in the south and east. The CIA analysts also invented a category to describe control by local warlords and strongmen, powerbrokers who owed no allegiance to either the government or the Taliban. Langley devised a charmingly utilitarian definition of control, as well: "the relative capability of the government, local leaders, or insurgents to mobilize resources in a defined geographic area to impose security, carry out organized violence, or credibly threaten violence to influence the population." It might have been tempting to give those studies a hopeful interpretation, arguing that the insurgents controlled or contested less than a third of the districts. But I was starting to understand that the insurgents did not consider all districts equal. The Taliban middleman seemed preoccupied with the roads and highways, always referring to a commander's power on the basis of his ability to regulate traffic.

After his departure, I rifled through my papers and stared for a long time at a more optimistic assessment of the districts, a map drawn up by Afghan intelligence and security services in August 2008. It was an absurd document, downplaying problems and touting success in places where none existed. But even that assessment showed red threat zones creeping up toward the capital. My eyes traced the four major highways that connected Kabul with the rest of the country: Shomali road, Jalalabad road, Logar road and Kandahar road. Only one of them, the Shomali, did not run through a red zone. The Taliban had not fully encircled the capital, but they appeared to be squeezing the supply routes.

This reminded me of the little message cards I'd noticed that summer on the cafeteria tables at Kandahar Air Field, announcing that supply interruptions meant some snacks were unavailable. The military base appeared to be running short of more critical supplies as well; aircraft landing at KAF in the previous months had been warned several times that they could not refuel there, forcing the United Nations to cancel flights to Kandahar. Entire buildings at the airfield shut down at the peak of fighting season to conserve diesel. The rubber bladders that served as fuel storage, which usually looked like giant water balloons, started resembling flat pancakes. The reasons for these so-called "supply interruptions" were obvious to anybody who saw the burned hulks of tanker trucks abandoned along the southern highways. The insurgents targeted aid shipments, too, stealing hundreds of tonnes of grain trucked into the south. But it astonished me that such problems reached all the way up to Kabul.

A few nights later as I drove around the darkened city with a police colonel, he complained that highway raids had reduced the fuel ration for his own vehicle issued to him by the Ministry of Interior. He also confirmed that only one highway into Kabul was not patrolled by insurgents. Glancing at my NATO press accreditation card, he said the small rectangle of laminated paper would become a death warrant if I travelled outside the city. "You're a foreigner travelling with this," he said, pointing at my badge, "and you can travel the Shomali road okay, but any other road they will capture you after one kilometre." He estimated that insurgent attacks on supply convoys in the ten central provinces around Kabul had quadrupled from the previous year. A Western security official called that a conservative guess. "They're cutting the arterial roads and choking the capital," he said.

It wasn't a siege in the traditional sense; traffic flowed on every highway. I visited all of the major gateways into the city and saw routes that still looked busy, sometimes jammed with lines of cars and trucks. What had changed, however, were the rules they followed. Truck drivers left doors open at the back of their tractor-trailers, securing their cargo with ropes, so that Taliban could easily look inside and check the shipment for anything forbidden. The insurgents even scrutinized customs papers to certify that the goods were destined for non-military customers, and gave receipts for the bribes paid at Taliban checkpoints. (The Taliban's bureaucratic approach to extorting the road-building business also extended, it seemed, to their methods of profiting from the traffic.) Truckers told me that the price for shipments to NATO military bases had climbed sharply, because nobody wanted to get caught helping the foreigners. At a gas station on the outskirts, a driver twisted his beard nervously as he described how a contractor had tried to persuade him to carry a load of diesel to a military base; he had refused, but his friend accepted—and got beheaded. The insurgents executed so many truckers, in fact, that the drivers had organized a noisy demonstration at a border crossing earlier in the summer to call for better protection from government forces. Some of that anger still simmered among the truckers in Kabul. One driver complained that his friend had been kidnapped for driving a truckload of chickens. How, he asked, could the Taliban consider chickens a forbidden cargo? He clearly thought I was a military spy, because he pointed his finger at me and asked: "Why are you not taking action?" Others seemed more sanguine. The next trucker I met described the local police as the real bandits, and said the Taliban territory gave him comparatively little trouble. Another driver said he stopped travelling at night in one district because of frequent robberies, but felt safer when the Taliban seized control and drove the brigands away.

A man in a white cap, selling bus tickets, said the insurgents also posed a cosmetic problem for frequent travellers between Kabul and the Iranian border: in Iran, men usually shave their beards or cut them short, but travelling there meant crossing Taliban territory, where too little beard could arouse suspicion. It was easy enough to get shaved before entering Iran, he said, but the beardless return journey could be hazardous. This threat hurt his business at a small ticket kiosk on the roadside, because anybody who could afford a plane ticket now avoided his busses. All the same, he sympathized with the insurgents: "The Taliban are not the problem," he said. "When people saw the bad behaviour of the foreigners and government, the Taliban stood up to protect them." A forty-year-old bus driver agreed, saying the police robbed him more frequently than bandits or insurgents. Another driver suggested that the cops in fact colluded with the robbers, ignoring them for a cut of the proceeds. He had fourteen years of experience driving busses on Afghan highways, and claimed he had never seen a worse situation on the roads than at the present. At a bustling ticket agency inside the city, a veteran salesman excused himself from the throng of passengers and sat with me inside a sweltering car, preferring the windows rolled up so nobody would overhear him talking with a foreigner. The core of the problem, he said, is that no single force controls the countryside. "During the Taliban government there was only one system, but now there are many opposing forces, so it's very dangerous."

For all of those interviews around the edges of the city, we drove a beat-up sedan and I disguised myself with the outfit I had previously reserved for dangerous parts of the south: loose pants, long shirt, sparkly cap. We did not tell anybody where we were going, and did not linger. None of the notes from those conversations run more than a few pages because there always came a moment when my translator would give me a look that meant we should leave. If I didn't catch his glance, he would become more forceful: "Mr. Graeme, please, let's go." He did not need to explain, and never had to ask twice. All journalists in the country understood that walking the streets involved risks, and the places we could wander were becoming fewer and fewer. Still, it felt wonderful to spend days outside, talking with ordinary people, and return to a comfortable guesthouse bed at night. I felt sorry for my colleagues back at Kandahar Air Field, sleeping on cots and unable to walk outside the perimeter. When I returned south in early October, I remember extolling the virtues of the capital, telling my journalist friends how comparatively easy it was to conduct on-the-ground research—not to mention how relaxing it was, showering off the grime at the end of the day, sitting on a terrace overlooking the hills, sipping a drink. I've always felt bad about speaking so enthusiastically about Kabul on those particular days. Within a week, I was proven wrong: my colleague Mellissa Fung, a reporter for the Canadian Broadcasting Corporation (CBC), became the latest kidnap victim. She travelled to a part of Kabul many other journalists had already visited, a camp on the outskirts for families running away from the war. That location was marked green on all of the security maps; despite the encroaching violence, nobody considered it a foolish risk. Her travels that day had been safer, in theory, than most of my days in the country. When she disappeared, I exchanged a flurry of messages with a Western security consultant:

> from: xxxx <xxxx@xxxx>
> to: Graeme Smith <xxxx@gmail.com>
> date: Sun, Oct 12, 2008 at 2:37 PM
>
> Just heard a rumor that a Canadian journo has gone missing (poss abduction) in Kabul. Any details you are privy to?
>
> from: Graeme Smith <xxxx@gmail.com>
> to: xxxx <xxxx@xxxx>
> date: Sun, Oct 12, 2008 at 3:46 PM
>
> Crap, really? Only one visiting Kabul right now—Mellissa Fung of CBC—and I'll check with her.
>
> from: Graeme Smith <xxxx@gmail.com>
> to: xxxx <xxxx@xxxx>
> date: Sun, Oct 12, 2008 at 3:51 PM

Shi*t motherf*ucker fu*k . . . yes, it's Mellissa. The kidnappers
have made contact. We're keeping it quiet until she's safe.
That's terrible. She's a sweet, beautiful girl. Terrible.

from: xxxx <xxxx@xxxx>
to: Graeme Smith <xxxx@gmail.com>
date: Sun, Oct 12, 2008 at 4:07 PM

Just got it mostly confirmed, female Canadian Journo out
visiting an IDP camp out by Karga Dam. Details are
sketchy right now.
I will forward you the report once I get something firm.

from: Graeme Smith <xxxx@gmail.com>
to: xxxx <xxxx@xxxx>
date: Sun, Oct 12, 2008 at 4:13 PM

We're trying to embargo the news until she's safe, but yes—
definitely keep me in the loop.

from: xxxx <xxxx@xxxx>
to: Graeme Smith <smithg@gmail.com>
date: Sun, Oct 12, 2008 at 4:31 PM

Looks like the info has already hit the tom-tom telegraph. It is
causing quite a buzz around town. We issued a threat warning
though we kept some of the salient details (nationality) out of
the report.
I will send it to you following this email.

from: Graeme Smith <xxxx@gmail.com>
to: xxxx <xxxx@xxxx>
date: Sun, Oct 12, 2008 at 4:41 PM

```
Thanks brother. I shouldn't be so shocked after all these years,
but I am.
```

Mellissa survived, and later wrote a book about how she was stabbed, raped and held captive for twenty-eight days. She spent most of the ordeal in a hole, a makeshift cell underground, surviving on cookies and juice. Afghan intelligence sprang her free, apparently after sweeping up her captors' relatives in a wave of arrests and trading them for her freedom. It had been a commercial kidnapping, intended to raise money, much like the business of the Taliban middleman I had hosted in my guesthouse. It was also a reminder that no safe place existed as the war spread northward. What happened in the rest of the country would disturb the peace of the capital, even the wealthy enclaves filled with birdsong and the squeak of tennis shoes. We were beginning to sense that, perhaps, we would not always have Kabul.

Afghan soldier patrols a poppy field

CHAPTER 15

A TOXIC TRIANGLE FEBRUARY 2009

The story that forced me to leave Afghanistan was something I'd been avoiding for years. Journalists often heard rumours about drug corruption, but like many of my colleagues I had been nervous about taking a hard look at the subject. It was radioactive, the most dangerous topic for research, involving serious money and deadly players. Few people were brave enough to speak plainly about the drugs, but their presence could be felt in everything. Drugs powered the south like an electric current, an invisible life-giving energy. The industry explained how enterprise thrived in the arid wastes: trucks full of fat-bottomed sheep trundling into town before festivals; jewellery filling the markets; money-changers sitting on carpets with strongboxes full of crisp currency; ornate walls of palaces climbing ever higher, resembling wedding cakes with their pastel colours. Drugs fuelled the opulence of a residence I visited one afternoon, where I sipped green tea from a gold-handled cup and marvelled at the thousands of tiny mirrors laid out in mosaic patterns on the vaulted arches of ceiling. Outside, beyond the brocade curtains, nomads were busy setting up tarpaulin shelters as their flocks grazed on the scrubby bushes. The herders' poverty matched the landscape, part of a rhythm thousands of years old, but the wealth of my host belonged to the modern economy. Nearly everything he bought—vehicles, gasoline, diet supplements, a state-of-the-art exercise treadmill—came from abroad. The money to purchase those things did not result from exports of Kandahar's grapes and pomegranates. Like so many others, he depended on the narcotics industry.

The drugs were everywhere, but the industry could be inscrutable. One afternoon I witnessed a puzzling scene in the border town of Wesh, a smugglers' haven on the contested boundary line between Afghanistan and Pakistan. Most of the town's activity concentrated on jostling crowds around the border checkpoint. Traffic clogged the road: cars, trucks, donkey carts, wheelbarrows, and tractors pulling stacks of baggage. The guards took bribes and did not search the packages, as usual, waving men and vehicles through the checkpoint with lazy gestures. So when the security officers perked up and started shouting, I couldn't immediately see what caused the fuss. Then I spotted him: an unusually dark-skinned man jogging onto Afghan soil with his arms raised above his head, like a marathoner at the finish line. He towered over the guards, wearing a red sweater despite the midday sun. Foreigners were a rare sight at that border crossing, and I was careful to disguise myself as a tribesman, but this guy seemed to enjoy his place at the centre of attention. He loped up to the passport office and roared a wild version of the traditional greeting, wishing peace upon the startled guards—"*Saaaaaalam Aleeeeeikum*!"—and awkwardly tried to give them high-fives. The guards ushered this strange creature into the office and summoned a clerk. The man slapped down a green Nigerian passport, waited a beat, and then opened a thick wallet and pulled out forty dollars. This caused a moment of confusion because the clerk had already found the man's Afghan visa and was reaching for his stamp when he caught sight of the bribe. "Baksheesh! Baksheesh!" the Nigerian shouted. The clerk shrugged, took the money and stamped. The Nigerian grabbed his passport and ran out of the office, pumping his fists in mad triumph. After a stunned pause, laughter echoed around the bare concrete walls.

I did not expect to understand the Nigerian's flamboyant entrance to the war; so many things escaped my grasp. Two days later, however, I got an explanation from a government official in Kandahar. I was visiting his office to drop off a book he wanted, *Goblin Market and Other Poems*, by Christina Rossetti—poetry is a popular enthusiasm in Afghanistan, and my friend was especially fond of Rossetti—and our conversation turned to the drug trade. "What do you know about Nigerians?" he asked, picking up a green passport from his desk and slapping it down on a scanner. The machine flashed. "The police brought me this Nigerian," he continued. "They hadn't arrested him, but they wanted me to check his documents." He handed me the passport. "Look at this. What do you see?" It looked like an Afghan visa. The official pointed out flaws: the paper didn't feel right, and the stamp was intentionally smudged. "You can buy much better forgeries in Pakistan," he said. "I wonder why he wasn't caught at the border." I flipped to the photo, and recognized the man. My acquaintance shook his head with astonishment when I described the scene at the passport counter. The Nigerian claimed that he worked for a trading company, but the company name did not match any listings on the Internet. The local authorities assumed that the Nigerian was a drug dealer (and possibly a drug user) visiting Kandahar with the same lust for adventure and profit that once drew prospectors to the gold rush. Perhaps he heard of the lawlessness and fast money, or maybe he saw photographs of the poppy fields that reached the horizon, churning out more raw opium than the world market could absorb. The Nigerian might have believed that no structure existed in the chaos of the south. He was wrong: he could bribe his way into the country, but he could not walk into Kandahar and buy a share of the drug business. It belonged to a small group of men, and they guarded its secrets jealously.

The drug trade hadn't always been so well organized, however. Smugglers felt wistful about the early days, when almost any entrepreneur could put together a team of men and call himself an opium dealer. I met two of those small businessmen in 2005, and heard their stories of freewheeling deals in the years before mafias divided up the market. Both interviews happened in a downtown restaurant in Kandahar city; back then, it wasn't suicidal for me to linger in public and speak English, and the drug dealers did not seem concerned about associating with a foreigner. We tore into roasted chickens with our fingers, and I took grease-stained notes about the basics of the industry. During the spring harvest, farmers scratched vertical lines in the green bulbs of their poppies, then later collected the gummy paste that oozed from the wounds. Dealers visited the farmers and purchased the paste, often packed into shopping bags. Smugglers collected these bags into shipments big enough to merit the risk and expense of a trip to the border, or to the nearest processing facility. Their routes varied, but the smugglers had essentially two options: overland through the desert, or by highway.

The off-roaders sounded a little crazy. A dealer told me he organized large convoys of Toyota Land Cruisers, moving several tonnes of narcotics at high speed. He preferred routes not controlled by any faction in the war, and carried enough guns to fend off bandits and reduce the need for bribes. They drove to rendezvous points near the Iranian border, or moved the goods into Pakistan's tribal areas. He could have been describing a scene from a Mad Max movie, and when I eventually saw a smugglers' camp it did resemble something from an apocalyptic science-fiction film. The makeshift settlement of Girdi Jungle started as a refugee camp in the 1980s, sheltering Afghans fleeing the Soviet invasion, but after a generation the camp had become more like a ramshackle city in the borderlands. Perched at the edge of a desert, where the dunes sank into flatlands, it wasn't immediately clear how the camp sustained itself. But the people weren't starving by any means; market stalls brimmed with fresh herbs and vegetables, and generous hunks of meat dangled from the butchers' hooks. The abundance might have seemed mysterious if I hadn't noticed the sport-utility vehicles roaring out of the shimmering haze, bearing unknown cargo from Afghanistan to this convenient spot just inside Pakistan. One night, in a nearby town, a fat drug dealer smoked a little hash and pulled a plastic baggie of opium tar from his pocket. He used the drug packet like a pointer, sketching out the shipment routes. I told him that the smugglers might, in theory, want to avoid places under control of any authorities, but they appeared to be crossing territory that fell squarely under Taliban rule. He smiled, and made a gesture with his fingers to indicate money: drug mafias funded the insurgents.

Other smugglers preferred the highways, and paid different tolls. I met a small businessman in Kandahar who hired metalworkers to carve hiding spots into the bodies and engine compartments of cars and trucks. His shipments moved unnoticed among the other vehicles on the roads; in case of trouble, each of his vehicles contained three unarmed men carrying wads of cash hidden on their bodies. His transporters did not usually need to pay bribes, however, because he took the precaution of keeping district police chiefs and checkpoint commanders on regular salaries. Even if they were caught, it was only a matter of paying extra to get his men and shipments out of custody. This so-called "government route" along the highways may not have been systematic in the years before 2005; the small businessman relied on personal connections and individual payoffs at checkpoints. He could name the police, army and militia commanders who controlled various places on the road where his vehicles might face inspection, and maintained strong relationships with them. The international community tended to shrug off this kind of low-level corruption, figuring that without such perks the Afghan security forces might have little incentive to accept jobs in the dangerous south.

As the insurgency grew, and Taliban grabbed more territory, it would have been logical to assume that the insurgents' share of the drug trade should have grown to reflect their increased power. But the insurgents appeared to face tough competition from mafias within the Afghan government, which became better organized as the years passed. It's unclear how much the international community understood about the threads of corruption that ran through all echelons of public and private life. It's possible that the Western allies, despite their informants and monitoring technology, never did find conclusive evidence that their Afghan partners ran drug networks. I met officials from the US Drug Enforcement Administration who seemed genuinely frustrated by their lack of solid information. They could not claim ignorance about the overall trend, however. A British narcotics expert illustrated the situation with a PowerPoint slideshow he gave to US intelligence experts. He showed them a drawing of weigh scales; one side represented the Taliban share of the market, the other indicated the government side. He clicked forward, and a stack of cartoon bills cascaded down to show the insurgents' windfall from protecting drug dealers. Then he clicked again, and a much bigger stack landed on the scales. The government's take far outweighed the Taliban's operation, he said. It was a blunt way of making his point, but the British expert felt a need to emphasize the message, particularly to the Americans; the US government was paying some Afghan strongmen for help with clandestine operations, after all, and the same characters were frequently the worst offenders in the drug trade. Nobody in the audience looked surprised as the British expert described the situation. A prominent US analyst, at the back of the auditorium, nodded and rolled his eyes.

Several months later, I sat down with a senior Afghan police official who had worked on counter-narcotics, and asked him whether that British expert was correct: Were figures in the Afghan government eating up the drug market?

"I saw the Toyota Land Cruisers coming out of the desert, the smugglers," I told him. "This is one way of moving drugs across the desert, in the open areas that belong to the Taliban. Another way is along the highways, the roads that belong to the government. . . . Which way is bigger?"

The officer looked at me like I was an idiot.

"The government routes are much stronger and protected," he said.

But in every other way, government influence in Afghanistan was waning. District leaders did not venture out to their rural offices, preferring to hide in major cities. Local officials pleaded for helicopter rescues to get them out of the Taliban-infested countryside. Security companies added dozens of extra men to protect convoys running through insurgent territory. How could the government mafias be strengthening their grip on the drug routes?

I may never know the answer, but one part of the equation seemed to be the way the government's anti-drug police attacked rivals and protected friends. The Ministry of Counter Narcotics lacked armed men, but a branch of the Interior Ministry known as the Counter Narcotics Police of Afghanistan (CNPA) had a presence throughout the country and commanded about three thousand officers. Its men had better equipment and training than regular police. Their leader, General Mohammed Daud Daud, a deputy minister of interior with responsibility for the CNPA, was considered the country's most powerful anti-drug czar. He was also widely believed to rank among the biggest players in the narcotics industry, as persistent rumours claimed that he used his position and his clout as a former militia commander to further his own interests. He vehemently denied any role in drug trafficking—"Your information is completely defective and deficient, and shameful for the prestige of journalism," he told my translator—and I never did put together what you might consider legal evidence of wrongdoing. But in the final months of my assignment in Afghanistan I started to assemble some fascinating information about General Daud, as one example of the way drugs reached their fingers into government. Asking questions about the general seemed safer than investigating other government figures, because his status as a northerner made him less dangerous to me in the south. I was also lucky enough to find the kind of paper trail that rarely surfaces in Afghanistan: letters that appeared to directly link General Daud with a drug dealer.

The letters were discovered by CNPA officers on June 19, 2005, during what must have been a really confusing narcotics bust. The takedown went smoothly at first, as the anti-drug team set an ambush on a road east of Kabul for a notorious dealer named Sayyed Jan. He refused to stop, and officers raked the tires of his new Lexus with gunfire. He tried to run away with two bodyguards, but the team captured them and found heroin in his vehicle. Accounts varied about the quantity of drugs; General Daud himself claimed it was 230 kilograms, but other counter-narcotics sources said it was somewhat less. (A British official joked, "Maybe some fell off the lorry.") More perplexingly for the CNPA team, the drug dealer was carrying letters of protection from their own boss. A letter from General Daud to a southern governor, dated three months earlier, introduced the drug dealer in respectful terms and urged the provincial leader to help him with unspecified duties. Two other letters show that the governor and local police chief obeyed the CNPA boss, writing their own guarantees of safe passage for the dealer. Reading those letters must have felt uncomfortable for the CNPA men, as they realized they had caught somebody with powerful connections.

It would have been convenient for General Daud to claim that the drug dealer had been operating as a double agent, secretly working on anti-narcotics operations—that could have explained why the anti-drug czar scrawled his signature on behalf of somebody caught with millions of dollars' worth of heroin. But the general did not offer that defence when a court convicted Mr. Jan. (He later escaped, under mysterious circumstances.) Nor did the general give any legitimate reason for helping Mr. Jan. When my translator confronted him, he touted his record of accomplishments and denied taking money from Mr. Jan—or any other drug dealer. I did not believe him. One of the trafficker's relatives sat down with me and explained how the payoffs worked, with bribes of $50,000 to $100,000 required for each major shipment. The most expensive payment, an additional $50,000 per shipment, went to the man Mr. Jan referred to using a Pashto word that sounds like *masher*, meaning *boss*. During my conversation with Mr. Jan's relative on a chilly day in November, he huddled deeper into his woolen shawl when I asked him to name the boss. "Who was his boss?" he said, looking at me seriously through the smoke of his cigarette. "His boss was the chief of CNPA."

Drug profits made government jobs worth serious money. Mr. Jan's relative estimated that officers would need to pay at least $200,000 per year for the privilege of holding some CNPA postings. A former provincial police chief told me the same thing, confirming that bribes worth tens or hundreds of thousands of dollars changed hands before authorities in Kabul appointed people to key postings. It seemed that among the government officials who controlled the gateways of the south, few cared about collecting a salary from Kabul. The money flowed in the opposite direction, as employees rented their positions and hoped to extract enough bribe money to make the investment pay off.

I showed my notes on drug corruption to an experienced United Nations official in Kabul. He told me not to mistake the government mafias for a seamless conspiracy, suggesting that the networks within the regime functioned more like interlinked, overlapping, competing factions. The United Nations estimated that the number of farm hectares devoted to opium cultivation during the first decade of the Karzai regime was, on average, more than double the number of hectares used for opium during the Taliban regime. For the sake of argument, I suggested that a cold-blooded observer might not see the corruption as entirely bad because it funnelled money into the impoverished government and created incentives for the regime to win territory. On an individual level, I suggested, couldn't the drugs serve as a motivator for Afghan police officers to assume dangerous posts that might otherwise get abandoned? My source from the United Nations didn't take this well. He responded:

"You're assuming it's a two-way relationship between the drug dealers and the government, but it's more like a triangle. It includes the Taliban." He explained that roughly two hundred light weapons were smuggled into Afghanistan every day during the peak of the recent fighting season. The insurgents used ammunition in industrial quantities, littering tonnes of bullets on the battlefields with their "spray-and-pray" marksmanship. Taliban were usually portrayed in the media as rugged frontiersmen, hauling guns and bullets through snowy mountain passes, but in reality the shipment routes were more efficient: just like the drug dealers, weapons smugglers took advantage of the roads paved by the international donors. The United Nations official quoted a statistic that nearly made me choke: about 50 to 70 per cent of the insurgents' weapons arrived by road, with help from corrupt figures in the Afghan government itself. (An intelligence source later confirmed this number, saying the percentages were even higher for ammunition.) The United Nations officials sketched out one drug route that took raw opium from Kandahar to a processing lab in the eastern provinces, then north to the border with Tajikistan. The same network of crooked officials, using the same trucks, smuggled guns back down the same roads for the insurgents in the south. A Kalashnikov rifle purchased for $100 or $150 in Tajikistan would be sold for $400 in Kandahar, a profit margin that made guns almost as lucrative as drugs. The fact that the rifles might be used to kill foreign soldiers—or even the corrupt Afghan official who sold them—did nothing to stem the trade.

My article about drug corruption appeared in early 2009, using the phrase "toxic triangle" to summarize the three-way relationship between the traffickers, insurgents and government figures. Within days of publication it became clear that I should stay away from the country for awhile. General Daud visited Kandahar soon afterward and seemed suspiciously curious about my whereabouts, as well as the identity of my translators, but fortunately he failed to discover their names. By then I had already departed. A US military intelligence analyst sent a message saying that Afghanistan "isn't healthy for you to come back to for at least a good, long while. . . . I don't want to be attending a funeral." I had expected that kind of backlash, in fact. My editors had approved a temporary leave from my job at the newspaper, so I would not need to go back to Afghanistan that year. I had already said goodbye to my local friends, who organized a farewell picnic at the last minute, throwing down a few woven mats in a parking lot near the airport. It had been a strange celebration, sitting cross-legged under a lone tree with barren branches, a little beyond the barbed-wire perimeter. Soldiers in a nearby watchtower paced back and forth as we enjoyed a final meal together. I promised to return someday.

Stray dogs at Tarnak Farms

CHAPTER 16

ANOTHER SURGE JUNE 2011

I stayed away from Afghanistan for two years, wary of the threat from General Daud. He probably forgot about me—just one of many annoying foreigners—but I'll never know whether he nursed a grudge: a bomb killed him in May 2011. His supporters wailed in the streets, and analysts lamented his death as a sign of instability. This was accurate; General Daud had been a dangerous man, especially for critics like me, but he ranked among the biggest of the pro-government figures who enforced a sort of order. The assassination was an indication of things going badly, of cracks in whatever structure existed in Kabul. His death allowed me back into the country, however, and I quickly made arrangements for a trip to Kandahar. I wanted to see old friends, and get a sense of how things had changed. News reports suggested that a radical transformation was underway: the United States had tripled the overall troop strength in southern Afghanistan. The surge of reinforcements was matched by a surge of violence, with insurgent attacks doubling in the province over two years. When I closed my eyes and imagined the war-ravaged place I had known, it was hard to picture Kandahar with dramatically more bombings, ambushes and assassinations. The city I left behind was a place where conversations often ended with a bang, as people rushed outside to gawk at smoke rising from the latest explosion. Now what?

Smoke from several bombings hanging over the rooftops at any given time?

Not according to my translator, someone I've known and trusted for years. I called him before booking my flights, and I felt relieved, as always, to hear his voice crackling over the rough mobile networks. He confirmed that many types of attack had increased, especially the targeted killings; the Taliban had become so precise in their selection of victims that they released biographies of the dead within hours after hit teams gunned them down, explaining why the insurgency had passed a death sentence upon some government staffer or aid worker. Still, my translator advised that downtown Kandahar was now less dangerous for journalists. Bombings and firefights on the main avenues were less frequent, making it unlikely that I'd get caught in the crossfire unless I went beyond the city limits. New guesthouses had been equipped with blast walls and reinforced guard posts to accommodate foreign visitors. Convoys of armoured vehicles no longer raced madly through the streets: the troops had learned how to drive more cautiously, drifting slowly through the city with their hatches sealed to avoid trouble. Afghan forces in the province were no longer a joke, my translator added, suggesting that a disciplined system of searching cars at every gateway to Kandahar city was helping to make the place safer.

These were practical updates from a friend who wanted to keep me alive during my stay, not the rhetoric of commanders. I had dismissed the claims of "fragile progress" in the south as more of the misplaced optimism we heard for years, but here was my closest friend in the city telling me that something positive was happening—at least in some neighbourhoods. This rekindled a theory I'd been thinking about for years, a hopeful idea about how the conflict might eventually simmer down. It seemed reasonable, after spending billions of dollars on the local government, to expect that the Afghan regime would become strong enough to survive on its own. The best historical precedent for this was the way the communist government under Mohammad Najibullah Ahmadzai—better known as "Doctor Najib" because of his medical studies—showed resilience after the Soviet troops withdrew in 1989. That period of history is often misunderstood, because many people assume that the administration set up by the Russians fell apart immediately after its sponsors retreated. But I've spoken with dozens of Afghans who remember those times, and they describe a situation that sounds remarkably stable. Kabul maintained control of the capital and key cities, offering bribes and territory for peace with rebel leaders. Moscow continued supplying hundreds of millions of dollars in cash, arms and equipment. Insurgents mustered a major attack on the eastern city of Jalalabad in the spring of 1989, throwing maybe ten thousand rebels at a government stronghold, but the offensive turned into a debacle and the rebel factions never showed that kind of unity again. Scholars who reviewed that period of history concluded that the insurgents weren't very good at the kind of organized warfare necessary to seize a country—and, without a common enemy, the rebel groups started fighting each other. Those factors might have allowed Dr. Najib to survive if the Soviet Union had not collapsed. His regime lasted only four months after aid was formally cut off in 1992, and by that point his citizens were starving without food deliveries. That kind of collapse seems unlikely to happen again, however, because the Karzai government does not depend on a crumbling empire; despite the economic troubles of the West, the regime in Kabul can still rely on sponsorship from many of the world's richest countries. My personal theory was that the foreigners would eventually withdraw their troops and the violence would slowly ebb, the way it happened during the Soviet pullout. I guessed that the withdrawals would sap the energy and unity of insurgents whose rallying cry has been the removal of foreign soldiers. I also figured that the Kabul elites, who had been reluctant to offer serious concessions in their long-running negotiations with the insurgents, would feel more willing to talk peace without protection from the troops.

That theory was about to get tested. Canada was pulling its troops from the south that summer, and the Netherlands had already withdrawn. Their numbers were small but symbolic, and reminded everybody about the bigger withdrawals in the coming months if the United States, France, Britain and other NATO countries went ahead with troop reductions. The declared goal of pulling "most" troops by 2014 was a vague target, but as I prepared for a return visit to Kandahar, the focus of all conversations was that the foreigners were actually leaving. That simple fact amazed people in the south. For years, many Afghans had suspected that the United States and its allies would keep their military foothold indefinitely; even the illiterate farmers understood why the US wanted bases near the borders of Iran and China. But it was difficult for my friends inside Afghanistan to pick up on the mood of war fatigue in the West, and hard for them to understand the depth of the recent economic troubles in the rich countries. Withdrawals had been discussed for years, but the reality did not hit people in Kandahar until the summer of 2011 as locals watched Canada's armoured vehicles pulling out, and listened to President Obama's televised speech promising to bring home thirty-three thousand soldiers within a year. All of a sudden, it didn't seem abstract to wonder if the local government could survive without them.

My first impression, after years away, was that the Afghan government looked a whole lot stronger. On my first visit, in 2005, I had to crawl along the baggage carousel and duck through the plastic curtain to find my bags at the Kabul airport, wrestling with dirty children who tried to slip their fingers in my pockets. By 2011, the local police had cleared away the beggars and porters, and the place felt more like a military airstrip than a civilian facility. Standing in the astonishingly straight line for a flight to Kandahar—no pushing, no jostling—I was surprised to meet a British journalist headed south for an embed with the Afghan National Army. This was the first time I'd heard of a reporter risking his life by going on patrol with a purely Afghan unit, without supervision by foreign troops, and we agreed it was a good sign. Even the airport itself looks better, I told him, gesturing at the clean marble, carved wood and freshly painted surfaces of the terminal.

"This place is beautiful now," I said.

An Afghan standing behind me overheard the comment. "Are you kidding?" he said. "It was much better during Najib's time." A muscular man with hooded eyes, he sat beside me on the plane and introduced himself as a Pashto-language interpreter for "OGA," an acronym that means "other government agencies," a shorthand for the US Central Intelligence Agency. He looked exhausted and did not harbour any great hopes for his own government, which he considered weaker than the communist regime. I asked him why the foreigners' good intentions amounted to so little, in his opinion. "Because they're idiots," he said, with his accent drawing out the first vowel of the word, *idiots*, into a long "eeeeee" sound. Then he cranked up something called "party mix" on his iPod and ignored me for the rest of the flight.

The final approach to Kandahar was choppy, with hot wind coming off the desert around the airfield. Even from the air, I could see progress: new roads, new buildings, new communication towers. Kandahar Air Field had expanded dramatically, like a sprawling dust-coloured city. An experimental farm greened a wasteland near the base, an arid tract previously littered with garbage. The expanded military airport now included a fleet of Mi-17s, part of the recently established Kandahar Air Wing, an Afghan air command that had started running basic transport and medical evacuation missions. Unlike their communist predecessors, the Afghans were not flying attack aircraft, however; the helicopter gunships that had helped Dr. Najib defend his regime were still considered too risky a weapon in local hands.

On my first day in the city, I woke early and drove south to the village of Deh-e-Bagh, a small settlement that was deemed safe enough to become a "model village," a showcase of development. The last time I'd driven that road it was a muddy track leading into dangerous territory; now my driver seemed relaxed, rolling down the freshly paved blacktop and easing to a halt at new checkpoints that loomed over the road like medieval fortresses. The town looked deserted, with no traffic and police standing guard every few hundred metres.

"No people, no problems," I said, half-unconsciously, and then noticed that my translator looked puzzled. I explained that I'd learned this phrase while living in Russia, that Stalin reputedly used those words to explain his brutal way of quelling unrest. I mildly regretted teaching him this expression shortly thereafter. We parked our car and started ambling through checkpoints, finally meeting a nervous American soldier who scrutinized my passport and seemed skeptical about allowing me inside; he became even less co-operative when my translator said, "No people, no problems," and laughed. I could see how the dark phrase would be unnerving, coming from a long-bearded Afghan who cackled wildly.

The soldier eventually let us pass, and I found myself sitting on a plastic lawn chair in the main hall of Deh-e-Bagh's administrative centre, a room decorated with the tasteless flair common to many Afghan government buildings: fake flowers, frosted glass lighting fixtures and a five-foot-high portrait of President Hamid Karzai. The district chief was holding court with a high-level delegation that included the governor and top NATO military commanders. I had seen previous such meetings play out like farces because of faulty translation, but this time the foreign troops had two interpreters mumbling into mobile transmitters that broadcast to small receivers worn by all foreign personnel in the room, with the Pashto-language proceedings smoothly recorded into a digital archive as if we were sitting in a United Nations conference hall. Other aspects of the meetings were surprisingly organized, too: Afghan officials for education, agriculture, public works and other departments stood up in turn and gave updates about their recent accomplishments. All of the local dignitaries appeared to have memorized some statistics about the number of schools opened, or kilometres of road constructed, which they stood and delivered with great flourishes. Public-affairs officers from the foreign delegations hunched over their notebooks and scribbled it all down. Their pens only paused during awkward moments, such as when the district chief announced that he planned to set up a website and Facebook page to inform locals about his good works—a strategy undermined, he acknowledged, by the fact that his own offices had the only Internet connection in the district. The district chief had been targeted by eleven bombings during the few years of his tenure, and one bomb had badly damaged his compound. Now rebuilt, the place looked more like a military camp than any kind of public facility. It was hard to picture the villagers dropping by to check their Facebook accounts.

After the meeting finished, I sat with the district leader as he chain-smoked Dunhills. The thirty-three-year-old was among the slickest of a new generation of Afghan leaders, capable of speaking in detail about the demographics and development profile of his area. He seemed intent on lobbying the foreigners for long-term project funding before the coming troop withdrawals, eloquently making a case that the modest industry of his district—growing crops and baking mud bricks—could be expanded to include fabric factories, wheat mills and processing plants for grapes, pomegranates, watermelon and other fruit.

As he spoke, the air conditioners died. The building lost power for perhaps the fifth time that afternoon. In the distance, we could hear his staff struggling to revive the diesel generator. He got irritated when I asked the obvious question, about how he would find electricity for his planned factories. He suggested that the foreign donors had wasted millions of dollars on modest upgrades to the nearby Dahla Dam that did not include power generation.

"You should ask the donors, why do they give their money to thieves?" he said, stubbing a Dunhill and lighting another.

"The big danger is withdrawal," he added. "They should wait for some time before starting this, maybe three years."

"What if they cannot wait?"

"If they leave, and the insurgency continues, will the Taliban come over these walls? Is that what you are asking? Yes, of course. Everybody knows this."

The walls had grown higher, but the officials who inhabited the government facilities had also become more paranoid. Over and over, in places where you might expect to find ardent supporters of the government, people expressed fear and anxiety. There was a sense of looming disaster, a fear that the foreigners built a system that would soon collapse. Nobody trusted that the Afghan government would be strong enough to stand by itself. I repeated my theory about two dozen times, asking everybody I met if the 1989 Soviet withdrawal scenario might happen again. None of the people I asked—governor, police chief, Taliban commander, hairdresser, farmer, people from all over the city—thought my historical parallel had much relevance. Many spoke about the tradition of revenge, the way conflicts can burn for generations in Afghanistan. A senior general from the Interior Ministry, whom I've known for years, invited me to his house for dinner and warned of an impending civil war. "This is just the beginning," he said. "It's only the trailer for the movie."

Other local officials said they sensed the movie unfolding like something they had seen before. I spent an evening sitting on cushions in the courtyard of Sarpoza prison with the facility's warden, a fifty-two-year-old who got the job after the tunnelling jailbreak a few months earlier. His prisoners now included his predecessor, the former warden, locked up on suspicion of helping the escape. The prison had been showered with international money, and looked stronger than ever. Huge concrete slabs protected the approaches to the main gates, and nearby roads were blocked off to prevent another jailbreak. Despite these improvements, the warden said, the ground underneath the prison remained soft and easy for tunnelling; another jailbreak could happen. When I suggested that the physical upgrades to his prison—costly, elaborate and futile—served as a metaphor for the whole international mission in his country, he said that many others had made the same observation. He waved off my idea that the history of Soviet withdrawal in 1989 might repeat itself. Having previously served in the communist regime and watched the Soviet troops depart, he remembered how the communists bought themselves a little breathing room in those days by making deals with their enemies. He predicted no such agreements with the Taliban. "It will be like Vietnam," he said, making a gesture with his hand to indicate a helicopter lifting off from a rooftop. I wasn't sure if he was referring to the iconic photograph from the fall of Saigon, of CIA personnel scrambling to escape, but he kept repeating the word: *Vietnam.*

The new Kandahar governor, Tooryalai Wesa, also served in the communist administration at the time of the Soviet withdrawal. His experience of those years stands as a testament to the surprising level of stability that followed the Russian pullout; in 1991, years after US diplomats cabled home their predictions that the communist regime would collapse in a matter of months, Mr. Wesa became the founding president of Kandahar University. By the time I met him at his office in the summer of 2011, he was feeling wistful about those days and anxious about the future. He remembered how the rebels used to fire rockets at the city twice a day in the early 1990s, but he still felt safer back then because he trusted his own men. Communist soldiers were not paid, but had better morale than the new generation of troops, he said, who are prone to running away from the battlefield. "They had belief, commitment," Mr. Wesa said. "At that time, communist political parties had real support." If the governor lacked faith in the rank-and-file, his men also seemed disenchanted. I ate lunch with one of the governor's bodyguards, and between mouthfuls of chicken the young man complained that he had not been paid in three months. When I asked if the government was as strong as Dr. Najib's regime, the bodyguard laughed so hard that he spit out his food. "No," he said, wiping up. "When the foreign soldiers leave, the Taliban will come back the next evening."

"Will this be a problem for you?" I asked.

"I will work for whoever pays me," he said. "Even the Taliban."

Other security men were less sanguine about the prospect of an insurgent victory. A few days later, as I was walking out of the police chief's headquarters, an officer flagged me down and demanded that I interview him. This was unusual; people associated with the government were regularly hunted and killed, so they did not stop journalists in the street and ask for publicity. Abdul Wali, twenty-one, gave his name, posed for a photo and declared that the foreigners should not give up. "They should continue," he said. "We're not able to stand without them. If all the foreign troops leave, Afghans will take revenge on each other. I will be killed." The young man was near the bottom of the pecking order in the police force, the first of eight security men who frisked visitors before they were allowed near the chief. Like many others, he alluded to the fact that senior officials could escape Afghanistan if necessary. "I don't have a 'Plan B,'" he said. "I can't move to Dubai." His fear of revenge killings was sensible: he served with a unit of the Afghan Border Police that had become notorious for alleged torture and extra-judicial killings, and it's likely that he had enemies.

I got a sense of how patiently some locals wait to take revenge when I met a farmer from Zangabad, a cluster of villages southwest of Kandahar city, nestled in the notoriously violent Panjwai valley. The forty-five-year-old said he owned about a hectare of vineyards. He claimed to have seen the bodies of women and children killed by NATO bombs on two occasions over the years; once he saw a charred half of a woman's corpse lodged inside a water well, tossed there by the force of an explosion. He also remembered the sparkly plastic rings on the fingers of children who died in another blast, heart-breaking little details that stick in the memory. But he spoke with the greatest emotion about the tragedy of his ruined vineyard, a piece of land that had been feeding his family for generations. Somebody called him during lunch on a cold winter's day and informed him that a Canadian-funded road crew had demolished his farm. The news shook him so badly that his wife mistook the phone call for news of a relative's death. He rushed to the scene but could not stop the armoured bulldozer. He could see the benefit of the road, in theory; it took over an hour to reach the city during the Taliban regime, and the new construction had reduced that time to only thirty minutes. He also understood the motivation of the foreign troops, who wanted to drive into the Panjwai valley without triggering bombs hidden in the dust of the rough roads. But the farmer became even more upset when he applied for compensation: he claimed that the damage would cost him $1,200 to $3,500 per year, depending on the harvest, but he received only a single payment of $350. He planned to quit farming and open a small dry-goods store in the city. After the blunders of the foreign troops, I wanted to know if he felt any relief at their departure. Would things settle down a bit? I spelled out my ideas about the 1989 withdrawal: fewer troops, less intrusion, diminishing violence, perhaps a surprising level of resilience by the government. He listened carefully, and shook his head.

"It will be more like 1992," he said. This was a sad prediction; he was naming the worst year in recent Afghan history, a time when rival factions carved up the landscape into a patchwork of fiefdoms, some no bigger than a few city blocks. The atrocities during that lawless period made the brutal Taliban regime look good by comparison. "I am an example of this," the farmer continued. "I will take revenge against the people who guided the foreigners." A Canadian officer told him that the local district chief had selected the route for the new road that smashed through his vineyard. The explanation was probably intended as a lecture about how things normally work in a democracy, but instead, the farmer emerged from the meeting with a belief that he'd been personally wronged by the local politician. Now retired, the politician still had enough influential friends that an immediate attack on his home would be foolish, so the farmer said he planned to strike when the troops leave and the government weakens. He talked about his murder plot with the kind of calm deliberation he might have used for planning the next harvest.

The optimists I met during that visit to Afghanistan fell into two categories: those in denial about the coming withdrawals, and those who still had hope for negotiations. A fair number of Afghans still refused to believe that the international forces could do anything except keep on escalating the war, after watching successive seasons of rising troop levels. Those who saw withdrawals on the horizon, but managed to stay optimistic, usually clung to the idea that their government would make peace with the insurgents. Depending on their opinions about the origins of the armed resistance, some emphasized that talks should involve cutting a deal with Pakistan—and, to a lesser extent, Iran. Most of the international community appears to have pinned its hopes on a ceasefire as well; but though talks continued in various ways during most of the years I spent in Afghanistan, they never produced solid results. The government and insurgent positions remained stubbornly far apart, with Kabul insisting that its enemies put down their weapons and accept the new constitutional order—and the Taliban, for their part, calling for a departure of the foreign troops before considering any other points.

If I had expected that the looming spectre of withdrawals would somehow bring the two sides closer together, there was no sign of it happening in Kandahar during the summer of 2011. I met the new police chief, Brigadier-General Abdul Razik, and reminded him that his own relative, a prominent anti-Soviet commander, had been among the rebels lured to the government side in the late 1980s. At that time, the communists had not bothered to make sure the rebels disarmed; if they were willing to keep order in their patch of territory, and avoid attacking the central government, then the Kabul authorities were ready to make peace. Maybe it was time to consider using the same tactic again, trading land and cash for a ceasefire? The young general was scowling and shaking his head before I finished the question. "The mujahedeen loved their country, just wanted the Russians to leave," Brigadier-General Razik said. "Now the insurgents want other things."

The Taliban usually disagree, saying their biggest aim is troop withdrawals, but Brigadier-General Razik was correct that the Taliban also want "other things" that do not sit well with the government: a new constitution, a new president. I hired the same researcher who had helped me with the Talking to the Taliban project, and he travelled into the Panjwai valley for meetings with insurgent leaders. The Taliban commanders had become more skittish than in previous years because US drones now whined overhead more regularly, picking up phone chatter and raining down Hellfire missiles. So my researcher brought his own phone to the Taliban leaders, meeting two mid-level commanders and calling my translator in Kandahar city so I could chat with them. One of them claimed to lead all insurgent forces in two districts southwest of the city. They were both full of triumphant rhetoric about the Canadian pullout and the coming US withdrawals. Somewhat chillingly, they were the only people I spoke with in Kandahar who predicted that violence would *decrease* after the foreign troops leave. They did not appear to think that the stability of 1989, *or* the chaos of 1992, were likely scenarios; instead, they expected to sweep back into power as they did from 1994 to 1996, leaving Dr. Najib hanging in a public square, imposing their brutal order. "When anyone doesn't want to accept the Koran as our constitution, we want to cut their necks," said the more senior commander. "The northern Afghanistan people, the Kabul people, they don't want our constitution and that's why we were fighting against them before." In the eyes of these insurgents, they have been waging a single continuous war for much of the last two decades; they did well in the 1990s, pushing the northerners out of the capital, and suffered losses in the following decade as the foreigners invaded, but looked forward to better odds in the coming years. My translator rolled his eyes at some of their fierce words, suggesting that they amped up their propaganda when speaking with foreign journalists. Still, most of it was standard fare for the Taliban. They did not sound ready to put down their guns, and neither did their opponents. It was hard to see them making peace.

The sense of impending ruin, of looming threat, was best captured by my return visit to an old acquaintance, the hairdresser whose small shop I had visited in 2006. Almost everything in his salon looked better than during my previous visit five years ago: the ripped grey linoleum had been replaced with blue tile, and waiting customers relaxed on a plush sofa instead of plastic lawn chairs. A television has been installed, tuned to news of the war. But the hairdresser pointed out a flaw that I'd initially overlooked: a deep crack in the arched ceiling, structural damage left by a suicide bombing a couple of years ago in the street near his shop. The hairdresser complained to his landlord that the jagged lines made him worried that chunks of concrete might break off. The landlord put masking tape over the cracks; when the tape breaks, he said, run away. The yellowed tape broke a long time ago, but Mr. Khoshbakht tried to ignore the warning sign. He avoided looking at the ceiling, and continued snipping, buzzing and trimming for the few customers willing to brave the dangerous streets for a haircut. He nodded enthusiastically at the idea that his damaged shop mirrored the way Kandahar emerged from the last five years: scarred by violence, with visible signs of improvement, but every day a little closer to the whole thing crashing down on everybody's head.

It's hard to live with that kind of fear hanging over you. The improvements to Kandahar city had spread all the way to the hairdresser's doorstep, as new blacktop replaced the dirt road outside his shop. When I asked him to talk about the legacy of the foreign presence, however, he focused on the violence. "They promised to bring security and stop the fighting," he said. "They did not keep their promises."

Graffiti at Kandahar Air Field

AFTERWORD JANUARY 2013

Many feelings propelled me back to war, but the strongest was curiosity. Or perhaps *curiosity* is too analytical a word to describe my desire to know. Imagine you're reading a novel and you misplace the book: the incomplete narrative becomes an ache. I quit my job, packed my bags and took a research posting in Afghanistan. "You came back . . . voluntarily?" asked a British diplomat. Yes, emphatically. My years in the south were marked by escalation: each surge of NATO forces, from 2006 to 2012, seemed to bring more trouble. What would happen as the troops withdrew? The early signs were difficult to read. We had rare inklings of positive trends in 2012, as civilian casualties declined for the first time in a decade. American military intelligence counted one or two attacks against civilians per day in the months before the first wave of NATO troops hit the south in early 2006; that number rose to an average of more than forty attacks per day in the summer of 2012. But then, like a minor miracle, in the last six months of 2012, the number of slain civilians started to taper off: each of the final months of the year were modestly better than the same period one year earlier.

Or, so we thought. Like so many other hopeful signs in Afghanistan, the violence numbers turned out to be less than clear. In early 2013, NATO said that a clerical error had flawed the previous year's statistics, incorrectly showing a decline in violence. In fact, NATO said, the violence remained about the same in 2012 as in 2011. Another analysis of the seemingly positive 2012 data suggested that any hints of the war cooling down might have been a result of an unusually cold winter, and not a dénouement in the conflict. This suspicion was confirmed in the spring of 2013, when a respected security group, the Afghanistan NGO Safety Office (ANSO), concluded that insurgent attacks grew 47 per cent in the first quarter, as compared with the same period a year earlier. The first sentence of the ANSO report noted that these numbers undermined the "linear logic" that fewer troops would mean less activity by the insurgents. In other words, the theory that I'd been floating—that withdrawals would drain the insurgency's momentum—was being challenged by ugly facts.

Despite the vicious war in the countryside, some officials in Kabul allowed themselves to feel confident. Their national army and police forces were stronger than ever in the last decade, making it seem unlikely that the Taliban could take the capital. In an interview with British media, President Karzai claimed that Afghan security forces would be better able to bring peace than the NATO troops. He also observed that, on the whole, the situation in the south deteriorated when international soldiers arrived in large numbers. "In 2002 through 2006, Afghanistan had a lot better security," Karzai said. "When we had our own presence there, with very little foreign troops, schools were open in Helmand and life was more secure." The president emphasized that he wasn't blaming the NATO forces, and he spoke without apparent animosity toward the international community—which, after all, had provided about 90 per cent of his national budget in recent years.

Karzai suffered criticism for his statement, but he was correct. The NATO surges into the south will almost certainly be remembered as a spectacular mistake. Many of the aims were noble: peace, democracy, rule of law. We thought that a sweeping program of armed nation-building might improve the lives of people in southern Afghanistan and simultaneously eliminate a haven for terrorism. Both of these guesses proved incorrect. Flooding the south with troops did not have a pacifying effect. The villagers were not, despite the assurances from experts, clamouring for the arrival of international forces. Many of them now hate the outside world more than ever. As the troops withdraw, they leave behind pockets of territory not controlled by the government of Afghanistan, and few guarantees that these will never again serve as incubators for international jihadists.

But how much guarantee did we need, that southern Afghanistan will not revert to a hideout for terrorists? I was never convinced that any military, no matter how large or capable, could roll into a swath of terrain and make sure that conspirators would never again use that location as a base for nefarious plots. I sometimes sensed frustration about the daunting task among the scribbles on the bathroom walls of Kandahar Air Field. Perhaps the only topic that united the men who wrote on the walls, besides their desire for sex, was their hatred of Afghanistan. They marked their days like prisoners. "Welcome to Shitnistan," somebody wrote. But the thing that really caught my attention was the bathroom door on which somebody took a knife or a razor and cut the words *NUKE AFGHANISTAN*, in capital letters. A maintenance worker tried to paint over the phrase, but somebody re-traced the letters in black ink. I had seen the same thing on other walls, sometimes accompanied by diagrams of how mass killing could be achieved: dotted lines indicating bomb arcs, sketches of mushroom clouds, little stick figures of Afghans frying in the nuclear blast. This was not an isolated idea, but something I kept seeing in military washrooms over the years. Maybe it expressed pure frustration. Maybe the soldiers wanted this long war settled, finally, and reached in their imaginations for the biggest weapon. But maybe it was a more sophisticated commentary on the absurd logic of the war, a Swiftian modest proposal that revealed the only way Western countries could feel absolutely certain that Afghanistan would never serve as a terrorist haven. Given that no sane person wanted to turn the country into a sheet of radioactive glass. perhaps this was the soldiers' way of saying the civilians at home had better get used to accepting risk in their lives, because there was a limit to how many people you can kill as a preventative measure. The phrase "never again," so often heard after 9/11, represented an impossible task for any military force.

This reminded me of a speech I'd heard years ago by the late American writer Kurt Vonnegut, in which he dissected Cold War logic by asking: "What fate is worse than death?" He argued that nothing could explain why countries need weapons capable of making the planet unfit for humans, because no scenario exists in which the best thing for humanity would be nuclear cataclysm. He was saying that the medicine was worse than the disease, in other words, and I wondered if the same applied to the fight against terrorism. Modern terrorists have rarely killed more than a few thousand people in any given year. Many times in Afghanistan, when my boots were stained with human gristle, I asked myself if the bloody effort could be justified by the hunt for small bands of madmen.

Defeating terrorism was never described as NATO's main goal in southern Afghanistan, however. Military interpreters sometimes heard Arabic on the Taliban communications intercepts, but for the most part the international jihadists had disappeared by the time NATO pushed into the south. Instead, the soldiers were assigned to improve the lives of ordinary Afghans. This wasn't entirely altruistic—military planners believed that the region would become more resistant to extremist ideology with a healthy dose of development—but it wasn't all cold calculation. Many prominent humanitarians were among those who called for a large contingent of foreign soldiers in the south. In July 2003, more than eighty non-governmental organizations declared a need for a bigger, tougher NATO presence in the provinces. "If Afghanistan is to have any hope for peace and stabilization, now is the time to expand international peacekeepers to key cities and transport routes outside of Kabul," the statement said. I'm biased in favour of one of the signatories—the International Crisis Group, which later became my employer—but it's fair to say that the organizations that signed the call to arms were some of the most respected voices in conflict zones around the world. Seasoned policy professionals genuinely felt that an influx of firepower would help the situation. Many of them still feel short-changed, that if only a larger NATO contingent had been rushed into southern Afghanistan, with greater haste, then perhaps things would not have gone badly.

I've had dinner party arguments about this, with people who know far more about Afghanistan and the conduct of foreign interventions, and I usually end up deferring to their claim that a bigger initial surge of troops might have resulted in success. But I can't help feeling that the right combination of tools and goals never existed for southern Afghanistan. Even with an imaginary contingent of perfect soldiers and development experts, with sufficient funding, deployed at the right moment, it's possible that we still would have been thwarted by our inability to understand the needs and desires of the local people. Our ideas for improving Afghanistan had ballooned into a utopian vision, an unrealistic and loosely organized set of goals. I keep a thick sheaf of papers that reminds me about those incredible ambitions. The grandiosely titled "Kandahar City Five-Year Municipality Strategic Action & Development Projects Planning" describes what the city leaders wanted to achieve from 2006 to 2011. Several months of discussion among Afghan officials and foreign donors had culminated in a two-day meeting at a palatial guesthouse; after welcoming remarks from the mayor and governor, policy experts presented the details. Public employees would wake up in the morning in houses built by the government, and ride to work in electric trolley buses or walk on paved footpaths because "people should not walk on the road." They would breathe easily during their commute, because of an air-quality program that fitted diesel cars and generators with smoke filters, and set up an engine-test workshop to check vehicle emissions. Beautiful scents would fill the air, too, thanks to the gardens and trees lining the streets, and the breezes coming through the new public parks. Workers would arrive each day at libraries, daycare centres, urban farm projects, new diagnostic laboratories, or one of the three hundred new factories. They could spend leisurely evenings in new gymnasiums, stadiums, playgrounds, cinemas, theatres, fitness centres and musical clubs. Or, perhaps they would spend their idle hours at one of the eighty public Internet kiosks around the city.

The mayor who spoke at that planning meeting was later assassinated, and the Kandahar governor narrowly survived several attempts on his life. The version of the city described on that day will probably never exist, partly because it was not rooted in the daily concerns of the people who struggle to survive in Kandahar and the surrounding districts. When I speak to local friends, they never mention Internet kiosks as their top priority. Usually, our conversations focus on the basics of survival.

There is still hope for southern Afghanistan. Electric trolleys seem unlikely, and it's unclear whether the local authorities will continue building girls' schools—or respect basic human rights. But violence declined in a few central districts of Kandahar province in early 2013, which suggests that the Afghan forces successfully kept the Taliban away from the provincial capital. If the Afghan government gets sufficient help from foreign donors, then I will remain skeptical about the insurgents' ability to overrun targets such as the major cities and airports. President Karzai could still be proven correct: Afghan forces could still win the war, after the terrible blunders of the international community.

For the Afghan government to gain the upper hand, however, the foreign money needs to continue flowing. If salaries aren't paid, local police could turn into insurgents or bandits. Problems with the pay structure would also threaten the integrity of the Afghan military, possibly breaking a key national institution into feuding factions.

Donors have promised to continue supporting the cost of Afghan security forces until 2017, but even the most optimistic projections show the donations shrinking in the coming years. The Afghan forces will also require help with air support and logistics, making sure that enough diesel, bullets and other supplies reach the front lines. Just as importantly, they need to refrain from beating people, stealing money and fighting each other. They need to behave in a way that inspires trust.

These are tall orders, but not impossible. Afghan security forces with a healthy budget from foreign donors may succeed in keeping the Taliban at bay. There's also a risk that parts of the country could fall into anarchy, or break into civil war. I keep thinking about the hairdresser in Kandahar city and the cracked ceiling of his shop, always threatening to collapse. I hope that the United States and its allies feel a sense of responsibility about leaving southern Afghanistan in that kind of peril. In his State of the Union address in early 2013, President Barack Obama predicted "by the end of next year, our war in Afghanistan will be over." Perhaps the war will be finished for many US troops, but the fight is far from settled. Afghanistan was an unsuccessful laboratory for ideas about how to fix a ruined country. It's morally unacceptable to claim success in a few limited areas—child mortality, access to education—and walk away. At best, we are leaving behind an ongoing war. At worst, it's a looming disaster. This is not an argument in favour of keeping battalions of foreign soldiers in the south, but a plea for continued engagement. Troop surges didn't work; the mission was a debacle. That should not discourage us. Rather, it should spur our work to repair and mitigate the damage in southern Afghanistan, and inspire a more careful approach to the next international crisis. The soldier who told me that modern civilization cannot tolerate empty spots on the map was probably right: we cannot write "Here be dragons" in the blank spaces, cannot turn away and ignore countries that become dangerous. That kind of neglect always bites us in the ass.

ACKNOWLEDGMENTS

If you've read this book, you know that the narrative has few heroes—except the translators. Several brave men risked their lives to collect the information in these pages. With their skills, they could have made a lot of money during the post-2001 gold rush in Afghanistan. Instead they chose a modest salary, and the difficult work of finding facts. They followed roads that nobody should have travelled, and dared to investigate figures who were powerful, corrupt and dangerous. In the spring of 2013, one of my former translators revealed how concerned he'd been about security. As described in Chapter 7, when our office was raided and I debated with my editors about buying a gun, we concluded that arming the local staff wasn't a good idea. But it turns out that one translator secretly went ahead and purchased weapons, stashing two Kalashnikovs in his house and a pistol under a seat cushion of our car. That wasn't much of an arsenal, by local standards, but it was a sign of his nervousness. I will always be grateful that our Afghan staff did not quit in the face of rising danger, and continued to tackle hard assignments. They cannot be named today, but hopefully in future they will get the recognition they deserve.

I started work on a book proposal in 2007 with encouragement from Dave Bidini and Dinah Forbes. Several friends recommended Jackie Kaiser at Westwood Creative Artists, and Stephanie Nolen kindly introduced me to her. Jackie has been the guiding force behind this project, going far beyond the job description of "literary agent" and becoming both mentor and fairy godmother. Humble thanks to Diane Martin, Louise Dennys, Anne Collins and Brad Martin at Knopf Canada for putting their faith in this book. It's been a special privilege to work with Louise, a literary legend. Paul Taunton handled the toughest part of the edit with such finesse that I found it hard not to add "Yes!" beside all of his marginalia. Thanks as well to others at the publishing house who contributed to this project, including Linda Pruessen, Shona Cook, Michelle MacAleese, Deirdre Molina, Brittany Larkin, Andrew Roberts, Sean Tai and Liba Berry. I'm grateful to Peter Jacobsen, yet again, for legal advice.

Many of the people who helped in Afghanistan must remain anonymous. That makes these acknowledgements rather lopsided; Afghan sources were my key interview subjects but naming them could put them at risk. Even my Afghan friends who have escaped often have families in the country that remain terribly exposed. For different reasons, most military and diplomatic sources also cannot be included.

Other important sources can be named, but with the understanding that they're not to blame for—and may not endorse—my view of the war. I had frequent assistance from the brightest young minds now writing about the south: Alex Strick van Linschoten, Felix Kuehn, Anand Gopal and Matthieu Aikins. Our group of observers was enhanced by Joshua Foust, Jean MacKenzie, Ben Anderson and Naheed Mustafa, among others, who contributed to e-mail chains that were enlightening and, often, sadly funny. A similar thread of conversation went on for years with Thomas Johnson, Chris Mason and a third person; all offered useful insights. Sami Kovanen was generous with his conflict data.

The camaraderie of journalists in a war zone usually defies the stereotype of reporters with sharp elbows. Murray Brewster took me under his wing, and I will always feel kinship with the temporary residents of the media tents at Kandahar Air Field. These included Al

"Big Daddy" Stephens, Stephanie Levitz, Michael Heenan, Stephen Puddicombe, Francis Silvaggio, Tim Lee, Sat Nandlall, Mellissa Fung, Paul Workman, Richard Johnson, Tom Blackwell, Sarah Galashan, Jonathan Fowlie, Peter Armstrong, Piya Chattopadhyay, Kelly Cryderman, Steve Chao, Lee Greenberg, Tom Parry, Peter Harris, Adam Day, Derek Stoffel, Jas Johal, Jeffrey Stephen, Colin Perkel, Tobi Cohen, Jonathan Montpetit, Sue Bailey, Martin Ouellet, Bob Weber, Dene Moore, Andrew Mayeda, Pascal Leblonde, Susan Ormiston, David Common, Laurie Graham, Susan Lunn, Brian Hutchinson, Mitch Potter, Matthew Fisher, Ben O'Hara-Byrne, Michael Heenan, Don Martin, Louie Palu, Mike Drolet, Paul Johnson, Lauren McNabb, Steve Rennie, Finbarr O'Reilly, Terry Pedwell, James McCarten, Bill Graveland, Fabrice de Pierrebourg, Agnès Gruda, Michèle Ouimet, Hugo Meunier, Bruce Campion-Smith, Rick Madonik, Rosie DiManno, Lisa LaFlamme, Tom Clark, Seamus O'Regan, Michelle Lang and many others.

Beyond the Canadian media, I was also lucky to meet intrepid journalists such as Kathy Gannon, Lyse Doucet, Carlotta Gall, James Bays, Tom Coghlan, Gretchen Peters, Yaroslav Trofimov, Tim Albone, Soraya Sarhaddi Nelson, Jason Burke, Anders Somme Hammer and Philip Poupin. Kathy, in particular, guided me through complicated issues.

Some of the greatest experts in the region were generous with their time and patience. Sarah Chayes welcomed me into Kandahar city and taught me the basics; Ahmed Rashid hosted me at his beautiful home and explained the region; Talatbek Masadykov, Eckart Schiewek, Michael Semple, Mervyn Patterson, Paul Fishstein, Barbara Stapleton and Barnett Rubin taught me Afghan politics. David Mansfield explained narcotics; Grant Kippen described elections. My wonderful friends, Georgette Gagnon and Nikolaus Grubeck, helped me understand human-rights issues. Antonio Giustozzi gave me my first taste of book-writing; Christine Fair showed me that it's possible to be a serious thinker but keep a sense of humour.

John Duncan, Mark Sedra, Amir Attaran, Roland Paris, Stephen Saideman and Kamran Bokhari offered expert perspectives from Canada. I also benefitted from the wisdom of Martine Van Bijlert, Peter Bergen, Anatol Lieven and Matt Waldman. More recently, I've also started to depend on Kate Clark, Fabrizio Foschini, Bette Dam, Megan Minnion, Heather Barr, Rachel Reid, Susanne Schmeidl and Riona Nicholls.

I gained profound respect for Joanna Nathan and Candace Rondeaux during, and after, their stints with the International Crisis Group, and feel grateful that they introduced me to the organization. I'm lucky to work under an illustrious group of bosses: Louise Arbour, Jonathan Prentice, Joost Hiltermann, Paul Quinn-Judge, Mark Schneider, Jim Della-Giacoma and, especially, Samina Ahmed.

This book would not have been possible without the resources and leadership of *The Globe and Mail*, a great Canadian newspaper. Stephen Northfield served as foreign editor during most of my years as a correspondent, and often my only job in Kandahar was to serve as a conduit between his brilliant mind and our talented Afghan staff. The rest of the foreign desk during that period—especially Susan Sachs, Philippe Devos, Christine Mushka, Linda Hossie and Shelley Cathers—saved me from embarrassment more times than I can remember. I had too many generous colleagues to list them, but I leaned especially hard on Paul Koring, Mark MacKinnon, Geoffrey York, Doug Saunders, Stephanie Nolen, Eric Reguly, Les Perreaux, Gloria Galloway, Steven Chase, Christine Diemert, Kathryn Mills, Karim Bardeesy, Jane Armstrong, Sue Andrew, Tim Appleby, Jeffrey Simpson, Murray Campbell, Sonia Verma, Jessica Leeder, Anthony Reinhart, Tu Thanh Ha, Colin Freeze, Joe Friesen, Patrick White and Greg McArthur. I also appreciated Christie Blatchford, my friendly adversary. Special thanks to Phillip Crawley and Edward Greenspon for approving the budget required to keep a correspondent in Kandahar. Thanks to Paul Knox, the foreign editor who first sent me overseas, and especially to Sylvia Stead, who watched over me.

I fell into journalism at *The Eyeopener*, the campus newspaper at Ryerson University, and my old colleagues feel like family: Liane McLarty, Kenny Yum, Sean Fitz-Gerald, Caroline Alphonso, Shane Dingman, Stephanie Bomba, Lori Fazari, Tim Fraser, Renata D'Aliesio, Ka Yan Ng, Michael Friscolanti and the rest of the gang. Nor could I have survived the newspaper trade without mentors: Tim Falconer, Lynn Cunningham, Julian Sher, Michelle Shephard and Rick MacInnes-Rae, among others.

I spent time with military forces from several countries, and was impressed by their hospitality, but the Canadian military stood above the rest because of its uniquely open system of embedding. Journalists could eat breakfast with the troops, walk off the base and have lunch with insurgents, then get back to the military mess hall for dinner. The fact that the Canadian military remained so helpful to journalists—in the face of political backlash—was a remarkable choice of principle over expediency. The military viewed me as a tough critic (my best friend among the officers called me "Darth Vader") but I can't remember a harsh word from any of the personnel. They remained polite, diligent and professional. I won't tarnish their careers by naming any of them, but I deeply admire many of the soldiers and officers who served in Afghanistan.

The same is true of the diplomats and United Nations staff. Chris Alexander, in particular, deserves thanks for explaining the optimistic view of the war with intelligence and rigor, no matter how much I disagreed.

Thanks to Asadullah Khalid for taking criticism with good humour.

Thanks to Richard Madan, Micaela White and Kiran Kothari for keeping my spirits up, and to Serif Turgut for her generous read of the book.

Deepest thanks to May Jeong—for the title, the careful editing and much else.

Most of the work on this manuscript happened at the Ritim Galata Cafe in Istanbul; the library of the Aman New Delhi; and the Dark

Horse Espresso Bar and Balzac's Coffee, at their locations in eastern Toronto. I'm grateful for their tolerance of a squatter with a laptop.

Most importantly, I would like to thank my family: my parents Stewart Smith and Lynn Gresham, and my sister Caitlin Smith, the brilliant music composer. It wasn't easy for them, getting occasional calls over crackling phone lines, or a few hasty e-mails. Thank you, thank you, thank you.

And apologies, to those I've forgotten.

INDEX

Pashto (language), 49, 84, 86, 98, 116, 120, 159, 191, 257, 265

Pashtoonkhwa (nationalists, Pashtun group), 98, 101, 102

Pashtun ethnic group, 19, 82, 98, 116, 120, 202, 203, 235

Pashtunistan, 19

Pashtunwali (code), 204

Peace Through Strength (PTS), 94

Petraeus, Gen David, 206

Pizza Hut, 118

Plato, 7

police. *See* Afghan Border Police; Afghan National Police; Counter Narcotics Police of Afghanistan; Directorate for Security)

"Popal" (name), 56

"Popal" (signs), 56

Popalzai tribe, 56, 202

poppies, 32–34, 155, 156, 164, 206, 251, 252

poppy field eradication, 206–8

pornography, 112, 158, 209

Portugal, 58, 79

prisoners. *See* detainees

propaganda, 98–100, 103, 108, 122, 141, 228

Prophet's Cloak, 9–10

Provincial Reconstruction Team, 51–53

"Quetta Council," 97

Qalat city (Afg), 51–52

Qassam, Haji Mohammed, 80–83

Quetta (Pakistan), 97–108, 111, 203

Quick Reaction Force, 225

rahbari shura (leadership council), 97

Razik, Brig-Gen Abdul, 82–83, 87, 272–73

Red Cross. *See* International Committee of the Red Cross

Registan, 114

religious prohibitions, 209

revenge, tradition of, 204–5

Romania, 58

Rossetti, Christina, 251

Royal Canadian Regiment. *See* Bravo Company; Charles Company

royal family (Afg), 172

Rubin, Elizabeth, 215–16

Rukiya (a young woman), 224

Rules of Engagement (ROEs), 31–32

Russia, 84, 207 (*See also* Soviet occupation; Soviet, collapse of; Soviet, withdrawal of)

"Safeguarding Afghanistan's Audio-Visual Heritage"(article), 14

Sangin Valley, 163–69

Sarpoza prison, 126, 133, 139, 142, 146, 216–31, 268–69

Savant, Jack, 38–39

security briefing, 116–20

Serena Hotel, 177

shalwar kameez, 116

Shaw, Capt James, 163–64, 166–69

Shomali road, 240, 241

shura, 101–2

Smith, Caitlin, 63

Smyth, Richard H., 210

Graeme Smith works as a senior analyst for the International Crisis Group, supervising a small team in Afghanistan. He previously served as a foreign correspondent for Canada's national newspaper, *The Globe and Mail*, with postings in Moscow (2005), Kandahar (2006–2009), Delhi (2010) and Istanbul (2011). He also worked as an adjunct scholar for the US Naval Postgraduate School in Monterey, California. His awards include three National Newspaper Awards, Canada's highest prize for print journalism, and the annual Michener Award for public service given by the Governor General of Canada. He also won an Emmy in 2009, for a video series that recorded the opinions of Taliban fighters. He lives in Kabul.